AIKIDO

and the
HARMONY
OF NATURE

Aikido To Shizen To No Chowa: *Aikido and the Harmony of Nature*

AIKIDO
and the
HARMONY
OF NATURE

MITSUGI SAOTOME

SHAMBHALA
Boston & London
1993

Shambhala Publications, Inc.
Horticultural Hall
300 Massachusetts Avenue
Boston, Massachusetts 02115

9 8 7 6 5 4 3 2 1

Design by Ruth Kolbert

First Shambhala Edition

Printed in the United States of America on acid-free paper ⊗

Distributed in the United States by Random House, Inc.,
and in Canada by Random House of Canada Ltd

Library of Congress Cataloging-in-Publication Data

Saotome, Mitsugi.
Aikido and the harmony of nature / Mitsugi Saotome.
    p.   cm.   ISBN 0-87773-855-6 (pbk.)
    1. Aikido—Philosophy.   I. Title.
GV1114.35.S26 1993   92-56440
796.8'154—dc20   CIP

Contents

著者寸感

合氣とは宇宙の根源的な生命活動力を表わす真理であって哲学ではなく割々として、この大自然界に休むことなく働いている調和を産み出しているところの現実の姿である。この真理の働きを体術や生活哲理に生かすものが武産合氣である。

人類のいにしえの文明の始めから〝武〟とは戈を止めるといって東洋においては世の中に平和な社会を建設するための祭り事の全活動の意味を指したのである。これを極言して私の恩師である合氣道の開祖植芝盛平大先生は「武は愛なり」と喝破されたのである。だからといって我々が武道に対して安易に理解した如くに認識することは真に〝さむらいの道〟として全生涯を献身的に生きぬいた実例としての植芝盛平大先生を正しく追慕することにはならないであろう。

人間の精神的な真実からの覚醒と世界の平和のために和合なさしめる道を探求しながら神に祈りつつ利他愛心に生きたのである。自己にきびしい修業を課して至誠と叡知の体現、宇宙心との調和、人類愛こそ合氣道開祖の教示された道である。

この著書を開祖の霊と関係者に捧げる　合氣道師範

Dedication

Aikido is not philosophy. Aikido is the true expression and revelation of the ever-evolving functions of the universe. Thus is derived the goal of Takemusu Aiki—experiencing the mechanisms of nature's truth in training and applying the theories in our daily life.

In Asia the word *Bu* means to halt the danger of the thrusting blade. Since the beginnings of human culture, this concept of *Bu* has implied a global advancement toward the construction of a peaceful society. "*Bu* is love," proclaimed O Sensei, Morihei Ueshiba, the Founder of Aikido and my mentor. Yet no simplistic understanding of Budo can in any way measure the life of unfathomable devotion and dedication O Sensei led in the Way of the true samurai. He strove for a human revelation of spiritual truth, and for world harmony through daily prayer and total unselfish concern for others. We must train hard for the attainment of wisdom, for harmony and an unselfish love for all humankind. Such is the path the Founder of Aikido has cultivated for us to follow.

I dedicate this book to the Founder of Aikido and to all Aikido followers.

SHIHAN M. SAOTOME

Translator's Note

Appearing in italics throughout this text are Japanese words and phrases which many readers will encounter for the first time. Often they have no English equivalent. Rather than try to give their literal meaning word for word, which is often misleading, we have tried to give the feeling and philosophy behind the word in the hope of presenting a clearer explanation. Some words will be defined more than once as the book progresses, so please do not accept the first explanation as the fullest. Each chapter builds on the preceding ones.

Most of the book has been written from discussions with Saotome Sensei and from his dictation in English. His usage of the English language, while not gramatically exact, is unique with a fresh and stimulating way of expressing his thoughts. To put some of these expressions into conventional English would make them much less effective. The goal has been to retain as much of his feeling and power as possible. If there are inconsistencies, errors, or misinterpretations, the fault is mine.

The Japanese names of persons born before the Meiji Restoration are written in the traditional Japanese manner, with family name first. Those born after that date, 1868, are written in the Western manner, with the family name last.

The use of the masculine pronoun to refer to both males and females has been avoided as much as possible, but because of the structure of the English language, flow and readability have often dictated its use. There is no such limitation in the Japanese language.

Deepest appreciation to Paul Kang, who freely gave of his time and energy to produce translations from the Japanese of the many difficult, complex ideas and O Sensei's speeches, and to Sara Bluestone, who added her professional touch to some of the diagrams and drawings. This book has gone through many changes to evolve to its present form, and many people, too numerous to name here, have helped in all its phases. Thank you all so much. And a special thank-you to Dr. David Jones for his guidance and support.

PATRICIA SAOTOME

Mitsugi Saotome (left) and Doshu Kisshomaru Ueshiba, son of the Founder

Preface

I think many people may have difficulty understanding *Aikido and the Harmony of Nature*. Some will be disappointed because there is so little explanation of the physical education of Aikido self-defense technique. In their search for technical information, these readers may miss the connection to Aikido in the discussion of science and the processes of nature. But the function of Aikido is different. It is not technique in the narrow sense, but the true meaning of the teachings of Morihei Ueshiba, the Founder of Aikido, that I wish to transmit.

Aikido movement must be understood from its roots deep in universal law. Its goal is to promote a deeper understanding and appreciation of the perfection of nature's balance, and to bring humanity back into harmony with God. I want to create in each person's mind a vivid flashback into our beginnings. I want to draw from your subconscious mind the memory of the very beginning of life and the struggle through time and space of the incredible evolution of humanity. I want you to feel the beauty and power of that evolution and give thanks to the Divine Creator.

We too easily forget our roots. In our selfishness we forget the delicate balance of the dependence of one life form on all others. If everyone applied to nature's resources a conservation born of respect, love, and understanding, and used them with an attitude of sincere thanksgiving to God, nature would be protected and the quality of life enriched. By protecting nature we protect society. By protecting society we protect ourselves. Self-defense is protecting and sustaining life. If nature is destroyed, the most fundamental requirement for survival is destroyed. To survive, we must nourish our body. If there is no food, if the water and the air are contaminated, there is no life, no society.

This is the essence of Budo. It is not the narrow art of fighting technique, but the art of saving life. And Aikido is first and always Budo. What help is fighting technique if there are one hundred starving people and no food? Many great Budo masters understood this. Many gave up the sword and returned to the land.

We live in a throw-away society of instant dinners and paper cups; every lazy, selfish act of excess is a crime of violence against nature. We are all criminals: we are killing ourselves.

Peace and harmony is not a game of logic. Only through peace and harmony and an abiding respect for nature's laws can we save our lives, and the lives of our children, and of our children's children.

This is O Sensei's teaching. This is my reason for writing this book.

Grand Master Morihei Ueshiba

FOREWORD
by David Jones

I would like to comment on Saotome Sensei's work, *Aikido and the Harmony of Nature*, from the perspective of my academic specialty, ethnology, the field of anthropology that focuses on the human cultural experience. One of my interests as an ethnologist has been the discovery of those aspects of the human adventure which seem to have near-universal expression under given cultural conditions.

In one sense, the thousands of recurring behaviors and responses described by anthropology present a picture of the universal human being. They may speak of the most ancient nature of the species and demonstrate those perceptions and actions that humans seem to find again and again to be apt and true. Aikido, viewed in its more sophisticated guise, is a modern facet of this endless wave of occurrence of those images of being, those codes of behavior to which billions of humans through many thousands of years have said, "Yes!" As the following brief survey will suggest, anthropology supports Saotome Sensei in his opinion that Aikido comprises a Way, or life model,

that can have meaning for the world citizenry.

One of the many important contributions that Saotome Sensei offers in this book is a presentation and explanation of Kannagara No Michi, the worldview of Aikido's founder, Master Morihei Ueshiba. Students of Japanese martial culture, and of Aikido in particular, will be very interested in the assumptions Ueshiba held concerning the nature of things, since these ideas form the bedrock of the structure of Aikido. Saotome Sensei tells us that *kannagara* means "the stream of God; the flow of creative energy that reaches from the past into the future." He adds that Kannagara No Michi is a "Way of life that strives for the truth and reality which is God." Saotome writes:

> Kannagara is a way of intuition. . . . Kannagara is a way of supreme freedom. . . . For the true follower of the Way, all actions arise from an unconscious and sincerely felt respect and appreciation for the perfection of nature's process and from the knowledge that all things have within them a living part of the Divine Spirit of Kami, the Creator of the Universe.

The mountains have God's name. The wind has God's name. The rivers have God's name. . . . The idea that many *kami* exist, as well as one original Kami, may seem a paradox; and the idea that *kami* govern the workings of the mountains and rivers, of the earth and the heavens, of trees and birds, may be incomprehensible to those who have received an education in modern science.

Kami might be seen as Master Ueshiba's experiential means of comprehending the singular immensity of Kannagara in the particulars of daily life. The basic notion of *kami*, that all things have a spiritual consciousness, an inner spark, is well known in anthropology. We use the term *animism* to describe a religious belief system in which every plant, animal, human, celestial body, earth form, and force of nature is felt to have this second self, soul, or spirit essence. Edward B. Tylor, the founder of cultural anthropology, coined the term *animism* and labeled his theory concerning the origin and nature of religion "the theory of animism" because his studies indicated that animism was one of the most ancient and pervasive of all religious ideas.

The "many *kami*/one Kami" view of Kannagara No Michi also resonates with the essential core of totemism. The most famous and influential of all sociologists, Emile Durkheim, in his classic *The Elementary Forms of the Religious Life*, described totemism as the original shape of religion. The totemic model, in a variety of forms and bearing a wide range of labels, permeates the human pilgrimage.

Another central aspect of Aikido is the Japanese concept *ki*. This is a notoriously difficult idea to translate for the West. Saotome Sensei succinctly states that *ki* is "the cosmic essence of life." In anthropology *animatism* is the term used to identify a belief in a nonanthropomorphic, free-floating force thought to exist all the time, everywhere, and in everything. (Some prominent early anthropologists thought animatism to be even more widespread than animism.) *Ki* is the word for this force in Japanese. The Chinese call it *ch'i* (*qi*), while the Indian yogi speaks of *prana*. The

Sioux word is *wakan*; the Comanche, *puha*. Each, to be sure, carries a particular and unique cultural gloss, but the basic belief found in each of these examples and many, many others is the same.

In connecting various strands of Aikido to certain belief modes such as animism, animatism, and totemism, I am not suggesting that Aikido is merely composed of a collection of ancient ideas. A large portion of "ancient ideas" may not be worth mentioning. I feel that animism, animatism, and totemism may best be thought of as labels for certain ways human beings think about the nature of existence. If one looks behind the Japanese word *ki*, the Comanche word *puha*, or the Sioux word *wakan*, one simply sees a human being understanding life in an apparently very, very human way. Though the words may change, and the particular animatistic concept may undergo certain structural modifications, the perception of some vaguely discernible "cosmic essence" is always, in both ancient and modern life-ways, somewhere present. I would say that all humanity embraces what the word *ki* points to and, in fact, lives by it.

In the practice of Aikido in the *dojo*, or practice area, the student is constantly being cautioned to move from the "center," to be "centered" in the execution of a particular self-defense technique, to "extend *ki* from the center." The Japanese use the word *hara* to identify this center, physically located in the lower abdomen. *Hara* is considered the concentration point of physical and spiritual energy, and to the mature student of Aikido its meaning may become cosmic. The core intent of the *hara* concept is expressed throughout the world. In English, we say that someone who displays courage, fortitude, or endurance has "guts," and in so doing we connect the lower abdomen with certain energy-demanding virtues. Once when traveling in Wyoming I heard an old cowboy tell a teenage boy who was about to ride his first rodeo bucking horse, "The only chance you have is to ride him in your stomach." And among many Melanesian peoples of the Southwestern Pacific, a common greeting asks, "How is your navel?" In the mountainous interior of New Guinea, the Dugum Dani have the belief that an *edai egen,* or "seed of singing," exists in the body's center and is the source of the individual's life power. The Chinese describe the *tan-t'ien,* or sea of *ch'i,* and locate it just below the navel. The *chakra* system of Indian Yoga also identifies a key *chakra* in this position. The "center" of Aikido is the ride in the young cowboy's stomach, the Dugum Dani's "seed of singing," and also the dictum of the Sioux medicine man Black Elk who said, "Anywhere is the center of the world."

If Aikido could be said to have an identifying shape, it would likely be the circle. Master Ueshiba stated:

> Aikido technique is structured on circular movement, for harmony is brought about and all conflict resolved through the spirit of the circle. . . . A circle encloses space, and it is from the perfect freedom of this emptiness that *ki* is born. From the center of this birthplace the creative processes of life are joined with the infinite, immeasurable universe by the Spirit. The Spirit is the Creator, the eternal parent giving birth to all things. . . . Within the circle the *ki* of the universe is guided in the processes of creation, evolution, and protection.

In *Lame Deer, Seeker of Visions,* the old Indian shaman says:

> To our way of thinking, the Indians' symbol is the circle, the hoop. Nature wants things to be round. The bodies of human beings and animals have no corners. . . . The camp in which every tipi had its place was also a ring. The tipi was a ring in which people sat in a circle and all the families in the village were in turn circles within a larger circle, part of the larger hoop. . . . The nation was only a part of the universe, in itself circular and made of the earth, which is round, of the sun, which is round, of the stars, which are round. The moon, the horizon, the rainbow—circles within circles within circles, with no beginning and no end.

To us this is beautiful and fitting, symbol and reality at the same time, expressing the harmony of life and nature. Our circle is timeless, flowing; it is new life emerging from death—life winning out over death.

In this book, Saotome Sensei urges the appearance of people with the spirit of the samurai: a spirit of courage, service, and compassion. Members of the Elk Warriors and Bow String Soldiers, Cheyenne Indian warrior societies, would accept the true samurai as a brother, as would the warriors of the African Nuer and Masai. Saotome Sensei discusses the meaning and importance of *marubashi,* "the bridge of life," a technique of a Japanese sword school in which one was advised to enter directly into the enemy's attack. This strategy could be understood by many peoples. Sanapia, a Comanche Medicine Woman I studied with as a graduate student in Oklahoma, told me that the course of action that gives the Comanche warrior greatest power, or "medicine," is found in facing the ghost directly, encountering and moving into this Comanche image of ultimate danger and evil. And we find that the story of the personal struggles of the Founder of Aikido, eloquently recounted by Saotome Sensei, is the universal tale of a sensitive, courageous, and determined man who confronts and overcomes many obstacles and hardships to experience a profound insight which he then sets out to expound. Master Ueshiba's story could be appreciated in almost any culture.

Saotome Sensei focuses in his text on the extension of Ueshiba's Aikido vision into the future by interpreting the basic philosophy of Aikido through the language of scientific method and research findings. In doing this, he gracefully avoids a flaw common with writers describing the "scientific basis of ancient beliefs." Saotome Sensei manages to combine *kami, ki, kannagara,* and many other difficult concepts so skillfully with the data of science that rather than one diminishing the other, they seem to be mutually enriching. He has amplified Aikido's voice without sacrificing its roots. After reading Saotome's work, the image of the thunderbird seems naturally coupled with a diagram of energy flow patterns in a thunderstorm; the storm becomes more sensual and alive, and the thunderbird is given more structural authority.

For me, this particular aspect of Saotome Sensei's presentation was especially notable. A subtle war is being waged all over the earth. Those who see the thunderbird and those who see the diagram are often in deadly conflict. The latter perceive the former as muddle-headed primitives, incompetents, and dreamers, while the former see the latter as rigid, simplistic, and inhuman. As is made very clear from Saotome Sensei's exposition, Aikido seeks harmony in conflict, not necessarily because it is a polite value of civilized people, but because harmony is creation's essential process. There is a common ground between antagonists, which, if joined, reveals a more powerful unity. The animists are shown in Saotome Sensei's writing that science basically supports and legitimizes them, and the scientists are instructed that they can be comfortable with the animists' view as a rich and suggestive continuation of knowledge. The anthropological philosophy can only applaud Saotome Sensei's Aikido, deftly demonstrated here in the realm of ideas.

In his preface Saotome Sensei writes: "I want to create in each person's mind a vivid flashback into our beginnings. I want to draw from your subconscious mind the memory of the very beginning of life and the struggle through time and space of the incredible evolution of humanity." As an anthropologist I see the individual's experience in Aikido as a microcosm of human biological and cultural evolution. Saotome Sensei may be speaking very literally. His Aikido ranges from the principles of energy acting in cosmic creation and identically experienced in Aikido to some of the most ancient and some of the most modern ideas and experiences of the human family. It is awesome to consider that Aikido is an art form that seeks to connect the individual with an intimate and personal experience of billions of years of creation.

A cross-cultural approach to Aikido can only be lightly touched upon here. For each example presented, dozens more could be added. Aikido is so harmonious with so many of the values, beliefs, and behavioral tendencies of most human life-ways that a point-by-point comparison could produce volumes. It is abundantly clear that Morihei Ueshiba touched a profound chord in the human spirit. His great contribution was in devising Aikido, a carefully crafted method designed to cultivate and lead the individual to his or her own confrontation with the Truth. Master Ueshiba, a Japanese man with a special kind of genius, made Aikido and its outer form bears the mark of the Founder's culture. However, Aikido's heart, its essence, is universal.

The basic themes of Saotome Sensei's book are delivered with great verve and success. Accessible yet poetic and invigorating language, well-conceived photographs, original and inspired drawings, elegant calligraphy, pertinent Japanese cultural and historical examples, clear organization of technical and scientific materials, a poignant portrayal of Master Ueshiba's life and philosophy, and the author's overriding literary and artistic sensibilities blend to produce a powerful and beautiful work.

In *Aikido and the Harmony of Nature*, Saotome Sensei, through the idiom of Aikido, makes a plea for global sanity. Aikido is the heart of a Universal Prayer. It is an eloquent statement of a basic human desire, expressed in countless ways since the beginnings of history.

AIKIDO
and the
HARMONY
OF NATURE

The kanji for Ai, when used alone, is translated as a meeting or joining; communication; confluence. Ki is translated as energy, power, vibration; the essence of life, of spirit. Together, Aiki, they mean to join the power; to become one with the power of the universal energy; to become one with the energy of the life force. Takemusu Aiki is the movement of truth, the protection and creation of life; a spontaneous and creative application that allows the dynamics and structure of the universal laws to be expressed in the human body, and the power of the universal energy to enter the human spirit. The first character, take, is the same as the bu in Budo. Takemusu is the spirit of the true warrior's Way.

1

HISTORY
of the
FOUNDER

"Saotome, that stone step must be moved a little closer to the house; it's difficult to step inside." Looking at the six-foot-long, one-foot-square solid piece of marble that my teacher had indicated, I knew it was too heavy for two men to move. I had returned from the toolshed and was rigging up a makeshift lever when I heard O Sensei behind me. "Saotome, what are you doing?" Impatiently he pushed me out of his way and grasped one end of the marble slab. With a small grunt he lifted it and moved it over the necessary six inches. He then went to the other end and, following the same procedure, completed the task. I stood staring, open-mouthed, as he mumbled in a disgusted voice, "Modern boys are so weak!" I was in my early twenties, and my muscles were strong and well tuned from many hours each day of hard Aikido training. But I could not budge the marble step that the four-foot-ten, seventy-eight-year-old master of Aikido had so easily moved.

As Morihei Ueshiba approached his mid-eighties, illness and time began to take their toll. He grew thin and his step was slowed. He needed help climbing stairs, and with each movement of his body he experienced severe pain. Yet throughout his illness he still taught Aikido. The moment he stepped onto the mat, he was transformed from an aging man enduring his last suffering into a man who could not be defeated by another man, nor by death itself. His presence was commanding. His eyes sparkled and his body vibrated with power. He effortlessly threw his *uchi deshi*, disciples, all of whom were young, strong, experienced from daily training, and at the peak of physical condition. Showing no sign of pain or discomfort, he laughed at our determined attempts to attack or hold him. In demonstration he would extend his wooden sword in front of him and encourage five of us at a time to push on it from the side with all our might. We could not move him or the *bokken* (wooden practice sword) an inch. It would have been easier to move a wall of stone.

One incident stands out from all others in my memories of this time. It happened shortly before he went into the hospital. I can still see

3

the Founder standing in front of me. As I faced him, my *bokken* poised to attack, the diminutive, frail old man was gone. In his place I saw a formidable mountain. His presence was awesome and his vibration filled the *dojo*. I looked into his eyes and was arrested by the powerful gravity of his spirit. The light shining there contained the wisdom and power of the ages. My body would not move. The palms of my hands were wet as I gripped the wooden practice sword, and sweat was breaking out on my face. My heart pounded and I could feel its rhythm throbbing through the veins in my arms and legs. O Sensei commanded, "At-

The Founder executing the ikkyo *technique.*

tack!" I gathered all my will into one *kiai*, one shout of supreme effort, attacking with all the speed and power I could muster. There was a flash of movement in front of me and O Sensei disappeared. I had made one fully committed strike. In the same timing, O Sensei had evaded my strike, and I heard the whistle of his *bokken* cutting three times. He was standing behind me. "Saotome, you attack so slowly." Just ten minutes earlier, I had supported a weak old man laboriously up two flights of stairs and into the *dojo* (practice hall).

The inevitable happened and his condition worsened. The doctors sent him home after a short stay in the hospital with the message that death was imminent. During the final two weeks of his life, as I took my turn sitting at O Sensei's bedside, I watched the familiar face beneath the wispy, white beard grow thinner day by day. I experienced a grief greater than any I had ever known as the many memories of his almost superhuman strength flooded my heart. Although his body was wasting away, his mind was sharp and his eyes had the clarity and peace of a child's. He talked very little at this time, but communication was strong and he was always thinking of Aikido.

Two days before his death he raised his frail body to a sitting position, looked at the students who were gathered there, and said, "You must not worry about this old man. All physical life is limited. Within the course of nature, the physical being must change, but the spirit will never die. Soon I will enter the spiritual world, but still I want to protect this world. That is now your task." He went into a deep meditation and after some time continued, "All my students must remember, I did not create Aikido. *Aiki* is the wisdom of God; Aikido is the Way of the laws which He created."

O Sensei looked up and indicated that he wanted to go to the bathroom. "I'm sorry, but after lying in bed all day this old man's legs are very weak." I quickly took one arm, and my close friend Yoshio Kuroiwa took the other. Slowly we proceeded down the hall, holding him tight lest he fall and injure himself. O Sensei suddenly straightened, pride flashing in his eyes. "I don't need any help." With a powerful shudder of his body, he freed his arms from our grasp. The weakened and dying old man had thrown two master instructors.

Our bodies flew until we pounded into the walls on either side. Step by step Morihei Ueshiba made his way alone. With each step his life was burning like the last brilliant flare of a candle before its fire disappears. Calm and at peace in the face of his approaching death, he seized the reality of each moment as it occurred. There was only that moment; each breath was infinity. How many memories did each step contain? His eyes were shining, his presence powerful. It was his final challenge.

A detailed account of the history of Aikido and its Founder would fill many volumes. It is impossible to give a full description in the limited space of this book. However, I believe that a short, basic history would be of great assistance to the reader in achieving an understanding of the art.

The event-filled life of Morihei Ueshiba is the process that gave birth to Aikido. It is the crystallization of his intense spiritual training and the creative expression of his strong and

The Founder, holding a white fan,
counters Mitsugi Saotome's bokken *attack with an* irimi *movement.*

ceaseless pursuit of truth. It is living evidence of the transformation of the selfish instincts of aggression through severe personal discipline, and through an attitude of devotion and reverence that leads one's life to higher levels of consciousness in order to receive the noble inspiration that causes one to rise above self-love, to a love and respect for humanity and society—a universal and Divine love that O Sensei called "the love of Kami," of God.

Samurai

Throughout his life, the Founder lived as a true samurai in the ancient Japanese tradition. He embodied a state of unity with cosmic forces that has been the spiritual ideal of the martial arts throughout the history of Japan. As one who brought this ideal to its ultimate completion and worked for the good of humanity and the world, his name and his life shine brilliantly in the history of Budo, the Way of the Warrior.

On December 14, 1883, in the Motomachi district of the city of Tanabe, Wakayama Prefecture, Japan, Morihei Ueshiba was born into this world, the fourth child of Yoroku and Yuki Ueshiba. A delicate and sensitive child, his early life was shadowed by illness. He often daydreamed, identifying with the miraculous stories of the great Buddhist teacher Kobo Daishi of the nearby Kumano region. At the age of seven he began studies in the basics of the Chinese classics at a private school of the Shingon sect of Buddhism. He studied deeply for one so young and possessed an extraordinary interest in the meditations, incantations, and prayers of that esoteric sect. Concerned that young Morihei was overly mental in his pursuits, his father, a strong and vigorous man, also encouraged him to discipline and strengthen his body through the practice of sumo wrestling and swimming.

During the years that followed, young Ueshiba received excellent instruction at Tanabe Elementary School. He developed a fine spirit, and his body grew healthy and strong. In intermediate school (for students between the ages of thirteen and seventeen) he took private lessons in the use of the abacus. In a little over a year he had made such rapid progress that he became assistant to the instructor at the abacus school.

Ueshiba moved to Tokyo in the spring of 1901 and established the Ueshiba Company, a stationery store large enough to employ several sales clerks. Meanwhile, a strong interest in Budo had awakened in him, and while he was in Tokyo, he studied both the Kito School of Koryu Jujutsu (unarmed combat) and the Shinkage School of Kenjutsu (techniques of swordsmanship). However, illness was to touch his life once again, and after giving his business to his employees, he returned home to Tanabe to convalesce. After his recovery Ueshiba married Hatsu Itokawa, whom he had known since childhood. The attitude of deep social responsibility that had been impressed on him by his father became stronger as he assumed the responsibilities of family life. Believing that change could occur only through action, Ueshiba became involved in many social reforms.

When a new fishing law was enacted that favored the large commercial fishing fleets, undue hardships were imposed on the smaller fishermen of the district where Ueshiba lived. Daring to oppose this law, he joined the campaign to revise it and participated in the "Iso Incident," a protest demonstration held in the small fishing village of Iso. With his help the problem was solved, and he became well known for his work.

At the age of twenty, Ueshiba enlisted in the military and served in the thirty-seventh regiment of the Osaka Fourth Division. His sincere and hard-working attitude and his extraordinary skill quickly drew the attention of his superiors. Easily regarded as the best bayonetist in the regiment, he displayed a technique so swift and clean that even the closest scrutiny of the judges could not detect how it was that each opponent was instantly sent flying.

During the Russo-Japanese War the stories brought back by Ueshiba's comrades of his great courage under fire made him a living legend, and among the troops he was respectfully called "the Soldier Kami." Recognizing his talent and his capability to become a future general, his superiors urged him to attend officer training school, but because of the situation at home, Ueshiba left the military after four years of enlistment. He took with him a certificate from the Yagyu School of Swordsmanship, obtained through study and practice during his off-duty hours, and the admiration and respect of all who had served with him. Upon his return to Tanabe, he channeled his skill and energy into social service and worked hard for the public good. He gained popularity among the people for his honesty and devotion.

In 1912, the Japanese government announced the beginning of the Hokkaido Project, encouraging people to settle in this northernmost, undeveloped island. The additional living space and farming lands were necessary to the welfare of the nation, and the Russians were showing an interest in its strategic location. The adventure of a new life and devotion to Japan were to challenge Ueshiba once again. So at the age of twenty-nine, he organized eighty people from fifty-four households in the area, and together they moved to the village of Shirataki, in Monbetsu County, Hokkaido.

The frozen land was harsh and inhospitable, unwilling to yield to the efforts of the new settlers. They were beset by storms and heavy snows, making their planned logging operations impossible. They tried to clear the land for cultivation, but the freezing rains drove them back into their hastily constructed shelters. Progress was slow, and the price paid in time and suffering was high. The first two years brought poor harvests and many hardships. Spirits were low, but Ueshiba encouraged the people, setting an example by his op-

timism and ceaseless hard work at the settlement, and his determined pursuit of negotiations for relief funds from every possible source.

Two years later, in the fall, the land yielded its long-awaited harvest and the people began to feel that a permanent settlement was feasible. Each of the projects they undertook—peppermint cultivation, lumbering, horse breeding, and dairy farming—was based on Ueshiba's plan and proved to be an important factor in the development of Shirataki. The village took on new life. People began to call Ueshiba "King of Shirataki," and when they had problems they came to him for advice and help. He served as a member of the village council and assisted in an exploratory excavation of underground mineral resources. In 1915 he met Sogaku Takeda, master of the Daito School of Jujutsu, who had occasion to pass through the area. Ueshiba was very impressed by Takeda's technique and continued in his quest for Budo with the study of Daito Ryu.

In November of his thirty-sixth year, Ueshiba received news that his father was in critical condition. Leaving Hokkaido, he gave his entire holdings to Master Takeda in appreciation for all that he had taught him. But on the way back to Tanabe, he was diverted by stories of a man named Onisaburo Deguchi of the new Shinto sect known as Omoto-kyo. Deguchi was a master of the spiritual practice called *chin kon kishin*, a Way of communication with the Divine Spirit of Kami through concentrated meditation. With the hope of a miracle, Ueshiba went to Ayabe, near Kyoto, to ask for prayers to alleviate his father's critical condition.

Upon his return to Tanabe, he learned that his father had passed away. His sorrow was deep, and he spent more and more of his time in prayer and meditation. Soon Ueshiba's thoughts returned to Deguchi's kindness and revolutionary approach to traditional spiritual teachings. He moved his family to Ayabe and entered the religious life of Omoto-kyo. Deguchi loved and respected Ueshiba and in-

vested him with much authority and responsibility. Deguchi told him, "You should make Budo your life. You have the strength to move mountains. Do it!"

Acting on this advice, the Founder opened the "Ueshiba School" of martial arts. He taught mostly those who had some connection with Omoto-kyo, but his fame as a martial artist quickly spread among other people. He cleared and cultivated the land near the main hall of Omoto-kyo, led the self-sufficient life of a farmer, and put into practice his idea of the essential unity of Budo and farming. The study of *kotodama*, the spiritual function of the vibration of sound, had become a key aspect in his search for the true spirit of Budo, and gradually he began to bring about the unification of spirit, mind and body. In 1923, the Founder officially named his art Aiki Bujutsu. *Aiki Bujutsu* is the blending of spirit based on classical martial movement. *Jutsu* is technique, as opposed to *do*, which is a path or way.

Kotodama   Aiki Bujutsu

The following year he accompanied Deguchi to Manchuria, seeking a place to serve as the spiritual center for "a world cooperative of people of five races and colors," a vision of Omoto-kyo based on the idea that all teachings evolved from a single origin. Their path led them into many tense encounters with armed bandits and professional soldiers. By this time the Founder had reached such an advanced level of spiritual awareness that when fired upon, he would perceive the aggression in the form of a small point of light immediately preceding the bullet. He described his experience: "Before the opponent could pull the trigger, his intention to kill would form into a ball of spiritual light and fly at me. If I evaded this ball of light, no bullet could touch me."

After returning to Japan in 1925, the Founder applied himself to mastering the art of the spear. He practiced day and night, utilizing his own unique methods of physical training and spiritual purification, and as his practice rose to higher levels, his martial skill took on an almost superhuman quality. At the culmination of a period of particularly intense training, during a meditation/purification practice, he had the realization he had been seeking all his life. At that moment, as the spirit of the universe enveloped his body with a shimmering golden light, he grasped the essence of *ki* (universal life force), he intimately understood the processes of the universe, and he knew that the source of Budo is the spirit of protection for all things. "Budo is not defeating the opponent by our force," he said; "nor is it a tool to lead the world into destruction with arms. To follow true Budo is to accept the spirit of the universe, keep the peace of the world, and correctly produce, protect, and cultivate all beings in nature."

While he devoted himself to further study and the establishment of this new Way of Budo, the name Morihei Ueshiba and word of his incredible skill spread in Budo circles throughout Japan. He traveled the country, teaching Aikido. People from all walks of life asked for his guidance.

With the help of many supporters, in 1930 the temporary training facilities were enlarged to include a mat space of over fourteen hundred square feet. This training hall was called *Kobukan Dojo* and was located in the Wakamatsu district of Shinjuku, Tokyo. (*Dojo* is the place where the Way is studied; *Kobukan* indicates a search for truth by transcending ordinary human consciousness.) That year, Jigoro Kano, the founder of Kodokan Judo, came to visit the *dojo*. Upon seeing Master Ueshiba's supreme skill, he said, "This is my ideal in Budo," and sent two of his students to study. Many young *judo* practitioners came to study at Ueshiba School. One of these was Kenji Tomiki, the leader of the Judo Club at Waseda University. Tomiki later developed an *aiki-jutsu*-style offshoot of Aikido that included competitive matches. At the same time, Gozo Shioda, currently the headmaster of Yoshinkan Aikido, studied as an apprentice to the Founder.

It was not easy for members of the general public to join the *dojo*. Only those with recommendations from two reliable sponsors were allowed to become students. The practice was so intense and rigorous that the *dojo* earned the nickname "Dojo of Hell." Many famous people, leaders in the military, government, business, education, and the arts, entered Ueshiba School, and through these contacts, the Founder taught the police force and those connected with the Imperial Court. The year 1932 found Master Ueshiba extremely busy teaching and giving demonstrations of the art. Branch *dojo* were established in other parts of Tokyo, Osaka, and Kyoto. Aikido was quickly spreading throughout the country.

In 1942, when the war effort was intensifying, Ueshiba was severely troubled by the disparity between his ideas of world cooperation and the actual state of the world relationships. Accompanied by his wife, Hatsu, he went to the town of Iwama in Ibaraki Prefecture, and once again he began to clear the land for cultivation. There he built an open-air *dojo* and an Aiki Shrine to serve as a spiritual retreat. The Founder has related that he said at that time, "There are getting to be more and more people in the military who are reckless and indiscriminate with their power. They have forgotten the importance of helping people, of relieving suffering. A bunch of fools, they strut about displaying their violence, their narrowmindedness, and wanton destruction of life. What idiots to go against nature, against the Will of Kami!

"The Way of *Budo* is to put new life into the original universal life force that gives birth to all things. Harmony, love, and courtesy are essential to true Budo, but the people who are in power these days are only interested in playing with weapons. They misrepresent Budo as a tool for power struggles, violence, and destruction, and they want to use me toward this end. I'm tired of this stupidity. I have no intention of allowing myself to become their tool. I see no other way but to go into retreat."

The Founder held strongly to his own belief and taught all who would listen, "The path of Budo is found in the union of Budo and farming. It is essential to actually put into practice the production of life force through Takemusu Aiki."

During and after the Second World War, the Founder devoted himself to farming and sought the perfection of the ideal of Takemusu Aiki. Abiding deep within his heart was the belief that the path of Budo is the path of compassion; that the task of a true samurai is to make the world fertile for peace and to protect all life. In his sorrow for the suffering and destruction caused by the conflict, he spent long hours in prayer. Master Ueshiba had reached levels of spiritual awareness attained by very few, but still he continued his search for the power of truth. Having virtually no income, he lived in extreme poverty, training body and spirit and working the soil.

In 1948, Japan was getting back on its feet after the chaos of war. Until that time, General Headquarters of the American Occupation had prohibited all teaching of Budo. But because of its emphasis on peace and the seeking of truth, Aikido was allowed to resume an active part in society. The name of the *dojo* was changed from Kobukan to the Aikikai Foundation, and it was headed by the Founder's son, Kisshomaru Ueshiba. Once again activity began, and the teachings of Aikido were spread among the general public. The Founder, respectfully called O Sensei (Great Teacher), was still in Iwama leading a life of Budo and farming while continually training and praying for world peace. From time to time he would come to Tokyo at his students' request, lectur-

Old Hombu Dojo

ing on Aikido principle and teaching technique.

In 1959, as public recognition of Aikido took root, O Sensei's fame spread both within Japan and abroad. There was a marked increase in the number of people coming to the *dojo* seeking instruction, and some of the leading students began to take an active part in spreading his teachings overseas. All who were touched by O Sensei, even for a short time, felt their hearts cleansed by his nobility and spiritual strength, and the radiant purity of his compassion and concern made us deeply ashamed of the selfish aggressions we found within ourselves.

While Japan was pursuing its policy of accelerated economic and material growth, there were many people who battled poverty in order to bring to the public O Sensei's Aikido, a living prayer for harmony, peace, and love on a universal scale unequaled in the history of Budo. Among these were Kisaburo Osawa, Shigenobu Okumura, Hiroshi Tada, and

Sadateru Arikawa, all of whom are now senior *shihan*, master instructors of Aikido. They worked devotedly behind the scenes at the main *dojo* in Tokyo, helping Kisshomaru Ueshiba. Special mention must be made of Seigo Yamaguchi, who abandoned a promising career and lived in poverty to aid in the expansion of Aikido. Another *shihan*, Morihiro Saito, served the important function of caring for O Sensei at Iwama. And Koichi Tohei first introduced the teachings of Aikido to the United States. Many *shihan* went to much time and expense to open branch *dojo* throughout Japan. There were also many famous and influential people of high social status and wealth who contributed to the growth of Aikido, and their assistance was invaluable. But we must not forget the efforts of the unnamed individuals whose dedication spread its light. It was the anonymous thousands of serious students, impressed by O Sensei's teachings, who provided the living base and support for the growing awareness of

Sugano, Chiba, Saotome, Doshu, and O Sensei

Aikido. That O Sensei treated all his students equally and taught us with great sincerity remains vivid in my memory.

On April 26, 1969, Grand Master Morihei Ueshiba completed the natural span of his earthly life. That same day the Japanese government conferred upon him the Order of the Sacred Treasure, the most highly esteemed of the many honors and awards he received for the founding and development of Aikido.

During my years of close contact with O Sensei as his personal student, I was profoundly impressed by his honesty and the depth of his reverence. O Sensei's reverence and understanding were born through directly experiencing the existence of God in a vast and indefinable universe. They could not be confined to any one particular religious sect or any one nation. O Sensei manifested a spiritual clarity greatly surpassing our ordinary understanding of the world. We were truly blessed to have been allowed the opportunity to study with such an enlightened being.

One day, during my years as his apprentice, O Sensei had just concluded his daily prayers at the Aiki Shrine in Iwama and began to speak in a soft and thoughtful voice: "Saotome, people often say that I created Aikido through my study of many other martial arts. But the Way of Takemusu Aiki that I am thinking of is different. It was born through the order of Kami that I only followed and conveyed to others. I didn't create Aikido. Aiki is the Way of Kami. It is to be a part of the laws of the universe. It is the source of the principles of life. The history of Aikido begins with the origin of the universe. Do you think a human being could possibly have created these laws? The shrewdness of human intelligence is not enough to understand this.

"If we forget gratitude to Kami, our lives are worthless. If we forget the processes and function of the universe, we are helpless."

When Aikido students think of O Sensei,

they often invest his life with the mysterious powers of the supernatural. However, looking back over O Sensei's life, I find this attitude incorrect. Clearly his martial technique was a miracle. It was the miracle of a spiritually enlightened man manifesting the justice and protection of Kami through a strong and highly trained body, a miracle of the abilities of the human body and spirit, of perception, of timing. His spiritual enlightenment was not magically bestowed upon him. It was earned through a lifetime of devotion to truth, dedication to society, and immense courage. It was refined through adversity and the bitter struggle of constant personal training. His was the spiritual attitude of the devout realist. To imply otherwise holds no respect for the principles he taught, for Aikido is reality. It has a vital function in this world as a tool to educate and refine society. It is a philosophy of action.

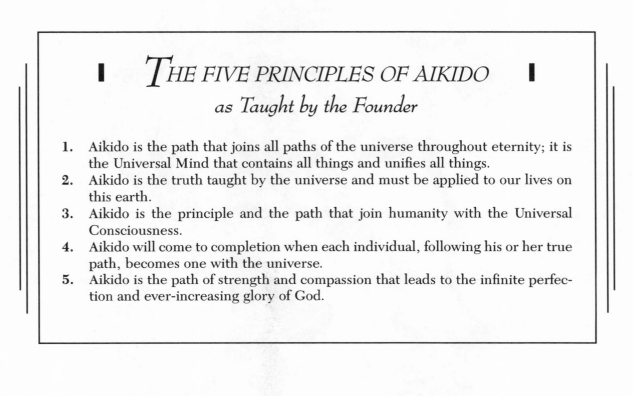

THE FIVE PRINCIPLES OF AIKIDO
as Taught by the Founder

1. Aikido is the path that joins all paths of the universe throughout eternity; it is the Universal Mind that contains all things and unifies all things.
2. Aikido is the truth taught by the universe and must be applied to our lives on this earth.
3. Aikido is the principle and the path that join humanity with the Universal Consciousness.
4. Aikido will come to completion when each individual, following his or her true path, becomes one with the universe.
5. Aikido is the path of strength and compassion that leads to the infinite perfection and ever-increasing glory of God.

Kannagara No Michi: Kannagara *is the stream of God, the flow of creative energy that reaches from the past into the future. Kannagara no michi, from which Shinto developed, is not a religion or a philosophy. It has no founder, nor has it any scriptures. It is a way of life that reaches for the truth and reality that is God.*

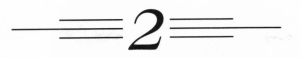

KANNAGARA NO MICHI

The development and refinement of tradition is a cultural process, formed by the spirit of a nation's people. Art, music, language, and particularly our relationship with God are developed from our experiences and needs, our basic consciousness. Tradition and theology, in turn, recycle to mold the spirit of a nation throughout the generations.

As there exist people of many different ethnic backgrounds in the world, the concept of "God" has many names. A primary factor in shaping lifestyles and attitudes in each cultural sphere, the perspective of religion has the power to control society's moral standards and influence our view of ourselves, the world, and the universe. When various peoples of the world hope for peace, freedom, and happiness, they do so in their own terms. Christians hope for a Christian world; for followers of Muhammad, it means the peace of Muhammad; Buddhists pray for Buddhist peace and happiness; and Hindus think Hinduism is the realization of truth. These are all concepts of peace on earth, but they come out of different contexts, and each one has a differ-

ent image. God has many faces.

It is not my intention here in considering the Way of Kannagara to criticize other religious ideas. Aikido is truth, and truth knows no religious or cultural boundaries. But the man who developed this particular Way to explore truth was Japanese, molded by the traditions of the Shinto religion. His art was the sword; his creative Way was Budo. His enlightenment is expressed in a powerful and graphic application of universal truth. An understanding of the basic attitudes and traditions that affected his life and the spiritual frame in which he functioned will give deep insight into understanding his art.

When discussing Japanese culture, Westerners most often mention the influence of Zen, one form of Buddhist thought. Clearly we can see the spiritual contribution of Zen to studies such as Budo, tea ceremony, flower arrangement, calligraphy, and garden landscaping. Indeed, there have been four religious philosophies that have made major contributions to the development of the Japanese consciousness: Shintoism, Confucianism, Bud-

dhism, and the Tao. However, there is an important point that is often overlooked. It is the flexibility of the Japanese people, cultivated over a long history and steeped in the intrinsic Way of Kannagara, to adapt and refine philosophies and ideas from other cultures and make them uniquely Japanese.

Because of this adaptability there is a great religious tolerance among the people. Many climb Mount Fuji every year, but not everyone takes the same path. Fujiyama has many sides, and each person climbs for a different reason, with differing abilities. There can be no argument over which way is the right way, for the top is the top, and all paths lead to the same ultimate reality. Who can deny that Jesus spoke of God's spirit? Who can say that the Buddha's teachings were not the teachings of God? And was it not to God to whom Muhammad directed his fervent prayers? All the great spiritual teachers were pointing a way to the top, to the ultimate reality which is the Universal Consciousness. The path is not important, but following and emulating a great spirit, a great teacher, and the sincerity and devotion with which the path is followed are all important.

Spiritual philosophies are not studied intellectually but integrated into the lifestyle and applied naturally in daily life. It can be said that in Japan one is born as a Shinto, married in a Christian church, and taken to a Buddhist temple when he or she dies. Of course, this is a generality, but it expresses the basic attitude that spiritual belief and activity are viewed as nutrients for the mind and spirit. Health and vitality cannot be attained by the digestion of just one type of nutrient; therefore one person will practice many different spiritual disciplines during his or her lifetime. Yet, underlying it all, the view of the universe and life as found in the ancient Way of Kannagara is a vital part of the foundation of the culture. Embedded deeply within the subconscious minds of the people, it extends an invisible influence and runs like life blood through traditional Japanese culture.

Kannagara is a way of intuition. There are no written laws, no strict doctrines of right or wrong. The only laws are the laws which govern natural phenomena and promote harmony. Kannagara is a way of supreme freedom, for the action appropriate to function in harmony with nature occurs spontaneously. For the true follower of the Way, all actions arise from an unconscious and sincerely felt respect and appreciation for the perfection of nature's process and from the knowledge that all things have within them a living part of the Divine Spirit of Kami, the Creator and Origin of the universe. The mountains have God's name. The wind has God's name. The rivers have God's name. Trees, grasses, animals, all things in nature are the consciousness of the Creator and manifestations of His boundless love.

The idea that many *kami* exist, as well as one original Kami, may seem a paradox; and the idea that *kami* govern the workings of the mountains and rivers, of the earth and heavens, of trees and of birds, may be incomprehensible to those who have received an education in modern science. But if we replace *kami* with the laws of physics, the laws governing natural phenomena, it becomes clear that the universe is tightly welded by the interre-

lationships, and the *kami*, the laws, do not exist separately. Einstein once spoke of the existence of a great Will in the universe, immeasurable by modern science, which governs the laws of physics. He was referring to the existence of a Universal Consciousness. Again and again, modern science is proving the intuitive wisdom of Eastern philosophy. All matter in the universe consists of the same material, the same essential energy. Whether a human body or a mountain, mass is the physical expression of energy, formed by the dance of vibrating molecules and atoms. And though the quality and the quantity are different, the Universal Intelligence is inherent in all things and produces order in all things.

The laws of the universe have been functioning since the beginning of time, billions of years before the age of humanity. Seen in this light, we must realize that science does no more than analyze and make use of these universal laws. Since ancient times, humanity has perceived a mysterious power that controls these laws and called this power "God." O Sensei called it the "miraculous function of *ki*." He taught that Aikido is the Way of harmony with the laws of nature. Aikido is the love and protection of all things. These teachings developed naturally from the idea of one original creative energy common to all things.

A rose slowly unfolds its mysteries in the warmth of the summer sunlight. Where among the branches of a bush that is bare in winter are hidden all those blossoms? Why this shape and color? And why is the air so sweet around it? O Sensei saw things with a different eye. For him these questions were answered when he looked at a rose, for he saw not just the surface, but the essence. With great clarity and insight he saw the love of God that produced that flower. The same love, the same creative essence, flows through all of creation.

We speak of love in abstract terms, but love is not an abstract idea. If for only one minute there were no love, there would be no life, no air, no water, no food. Love is reality. We live and function on this earth as an expression of God's love; it is not an abstract, sentimental love, but a love as vital and strict as all of creation. God is not logic; God is not philosophy; God is love.

Harmony and unity are the essence of love. Universal love is not selfish love. Universal love is justice. It has no prejudice; it embraces equally all of creation. Love has no expectations. It penetrates and fills its object, and dynamic opposites become one and grow together. The nerves of God fill the void. His sensory awareness reverberates in the unseen world where all action and phenomena have their origin. The invisible world of vibration, the void between the stars and the vacuum within the orbit of electrons, is charged with His pulse. This is the spiritual world, and visible matter is created from its energy by the movement of His breath.

The harmony of elementary particles is based on love. The laws of electromagnetism upon which all of creation is structured gives the universe its great richness and variety of form. They are laws of dynamic activity, for lying deep within all matter is the perfect rhythm of the universal vibration. The polar opposites of yin and yang, of electron and proton, of centrifugal and centripetal forces, are but two images of the same reality. Within this rhythm infinite creativity arises as fire and water are combined, opposites united. The Creator and creation are one, not separate, and we are not apart from the perfect rhythm that is an expression of Holy Wisdom.

Unity is the power of God and resolves all conflict. The process of the unification of opposites is *musubi*, the reunion of the two faces of God. Centripetal forces, yang and center-seeking, fused with centrifugal forces, yin and center-fleeing, create the perfect balance of the galaxies. *Musubi* is movement, for without movement there can be no joining. Its symbol is the spiral perpetually recycling its energy, a process that has no beginning and no end. It is continuity and it is change, a pattern of duality seeking the one, and the one seeking its extreme.

Our rational judgment sees extremes as sep-

結び

Musubi

arate, a dichotomy in which opposites are in conflict. The false illusions of this duality must be realized before the spontaneity of truth can be experienced. The extremes of happiness and sadness, love and hate, morality and immorality, each have meaning only in relation to the other, their determinations valid only in relation to the observer. Until we know sorrow, we cannot know joy. In the creation of beauty, we recognize the absence of the beautiful. In pleasure there is pain. We cannot know the one independently of the other. To see the one in all things implies the recognition of opposites, but it excludes judgment; and opposites appear only as the dynamic unity of change.

All of life, all universal activity, is process, *musubi*. A cycle of becoming, it is the process of dynamic movement between the polar extremes of universal law, and the only constant in the universe is change. Nothing stays the same for a day, an hour, or even a second. Night turns into day; the snows of winter bring forth the blossoms of spring. We are born and we die. Birth and death, decay and rebirth, the cycle of life—all is change. Change is life, and the ability to change is the essential element of growth. The freedom founded upon the realization and acceptance of this truth, that nothing stays the same, is the source of the power of true creativity.

To talk of harmony, unity, and the principles of *musubi* is simple, but to apply these principles to the conflicts faced in everyday living requires a deeper understanding and sincere trust. Logic may tell us that within the process of *musubi* lies truth, but the moment something of value rests on the outcome of a situa-

tion, we no longer trust that logic. The beautiful ideas and flowing phrases are forgotten under the pressures of reality. In philosophy a theory of truth is expressed in words, but the truth of Aikido lies in action, the theory proven in practice. By the physical application of *musubi* we develop a deeper understanding in the heart instead of the mind. Through *keiko* and experience we learn to trust its power. The term *keiko* refers to practice or training, but the deeper meaning of *keiko* is reflection and refinement, to return to the origin and discover reality. Only through the study of the past and an appreciation of its experience can we understand the present and refine our spirit.

Without the experience of conflict we cannot know harmony. Viewed without judgment, conflict is neither good nor bad. It is only the opposite of harmony and a stepping stone to creativity. We must challenge our concepts, grinding the negative edges from our attitude so that negative fighting spirit becomes creative fighting spirit. The stress and pressure of Aikido training brings this spirit to the surface and exposes it so that it can be examined and refined. Discovering our physical limitations causes us to reflect on the deepest meaning of harmony and conflict and to strive for a level of consciousness above the ego, closer to the Creator.

Satori

To achieve *satori*, enlightenment, means to draw nearer to God, to take away the gap, to tear down the fence between us and the natural world. Our personal struggle for refinement will lead to the realization that our lives and the workings of the universe are one. This

The rhythms of koshinage are the rhythms of the waves breaking across the rocks.

Koshinage, *the living symbols of yin and yang.* Hiroshi Ikeda, Shihan, nage; *Paul Blackwood,* uke.

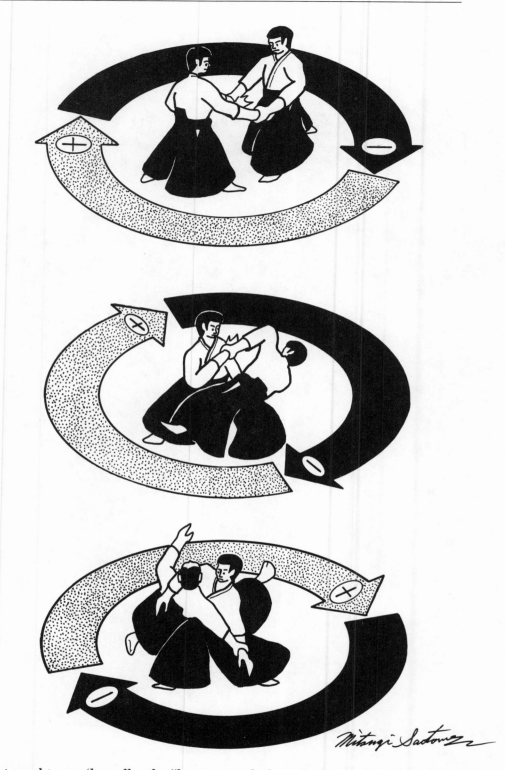

Ryote dori tenchinage (literally, the "heaven-earth throw") clearly illustrates the rhythmic wave of polar opposites: balance created by centripetal and centrifugal forces.

Bruce Merkle, uke

is the active and living *satori* of Aikido training.

Only sitting in meditation selfishly awaiting personal *satori* has no meaning. To truly achieve *satori* is to understand the great responsibility we have to God, to His creation, and to society. With this understanding, an appreciation for all life will fill the heart, and modesty will replace selfish egotism. True *satori* is forgetting *satori*. True *satori* is understanding responsibility, not selfishness. Many people misunderstand Zen training and think they only have to sit in meditation hour after hour to become enlightened. Sitting is an important part of Zen training, but more important is to understand reality, the reality of sweat, of work, the reality of responsibility. In a traditional *zendo,* one day without work is one day without food. Often there is no talking for a week, a month, or even a year. Silence and action are modes of training that teach us to still the mind and see inside. The training of *nai kan gyo* is a meditation in which we look deep inside our consciousness and join the spirit of God. *Satori* means truly developing God's spirit within and embodying the function of God without.

O Sensei's life was one of freedom, of living in this moment, and he believed that freedom is responsibility. O Sensei was always thinking of bettering this world, never of escaping it. He despised the weakness that makes people want to forget reality, to blindly ignore the pain in the eyes of a starving child—people who say, "It's just *karma;* this body is a jail, this world a prison. I'll search for my own personal salvation and build a better situation in the next life." How can this be spiritual thinking? This attitude holds no respect for God. Forget *karma,* forget the next life, forget *satori*. Now is now! A baby is hungry; give it food. This is spiritual. A man's tongue is swollen from thirst; give him water. This is God's love.

In Japan, people say that they can see the shape of a rabbit in the surface of the moon. This comes from a children's story of an old Buddhist priest living high upon a mountain

to spend the remainder of his life in prayer. This gentle priest was much loved by all the mountain creatures, who were his only companions. But times were very hard, food was scarce, and the old priest was weak with hunger. When word of this reached the animals, they dug into their meager stores and scoured the mountainside in search of food. At last they gathered outside the mouth of the old priest's cave and laid their gifts before him. The squirrel brought nuts, the bear brought sweet wild berries, and the racoon brought fish, fresh from the icy mountain stream. Everyone had brought a gift of food to the starving priest. Everyone, that is, except the rabbit, who was very, very poor. All the animals were astonished, and there was much gossip about the uncharitable rabbit. Unconcerned, the rabbit quietly built a blazing fire, and as the flames began to lick the sky, he turned to the priest and said, "I'm sorry, but I am very poor. I have no food. Please, eat of my meat." And before he could be stopped, the rabbit jumped into the fire. Whose was the greatest love? Which animal made the true sacrifice? This story embodies the spirit of the true samurai. O Sensei was a great samurai, a mountain, not a cloud. His philosophy and his love were steeped in the very highest ideals, yet with a broad base and deep roots grounded in reality. O Sensei is the Himalayas. O Sensei is Everest.

Heaven and hell are now. We create our own heaven or hell by our actions, our thoughts, and our words. One of the deep spiritual symbols of the Shinto religion is the mirror. It is believed that by looking into a mirror we will see the face of God, for the face we see is the image of our own personal reality. If it is a smiling face, our God is a happy God, a God of love. But if the reflected image is one of unhappiness or of hatred, the face of hell stares back. Physical attitude reflects the spirit, for they are one. If we do not train and cleanse the foundation of the body and the mind, truth cannot be expresed and we cannot help society.

As the earth was created by fire and water, it is also cleansed by fire and water. The natural phenomena of rain, wind, and snow purify the earth and its atmosphere; its internal balance is restored by volcano and earthquake. Natural processes drain the body of excess and waste. The symptoms of illness—fever, swelling, and sweat—are the body's natural purification techniques to restore balance. Cleansing is a fundamental part of the natural order of life. The spiritual world and the material world are not separate, but only different forms of the same reality, each influencing the other. To truly become one with the Creator and experience *satori*, we must follow the laws of nature and purify the body, the heart, the spirit, even our physical surroundings. Cleaning is an active prayer of gratitude. The body is washed; the toxins within the body are flushed by purifying the blood and bowels through proper diet, sleep, and strenuous activity. The environment is kept clean and orderly, free from the vibrations of negative thoughts, words, and actions. By the sincere attempt to recognize the God that is within us and without, the living sea of energy in which we move and that moves within us, and by the effort to embody His function, a deep inner peace cleanses the heart.

The many special ceremonies and techniques of purification are called *misogi*. *Misogi* removes the outer layer, takes off the cover, scrapes off the dust. If your eyes are closed, you can't see the light. If you are wearing gloves, you can't feel the earth. *Misogi* cleanses and refines; it opens the eyes and peels off the gloves. Fasting is *misogi*; meditation and prayer are *misogi*. *Keiko* is *misogi*. The path of Aiki is the path of *shugyo*, the day-to-day struggle, the work of education to refine and purify the quality of life.

Originating with the One which split into two, the follower of Kannagara believes that all of humanity is the direct descendant of the gods. The whole world is truly one family. From a lineage of *kami* beginning in the spiritual world of energy and continuing into the material world of matter, man and woman were begotten by the gods and created from their essence. Truly a child of God, each person's bloodstream is His bloodstream; each person's spirit is His. Born of Kami, we return to Kami upon death, the body an impermanent temple that houses the spirit of Kami in the material world. This idea is expressed in the Chinese character for "person," *hito,* which means "to contain the light of God"; and the character for "body," *iki miya,* which literally means "living shrine." As a piece of iron is magnetized by a change in its electrical alignment, love magnetizes all the cells, all the atoms in the human body, and the light of Kami is drawn within.

This gift of life, the light of God, carries with it a profound responsibility. To polish and refine the human spirit so that the world around us may be more clearly reflected, to care for and protect all of creation, is the responsibility shared by all humanity. *Reigi* is often translated as "courtesy" or "etiquette," but the meaning is much richer. *Rei*, also a term for bowing, translates as "Holy Spirit"; *gi* is "manifestation." Bowing to another is the recognition of this responsibility and of the spirit of Kami within each person. In essence it means that although we are different, we are one in origin. Our bodies are different but our spirits the same. Our functions are different, yet we share the same responsibility to God. For the follower of Kannagara it is a responsibility accepted naturally with gratitude and joy.

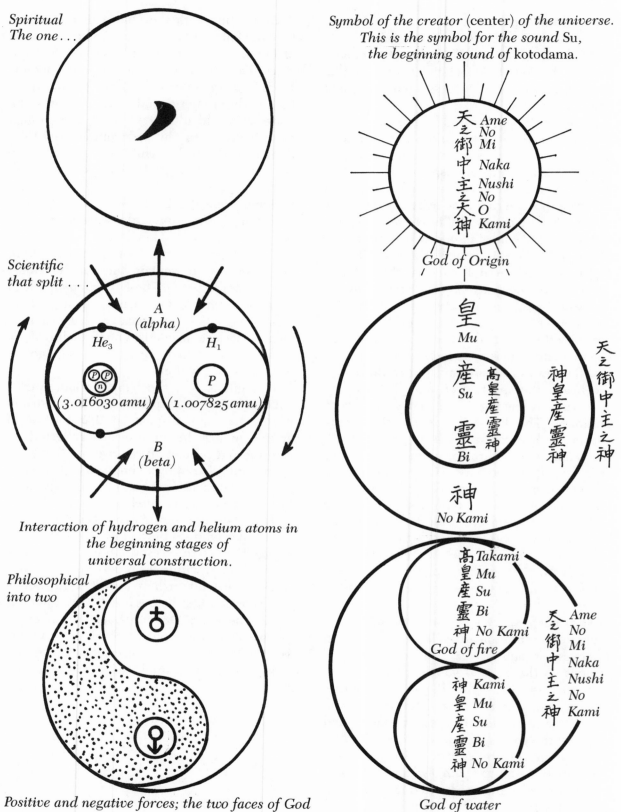

Spiritual
The one . . .

Symbol of the creator (center) of the universe.
This is the symbol for the sound Su,
the beginning sound of kotodama.

Ame
No
Mi
Naka
Nushi
No
O
Kami

God of Origin

Scientific
that split . . .

A
(alpha)

He₃

H₁

P P
n

P

(3.016030 amu)

(1.007825 amu)

B
(beta)

Mu

Su

Bi

No Kami

Interaction of hydrogen and helium atoms in
the beginning stages of
universal construction.

Philosophical
into two

Takami
Mu
Su
Bi
No Kami
God of fire

Ame
No
Mi
Naka
Nushi
No
Kami

Kami
Mu
Su
Bi
No Kami

Positive and negative forces; the two faces of God

God of water

THE HARMONY OF LOVE
A Lecture by the Founder

Aikido is none other than the manifestation of the workings of love. Love gives form to the universe and purifies all things. The universe scatters the seeds from which all things grow; it contains the infinite power which nourishes and allows them to prosper. I gave the name Aiki to the manifold laws of the universe brought forth from love which govern the destiny of the intricate tapestry of life as it is woven on this earth. To carry out the mission of universal compassion on earth, to protect and cultivate all things in nature, this is the task of Aikido.

What is the source of the materialization of life in the universe? It is the expression of the Infinite Spirit and of love. Aikido is a pure expression of that source. It is the original path to the blessed harmony of all humankind with the universe. Only if we follow the Aiki principle of unity with Kami and bring humanity back into balance with all things will we be a part of the infinite growth toward perfection. To bring about the end of malice and suffering is the vital mission entrusted to us by the universe.

The actual forms of the universe are revealed within the human body. We must begin to see the universe within us and awaken to the principles of balance and of love, sacred principles given to us by the universe. The universe unfolds in a never-ending mosaic of many forms; each one a different aspect of its fullness, each one in balance with all others. Just as the universe expresses love in different ways, we must express through our own lives the dynamic balance and harmony of the universe in all of our many relationships. Through this process the universe itself will enter into the human body and spirit, giving nourishment and true power.

All things in the universe come from one source, one creative energy. All things on the earth are the expression of this universal love. The heart of the universe beats in harmony within all of creation and bows in reverence to all of its glories. Each one of us must strive to understand this rhythm and experience the heart of the universe which brings about the harmony of perfect balance. The mission of Aikido follows the absolute path of universal love. Its teachings are the teachings of Kami. Its principles are the laws of harmony and balance in all the elements, in the creation of life on earth. Its function is to join with the heart of the universe and give love.

"The mission of Aikido follows the absolute path of Universal love."—*Morihei Ueshiba*

Ban Yu Ai Go is the mission of Aikido, to love and protect all things. Ai is love. It is not a weak, sentimental love, but the all-powerful universal love.

In Kannagara the counterparts of yin and yang are aramitama, *spirit of firmness and strength, and* nigimitama, *spirit of flexibility and gentleness.*

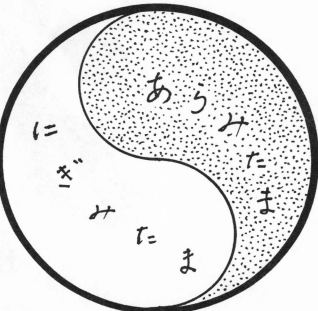

Kami No Hikari: *the Light of God*

The
BEGINNING
of the
UNIVERSE

O Sensei said, "If you want to study Aikido you must study the creation and movement of this universe, the principles of the forces that created it, the flow and function of nature's energy, the movement of the galaxies. All is related, all part of the universal law. The energy forces of life—nuclear reaction, electromagnetic current, gravity—these are Aikido principle and the basis of technique."

The universe did not originate with physical movement. There was no form, only an immense cloud of gas and dust suspended in the darkness. Occasionally a random exchange occurred between atoms, but it held little significance. The power that sent proton colliding into proton with sufficient violence to fuse them into atoms of new elements began with vibration. A tidal wave of creative energy seared the darkness with light and began an infinite process of change and refinement destined to continue for billions of years. In the beginning was vibration; then there was light. An incredible light, it first exploded the aimless movement of subatomic particles and matter into chaos, then began to weld it into

order. In a fever of atomic reaction, an unstoppable wave of power generated enormous heat, and that heat, that energy, that dynamic universal action gave birth to the stars and the galaxies. The breath of God, inhaling and exhaling through centripetal and centrifugal forces, stirred the universal plasma. Formed and bridled by the forces of gravity, the stars in the galaxies and the planets from the nebula around the stars inscribed the signature of their orbits into the void. *Ki* is the essence of that creative energy, the supreme justice that rules that all creation obey the same universal laws.

In the beginning, before the beginning, all matter, all radiation, all space was concentrated in a curved sphere, a celestial vacuum from which the radiation and the matter could not escape. The temperature of the universe was so high that nuclear and electromagnetic forces could not function to bind the basic particles into nuclear and atomic structure. It was in a state of thermal equilibrium in which the dominating force holding the material of the universe together was the force of gravity.

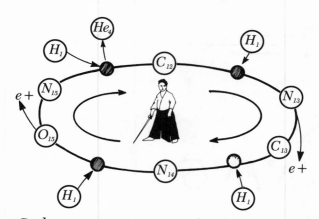

Carbon-nitrogen-oxygen cycle of nuclear energy production at high temperatures in stars

Then the condensed primordial ball of fire exploded, charging the depths with the energy of light, radiation. As the hot, fiery ball began to expand, the existing matter was dissolved in the light as salt dissolves in water. Elementary particles were continuously created and destroyed, forming and annihilating neutron, proton, and electron as the universe rapidly expanded. There was a far greater amount of energy in the radiation than in matter, and the nuclear force was quickly taking control. As the energy of the intense heat supplied the power for the expansion, the temperature of the universe dropped and the speed of the expansion began gradually to decrease, controlled by the gravitational forces acting upon it. The amount of energy in the light relative to the amount in matter decreased, and neutron began to fuse with proton in a fever of nuclear reaction.

Radiation was distributed evenly throughout space, but as the greater amount of energy came to be contained in matter, matter began its domination of the universe. And the power of attraction that causes matter to draw together, the force of gravity, once again became the dominating power controlling the direction of its evolution. The expansion of the universe is thus not infinite, but finite. Matter, too, is finite, for there is no new matter being spontaneously created. A closed cycle, it is believed that our universe will eventually reach

its extreme and begin to contract, condensing energy and matter back to its original fiery state.

We can still witness conditions much like those that existed at the time of physical creation, stretching across our vast and changing universe. Hiding the more distant stars from view, the ever-present clouds of gas and dust, forming a rich, creative medium of the universe, have existed since before creation. Only hydrogen and helium comprised the raw material from which the first generation of stars was created. But during their evolution, the extended time of intense nuclear reaction released at their death an even more creative medium into space. It was material rich in carbon, oxygen, magnesium, calcium, iron, all the material necessary for the miracle of the eventual evolution of life on earth. Floating between the stars, this sparsely distributed matter was the material from which the second generation of stars was formed.

Hundreds of millions of years following the explosion, the universe had grown much brighter, illuminated by countless stars and nebulae. Although endlessly evolving in form and function, the universe was very much the same as it is now. But the individual star never stays the same; it constantly evolves through the changing cycles of development as it processes the raw materials for universal construction. Its core continuously exploding through a chain of violent nuclear reactions, it converts hydrogen to helium to the heavier elements. The greater the mass of the star, the more fevered is the reaction speeding up the process of its evolution. As it completely exhausts its nuclear fuel, there is no way to replace the rapidly escaping energy, and death is inevitable. The internal temperature and pressure of the star drop until it can no longer support its own weight, and the gravitational energy created by the collapse causes intense shock waves to surge from the inside outward. The death takes many forms. The star may explode into a bright, giant star, becoming thousands, even millions of times as luminous, and blow its outer layers into the surrounding space. It may be reduced to a white dwarf, a quiet reminder of its former glory, or, consumed by its own gravity, disappear into an inescapable vacuum in time and space. Whatever form it takes, the remains of what was once the awesome spectacle of a star silently abides in its celestial tomb, awaiting rebirth and a renewal of evolution according to the laws of the Creator.

With the same spirit and observing the same laws, Aikido technique is created. It must begin as all of creation began, from the physical purity of no-form, no-time, no-space, originating not with the detection of physical movement, but with the perception of vibration. An open, flexible attitude, receptive to change, is essential. Only a reflecting surface of intense clarity, extending pure spiritual vibration into space, will catch the enemy's spirit in the returning echo. No thought, no ego, no opinion or judgment must cloud the surface, for it is this reflection, charged and influenced by both vibrations, which creates a reaction and defines the physical form. The resonance of spiritual breathing, expansion-contraction, the exchange of vibration and energy, produces the fever that spontaneously creates, through a strict adherence to the laws of God, the exact application to bring harmony and order. In one immeasurable micro-unit of time, everything fuses—spirit, mind, and body—in answer to the enemy's vibration.

"*Katsu hayabi*—in a single instant, perceiving the movement of the enemy's spirit, I understand exactly. There is no time, no space, only the universe as it is," said Morihei Ueshiba. In that instant, as the explosion of spiritual power manifests itself, the physical laws of the universal movement are embodied. The unseen essence of *ki* becomes a visible reality, assuming the dynamic shape at the foundation of all the energies of existence, the spiral. The movement of the spiral is revealed at the beginning of physical creation in the electromagnetic vibration of light. Any given point on a photon, a spinning orb of light energy, will describe the shape of a spiral helix. The earth

around the sun and the sun as it moves in the galaxy follow this path. The rhythm of the spiral is expressed in the influences of the moon upon the earth in the movement of the waters and the changing of the seasons. It is inherent in the continuing process of evolution and the cycles of ecological existence. We discover the spiral helix in the structure of amino acids and in the proteins that result from their combination. And found in the nucleus of every living cell is genetic material capable of reproducing itself, the DNA molecule. The physical essence of life functions in the shape of a double helix. From the circulation of blood in the human body to the burrowing of a mole into the earth, the shape of the spiral is obvious in the movement patterns and structural patterns of the natural world that surrounds us. A chilling gust of wind lifts powdery snow from a mountain peak in soft, swirling clouds. Falling in slow, spinning arcs, a withered leaf ripples the surface of a quiet pond. The seas are lifted and the boundary between land and water disappears as the tensions of the atmosphere are released in the awesome power of a hurricane.

O Sensei recognized the harmony and power of this movement. He saw and understood the creative process from which all things evolved. Aikido is creation: the creation of harmony and justice from violence, a positive energy creating light from the darkness. The physical movement must embody the principles of the spirit. Negative power is to be met, not with conflict, but joined, interpreted, and redirected through the power and balance of spiral movement. When the enemy attacks, meet him with the confidence of insight. Draw him into your center and re-create the dynamics and power of the galaxy's movement. Through the dictates of the spirit, the body can create the force of gravity, it can create a vacuum, surround itself with a magnetic field of energy. This can be accomplished only through an intimate and functioning knowledge of the principles of balance, the reactions and relationships of energy, universal law. The critical timing and control can

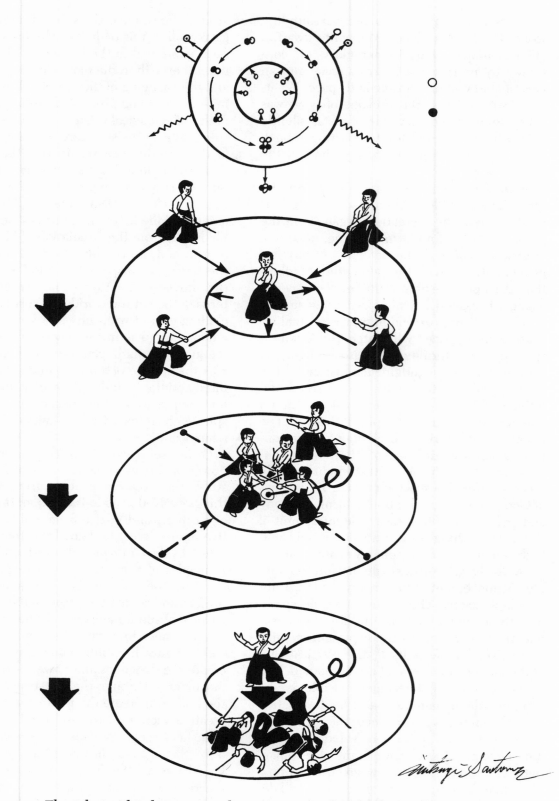

The relationship between nuclear reaction and multiple attack

In this sequence nage *gains possession of one of the weapons and uses it on the remaining attacker. Ken Nissen and Ellis Amdur, uke. Photo by Carl Shiraishi.*

The movement of a comet and ryote mochi kokyu nage

Kevin Choate, uke

Solar flare

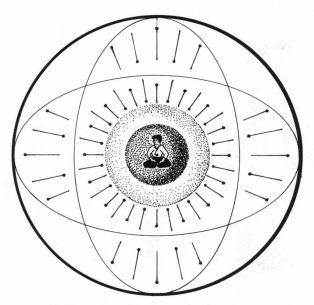

The echo of spiritual vibration

only be achieved through a body that is strong and liberated by constant study and training.

Almost every day I received *ukemi* (the techniques of falling, the act of receiving the force and saving yourself from injury) from O Sensei, and through those experiences I slowly began to grasp the connection of the movements of Aikido with the movements of the universe. Many of those times remain vivid, a flashback as clear as this moment and deeply remembered; every nerve in my body contains its own individual living memory of the feel of his power. It is not an intellectual memory, but one of emotion and sensation, and in the attempt to give it voice lies the danger of misunderstanding.

The Founder's signature.   Katsu hayabi.

Ukemi

In the earth's movement around the sun, the sun's movement through the galaxy, and other patterns of the natural world, the shape of the spiral is evident.

Yokomenuchi kaitennage. *Bruce Merkle*, uke.

The dynamic structural pattern of the spiral and its application in the nikyo *technique.*

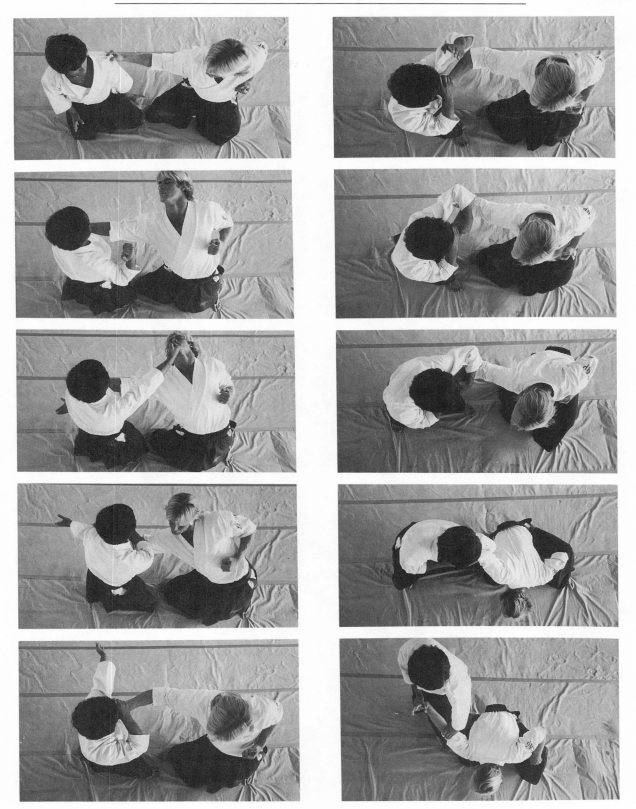

Robert Moller, uke

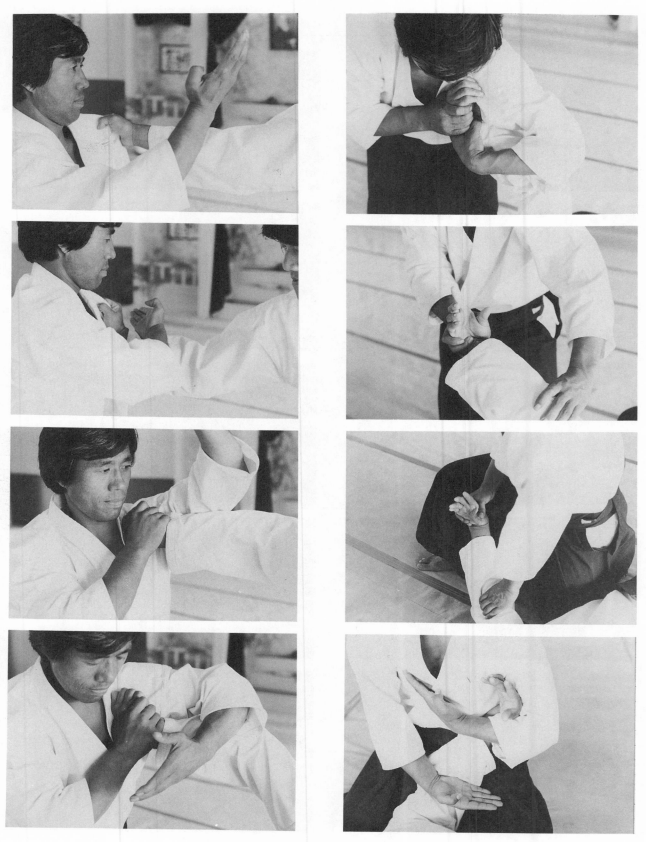

Kata dori nikyo. *Ikeda*, shihan, uke

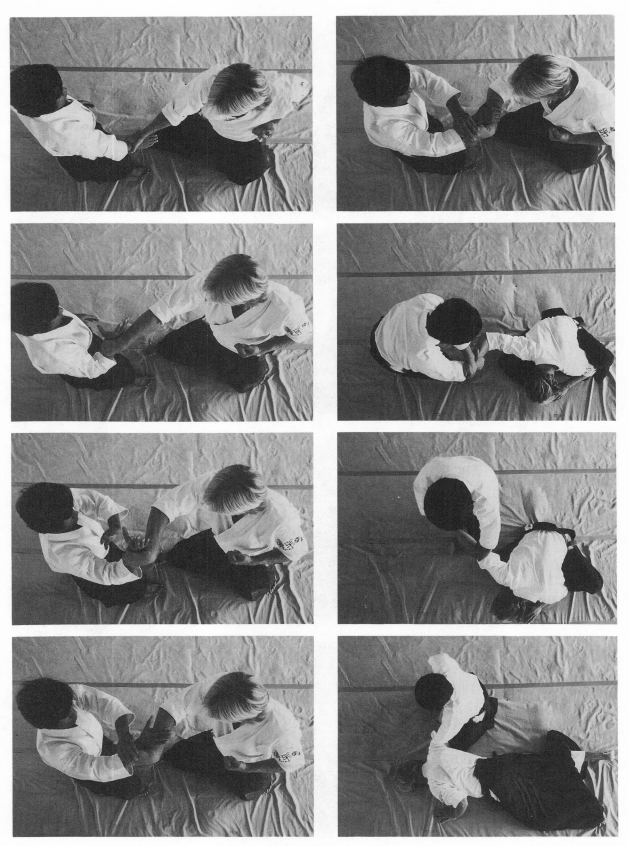

Kata dori nikyo. *Robert Moller*, uke.

The negative force joined and redirected, shomenuchi iriminage. *Bruce Merkle,* uke.

If a child who had never tasted sugar should ask, "What does it taste like?," your reply might be, "It is sweet." But what is sweetness? How can a taste be explained in words? Each person tastes differently. Past experience, knowledge, and personality are all determining factors in an individual's reaction to a particular taste. It must be experienced to be fully understood.

Do not see my experience through the clouded eyes of a mystic, but with the clear, crisp vision of a seeker of truth. The experience, and my interpretation of it changing and growing with time, has been so vital and is still so vital to my search for Aiki that I must try to give it voice.

During the demonstration of a technique at practice as O Sensei's *uke,* I attacked him with all my power, and my only thought was to strike him down. The walls of the *dojo* shook as his *kiai* shattered the air, and my entire body was imprisoned by the shock. (*Kiai* is the release of spiritual and physical power in the form of a piercing scream originating in the lower abdomen.) I perceived the power of a hurricane; the violent winds of a typhoon

Kiai

lashed my body. And the force of his gravity, drawn from the energies of the universe, sucked me deep into the vacuum of a "black hole" from which there was no escape. Deep within my core a bomb exploded, and the whole universe expanded. There was nothing but light—blinding, searing light and energy. I could not see or feel my body, and the only reality was the enormous energy expanding

"And the force of his gravity sucked me deep into the vacuum of a 'black hole' from which there was no escape."

from it. For those watching, it happened in the split of a second, but for me time had stopped. There was no time, no space, no sound, no color, and the silence was more deafening than his scream. In the light so completely, I was the light, and my mind and spirit were illuminated and completely clear. Then I was unconscious. As my body connected with the tatami mat, I was revived.

Still now, I don't completely understand receiving *ukemi* from O Sensei. My consciousness returns to those experiences time and time again, the flashback vivid and total. But sometimes I'm immersed in blinding light, complete light, and sometimes it is a complete dark, black world—in the same way that a piece of dry ice is so cold that it burns you when you touch it. Maybe my physical and spiritual situation is different and that affects my memory of the light or darkness. But the memory is always breathing and full of life.

I would often receive *ukemi* from O Sensei at early morning class, sometimes being thrown as far as thirty feet, and the rest of the

O Sensei's irimi *movement three years before his passing. M. Saotome, uke.*

day the stiff pole of my backbone would be loosened and flexible. Physically and spiritually I was very clear: no confusion, almost no ego, cleansed and refreshed, my demons purged.

O Sensei taught, "The principles of the true harmony of Aikido can be found by training in the principles of gravity." Gravity is within all things and affects all things; there is no escape from its force. It cannot be altered or interrupted by any presence or counterforce. It controls energy as well as matter; time slows down and space is warped by its pull. The great organizer that made possible the reactions of nuclear and electromagnetic force, it creates order from chaos in the structuring of the galaxies, the stars, and the planets.

In that first great explosion of creativity, the universal energy was shattered in two; the richness and diversity of the universe began as a new order, and unity was created. This is the respiration of God, the universal flow between the extremes of unity.

God is fire and water, light and air. He is centrifugal and centripetal, yin and yang. God is dynamic movement and God is unity. From the origin to now, the universe has been con-

tinuously creating and refining according to the principles of universal creativity, the principles of opposites. These principles working within the body make life. In order to truly understand this we must empty ourselves of ego, for ego is the boundary that sets limits on the human spirit.

Often we misunderstand and think that we are controlled by gravity or that gravity is attachment. But, as witnessed in the power of the collapsed star, the greatest force of gravity is emptiness, the gravity created by a vacuum. True emptiness is the absence of selfish ego. Not understanding this principle, we try to refine our physical strength. This is narrow strength. It is not the strength of reality, but a transparent covering that is easily penetrated. No ego is the character of God, and character emptied of selfish ego draws love, respect, and trust. This is true power.

When you have no ego, no commands, no orders, no selfishness, then your life and the universe are the same world. When you stand at this point of emptiness, there is no fence between you and the universal power. There are no territorial boundaries, so the energy flows freely, unobstructed, not from the self but from the infinite power of the universe.

O Sensei said, "My energy, my power, is not controlled by me. I am empty, but through my body flows the energies of the universe. My power is not my power. This is the universal power."

"Saotome," he told me, "you attack a typhoon, a hurricane, a tornado. You are punching air, the clouds, a mountain. What do you feel when you strike the sun?"

When people think, "I am free," they usually think so for selfish, cunning reasons. They want to do something, or want to have something, or want to be something. Attachment to desires is not freedom. True freedom is emptiness. If you are completely empty, God's spirit will bless you, for then you are one with the universe and one with the Creator.

The Way of harmony is not an easy path. Truth will not enlighten a lazy spirit. It is a Way filled with the hard work, sweat, and pain

"I am not a man, I am the universe itself." — *Morihei Ueshiba*

of reality, for conflict must be experienced and understood. The physical experience of conflict is frustrating and demanding, but the greatest frustration, the most exhausting demand on the spirit, is the struggle to subdue the ego as you strive for personal refinement and ultimately the refinement of society. But it is also a Way filled with the intensity of challenge as the spirit is made fertile for the joys of growth.

"I am not a man, I am the universe itself," said Morihei Ueshiba. This is not theology. It is truth. We are truly created from the material of the stars, the light of God, for we too began with the great explosion of light. All the known elements were created from the reaction of that surging energy. And as the death of a star releases the substance of its creation back into the universe to be used yet again, our bodies will return to the dust of the earth to await their ultimate release at the death of the sun.

Aikido energy flow and the movement of energy in a quark

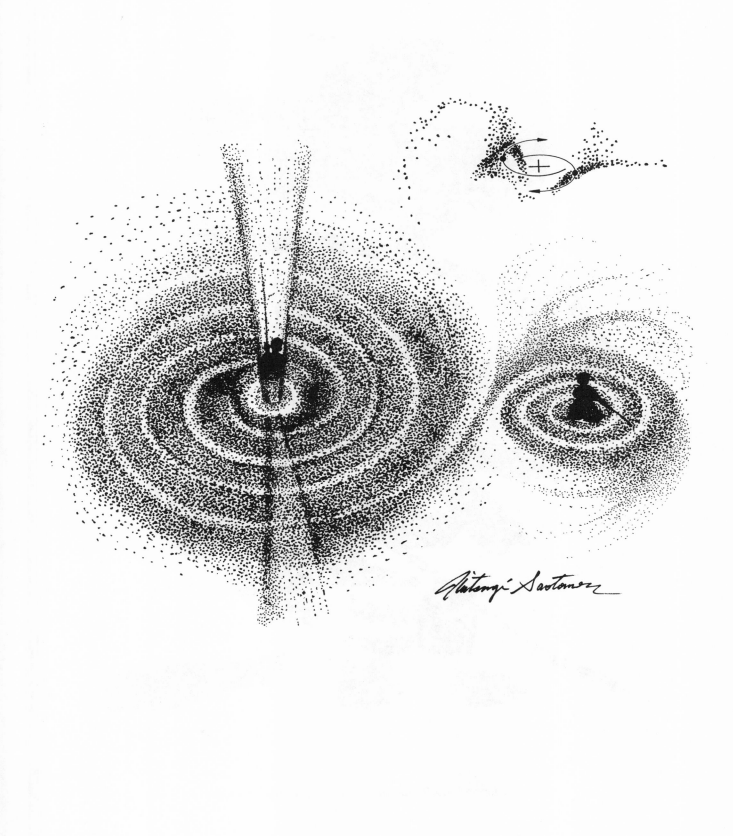

Takama hara *is the all-encompassing universe.*

4

PERSPECTIVE on TRUTH

We are in the universe, and in fact we *are* the universe. Yet, blind to its reality, we see a vast and lifeless expanse in which a realm of living organisms maintains its separate existence on the earth. The evolution of the earth and of life on the earth is a continuing cycle of the same laws and the same material that created the universe. Organic matter cannot be separated from inorganic. From the time of the ancient scholars and philosophers to today's molecular biologists using modern technologies, we have, each in our own way, tried to solve the mysteries of the reality and the function of life.

O Sensei was a deeply spiritual man, and when he spoke, he spoke in spiritual terms. His lectures on Aikido philosophy and the responsibility and meaning of life were filled with the names and images of God. Most people found it difficult to understand the ancient Shinto names for the many gods and the spiritual concepts contained within their utterance. But O Sensei said, "Religion is science." He spoke of universal law, and the names of the gods were the names of natural phenom-

ena: centripetal and centrifugal forces, fire, water, the wind, the sea. I realized that to understand the true spiritual meanings, I must also study science. It was through this study that the spiritual meanings were made clear. Had my search been confined to the study of Shinto and spiritual thought, my thinking would have narrowed more and more, and I would have been lost in the echo of God's name, buried in symbolic truths without understanding the reality that they symbolized.

The religious myth is the first form of science and has served humanity well. It fostered, through necessity, a moral code of conduct that fortunately lives in our subconscious still. The dawnings of civilization and of creativity are inexorably tied to religious myth and to our great need to believe in our own divinity. The biblical account of the Creation has its roots in early Egyptian and Babylonian myth, the ancient word *adam* meaning soil or clay. According to Genesis, God molded the dust of the earth into a figure of clay and by His breath filled it with life and a Divine Spirit. This was Adam. In this context man was made;

he was physically sculpted by a personified deity, an act of creative love that the primitive mind could more easily understand.

Stories such as these were beginning exercises in intellect and creativity. Unique in our drive to define existence and in some way ensure our individual immortality, we tried to uncover the explanations for a world we did not understand and could not control. These myths and legends are certainly not wrong. They are symbolic truths and should be understood as the intuitive and poetic wisdom of ancient peoples as they looked upon nature, as their attempt to communicate their understanding that life is a product of the natural world. Yet from many of these ancient civilizations we have found evidence of deep knowledge and incredible accomplishments that could not be merely accidental: the geometry of the Alhambra, the mathematics and startlingly accurate astronomical calculations of the Maya, the incredible sophistication of the Pyramid of Cheops, the engineering marvel of the Great Wall of China. But most of this knowledge was destroyed and buried because of narrow-mindedness and fear, sentencing humanity to ignorance for centuries yet to come.

The great spiritual leaders and prophets throughout history have been men of deep wisdom and enlightened knowledge, yet their teachings have always taken the form of parables and myths. Perhaps the limitations of the spoken form of communication and the limited knowledge of the people forced them to use the myth as metaphor. Then, as the teachings were handed down from generation to generation, translated from language to language, the true and intuitive meaning was often lost in the telling. Perhaps it is as written in the New Testament (Matthew 13:10–14):

> And the disciples came, and said unto him, Why speakest thou unto them in parables? He answered and said unto them, Because it is given unto you to know the mysteries of the kingdom of heaven, but to them it is not given. Therefore speak I to them in parables: because they seeing see not; and hearing they hear not,

neither do they understand. And in them is fulfilled the prophecy of Esaias, which saith, by hearing ye shall hear, and shall not understand; and seeing ye shall see, and shall not perceive.

Unfortunately, later generations took these deeply symbolic stories as literal fact. The stories were comfortable and gave us a spiritual formula to follow, freedom from responsibility and the ever-present possibility of escape by miraculous intervention. A man scrambles up the side of a mountain; a rock breaks away and he falls. The final seconds of his life will be spent desperately praying for the miracle of the hand of God to reach out and rescue him from the unyielding earth below. Never mind the law of gravity; the individual wants a personal miracle. Stubbornly clinging to the spir-

itual concept of God's "right" to govern the universe by miracle rather than by natural law, we subconsciously want to believe that "I and I alone" am above and exempt from the laws that govern nature.

New ideas and continual challenges to the accepted definitions of life have jolted our consciousness time and again as new methods of scientific inquiry are developed. Filled with complexity, the questions of life and of humanity's relationship to the universe are closely connected to our ego, the way in which we perceive ourselves, and the spiritual and philosophical truths by which we live. The old ideas, comfortable and deeply rooted, do not die easily.

When Copernicus first advocated the heliocentric theory that the earth revolves around the sun, it shook the very foundation of religious belief and became a heated issue in the religious courts. People believed that it threatened the idea that an almighty God had created nature, that it threatened their firm conviction that the glories of the heavens must spin around the earth, with man at the center of the universe. But it was Galileo Galilei with his telescope and his innovative scientific methods who became the real victim of their prejudice, for he believed that the laws that rule the universe and the laws that govern life must be the same. In *The Starry Messenger*, the 1610 publication of his astronomical observations, he sought to prove that Copernicus was right. Caught up in the religious conflicts and struggles for authority and power of the time, Galileo was persecuted, threatened with torture, and forbidden to ever speak of his beliefs again. It would take almost three hundred and seventy years for the church to officially absolve him of his guilt.

Darwin's concept of the origin of the species by natural selection was met with ridicule and anger. People once more felt that it threatened the divinity of humankind and challenged the very existence of God and a Divine Creation. In a 1950 BBC broadcast the Anglican canon C. E. Raven explained, "That creation was a process, not an act, continuous, not intermit-

tent, operating through the orderly sequence of natural events, upset the whole idea of a God outside the world who set it going, and then on special occasion intervened by miracle to alter its course. We can now see that such an idea was never satisfactory; and in fact, was not the belief of St. Paul or the first great Christian theologians."

The study of the cell has shown that there is life in every organ, tissue, and individual cell, as well as life processes in each phase of their existence. The cell is our role model, and the requirements imposed by our limited knowledge, which distinguishes living from nonliving, have separated organic from inorganic, animal from mineral. But now, as we are coming to understand universal phenomena and the phenomena of life itself through the same atomic structure of matter, we have discovered that there are processes of birth, growth, and death even in molecules, atoms, and elementary particles. The presence of these processes signifies that life of another definition does exist. As we explore the microscopic realms of inorganic material, we find a world

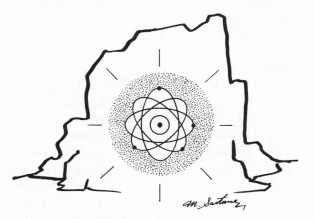

of intelligent activity in the functioning of those tiny particles of matter (energy). We must admit that in their orderly movement, there is consciousness. In considering life more deeply, we find that it is an essential component of all the natural world. All mass consisting of the vibratory activity of atomic structure has consciousness. Inorganic materials, rocks, minerals, and soil, all serve to nourish life and have played a vital role in its evolution. The progressive development from inorganic to organic and the evolution of life from simple to complex forms must be acknowledged as one continuous living flow that connects the past with the present and leads us to an appreciation and understanding of the natural generation of life.

Perhaps in another system, with other planets circling a different sun, there is also life, maybe in a distant galaxy, possibly in another part of our own galaxy. There may even be a life form that we are as yet unable to recognize on one of our neighboring planets. The discovery of extraterrestrial life of a different form would be of enormous value in understanding our own life systems. Opening our minds, it would give us the gift of another perspective, a new way of seeing, as we examine our own world and our relationship to it.

The whole universe is alive; every atom is alive with its own form of consciousness. But, as far as we know, the incredible circumstances that brought about the maturation of life forms of a higher consciousness, life as we recognize it, gave its expression to only one planet in the system of the sun. Why was only the earth blessed with these elements? Was it chance, a miracle? Or was it the product of a great design, of natural laws written by an unimaginable intelligence? The actual formation of the sun and the development and evolution of life on earth is filled with unsolved questions. There have been many theoretical answers that become more and more sophisticated as humanity continues to evolve. At best, they are only theory, educated guesses set in a statement concerning the probability of consecutive occurrence. We understand the sequence in which various chemical components condense out of a hot gas as it cools. We believe that only specific densities of condensed matter could survive the tidal disruption of the sun at a given distance. In ways such as this we try to understand the formation, position, and chemical structure of the earth, and the conditions that made possible the evolution of fragile life processes. We will

probably never know for certain, but if we lose sight of these questions and no longer try to understand the special qualities that promoted life, nor try to understand the delicate balance in which we exist, we are doomed.

The phenomena of life are a part of the miracle of the universal drama. The stage of this drama is the earth, and the source of energy for its production is the nuclear power of the sun (fire) and the primeval oceans (water). The Oparin "coacervate theory" of the spontaneous generation of life from inorganic matter is widely supported. This development is now understood as one small part of the history of the earth's development, which is an even smaller part of the history of universal evolution. Scientists have explained most of the life processes as a result of chemical action and reaction. The changing of the elements of sun, water, and earth into vital, life-sustaining nutrients, the very beginnings of life on earth, have been so defined. But then, is that the whole answer?

It is believed that the life history of the universe occupies some thirteen billion years in time as we measure it. Our own evolution through time, space, and matter, originating with the simplicity of the single-cell protozoans and ascending to the deep complexities that define *Homo sapiens*, is worthy of awe and wonder. The functioning of millions of cells and their interaction to create a living, functioning entity is a profound and holy miracle. You must think deeply, not only with your mind, but with your heart, your spirit. Who wrote the laws that control this great evolution of energy? From what inscrutable source comes the energy that permeates this universe and gives it life? And what is life? Is it only the narrow definition of organic process that we have given it? Science can attempt to explain, but looking to science alone is as narrow as clinging only to parables. According to the nature of science, further research is done, more questions arise, and gradually the original question is buried by specialization. Finely divided and specialized knowledge does not necessarily give an objective insight into life, for its parts cannot be divided if it is to function as life.

A plate is dropped and shatters. You can put the pieces back together again to obtain the original shape, but its function is not necessarily restored. The plate has been changed by your interference and can never be the same. Life must be understood in its original state as part of a living environment. The moment we isolate, measure, and judge, we have become a part of its reality, effecting change, and we cannot know its truths. In order to understand nature and the universe, we need to realize the limitations of science. Performed by mortals, understanding is incomplete, for there can be no objectivity. The science of humanity can only serve to illuminate God's love. Between scientific truth and spiritual truth there must be no separation.

Once a theologian asked O Sensei, "How do you account for the fact that no matter how hard we pray for peace in this world, we witness so much conflict all around us?" The Founder replied:

"There is an imbalance between the discoveries of physical science and the discoveries of the spirit. For a long time now, great emphasis has been placed on technological advances, while spiritual growth has largely been ignored. This enormous gap must be closed for the universal mechanisms to operate smoothly on this earth. There must be balance. The two factors, the physical and the spiritual, must feed and enhance each other, working together in harmony.

"God has given us a physical expression to serve for the refinement of our spirit within this world and the universe. To this end, we must nurture the body, but the body in turn must follow the conscience of the spirit with total obedience. The body must be trained as the guardian of the soul and as the guardian of the light of God on this earth. We must polish the vehicles through which we experience the wisdom of the universe. By hearing and seeing clearly, by smelling, tasting, and touching with sensitivity, and by opening the heart, mind, and spirit, we shall experience and per-

ceive the full truth of God. In this way, we shall cultivate the virtues of the universal spirit on this earth. We shall bind together as one, the divine essence, the universe, and the expression of our lives.

"It is my belief that physical science can be advanced for the enrichment of humanity rather than its destruction only through further developing the science of the subconscious mind and of the spirit. Only by the interwoven growth of the two shall we approach a closer relationship between heaven and earth.

"People argue about which God should be worshipped and disagree over what name He shall be called. This is not spiritual development, but spiritual stagnation. This kind of debate will never lead to an understanding of the workings of the universe nor to the discovery of the uncounted manifestations of Kami. No understanding of the Creator is possible without an understanding of compassion and of the Creation. Without an intuitive perception of the intricacies of the process of creation, one cannot experience the truth of Aiki.

"Every life, every speck of matter, every element or vibration is an integral part of the whole which is the Creator. As children of the Creator and a part of the Creator, we must not pollute, nor destroy, nor distort, nor damage in any way even the smallest part of that which He created. We are responsible for nurturing the riches of this earth; we must cherish all the delicate jewels of life entrusted to our care. If even one person will see this clearly, the *ki* of the universe will naturally permeate that enlightened being. He shall be the echo of God generating positive vibrations and actions to influence others.

"And Takama Hara, the spirit of the universe, will be found within. You will search the farthest reaches of the earth and explore the endless expanse of the skies in vain, for you will not find it. Takama Hara is with you al-

ways. You need only realize that Takama Hara, the creative structure of the universe, is the creative structure of your own body. All the elements and patterns of the universe are within the human form, charged with the spirit of God's creativity. Why must you seek elsewhere for Takama Hara?

"Such is the Way of true Budo. Understand the universe as the masterpiece of Kami. Understand that all things are the reflections of Kami's many forms. It is the science without equal. It is the science of Truth. The future of humanity depends on such wisdom. The prayers for peace and prosperity will be answered if we but perceive this earth as a reflection of the universe itself. Aikido must share the burden and the joy of establishing a world in which all things are respected and all things are honored for their true spirit, where all things are allowed to express their true nature, each with its own value, within its own time and its own space. Without this spirit of chivalry for all things, Aikido will cease to exist."

During a worldwide tour after his flight into space, the American astronaut John Glenn and his son visited Japan. In his honor a special demonstration of Aikido was given by O Sensei at Meiji Gakuin University. After the demonstration Master Morihei Ueshiba and Captain John Glenn were introduced and shook hands. O Sensei was profoundly interested in Captain Glenn's impressions and thoughts as he traveled through space, so he asked through interpreter Keijiro Nunoi, U.S. Ambassador and Immigrations Officer, what in fact he had felt. Glenn replied that as he looked at the earth and the cosmos that surrounded him, he deeply believed that this universe is God's living garden. O Sensei smiled and said, "Spiritual teachings and modern science are exactly the same. Science bears witness to the power of God."

(Left) *The author prepares to attack O Sensei in a special demonstration for Captain John Glenn.*

John Glenn (far left) and interpretor Keijiro Nunoi (far right) look on as O Sensei shakes hands with Glenn's son.

Shizen tota *is nature's adjustment.*

5

The HARMONY *of* NATURE'S JUSTICE

My *dojo* is nature; it is the universe. It is truly a dwelling, a *dojo* and a temple built by Kami. It you look with the eyes of your heart, it is the teacher that possesses the scientific and spiritual truth which will lead you to enlightenment. It is all the sacred scriptures. The laws of nature have come into being through the function of love, the absolute harmony found in the unfolding process of creation. It is imperative that those on the path of Aikido practice with these things held deep within their hearts. — Morihei Ueshiba

The earth is a living organism, and life as we recognize it is only a part of its process. It breathes in a twice-daily tidal motion controlled by the gravitational influences of the sun and moon as it speeds through space. The land on which we carry out our lives is structured on the flowing framework of the earth's dynamic interior as the many strata of rock between the hot liquid core and the surface shift and change. Acts of creation and destruction, birth and death, continue unseen and often unnoticed by the relative insensitivity of human perception. But the results become evident as the powerful crustal plates are driven against one another, crumpling billions of tons of rock into great mountain chains. At one location on the planet, a volcano breaks the surface of the oceans, belching the fiery material from the center of the earth to form new land masses, while in another, the earth trembles from seismic shocks as earthquakes split its crust. Earthquake and volcano are the yin and the yang, powerful physical expression of the same process. The ocean surface interacts with the atmosphere affecting climatic conditions around the world. This constant exchange of the energy of the sun results in the rise and fall of the great ocean swells and the quiet power of the circulation in the depths of the seas. It is expressed in the erosion of beach and cliff as the surf assaults the shore, in the sudden exploding force of screaming winds and pounding rains, and in the giant waves that sweep across an entire ocean to devastate the lands within their path. Labeled as destructive violence by the narrow vision of humanity's ego, the natural phenomena of volcano, earthquake, tidal wave, and typhoon are nature's immaculate system of adjustment, the mighty force of harmony.

The earth undergoes its endless cycle of growth and decay, causing continually changing patterns of sea, mountain, and plain. It builds and develops but at the same time balances this activity by constant erosion of that which it has created by water, ice, and wind, chemical action, and life. In this unique thin zone where the high-density material of the geosphere, soil and rock, and the hydrosphere, water, meets the low-density atmosphere, all things are extremely unstable and change rapidly to promote the balance of the whole, from extreme to balance, always back to balance. The earth, its oceans, and the atmosphere meet and influence one another through their mutual contact. Temperature and pressure undergo kaleidoscopic changes. A delicate membrane pulsating with life covers the earth, where innumerable beings are born, live, and in time are returned to the earth. They develop and change, constantly refining their existence and the existence of their successors. Here nature's laws are harsh and without exception. If a life form, any life form, cannot change and adapt, it will perish, for the balancing of nature will continue. This, the biosphere, is a place of endless development, creation, and destruction.

We talk of nature's harmony, our eyes soften, and we see in our imagination a blue sky with fleecy white clouds reflected in a quiet pond. The song of the birds echoes from leafy branches. A soft, warm breeze lightly brushes our face as it waves the tall grasses, and we smile as the lion lies down with the lamb. This image contains the too-sweet smell of decay. The lion will die of starvation. The sheep will overpopulate the area and destroy the tall grasses that anchor the soil. The rich topsoil will be washed away, the pond will dry up, and the sheep will die unnourished. The trees will die, and the only sound, the sound of the wind, will echo in a parched and lifeless desert.

Every impression, every idea flows through the distorted filter of individual ego, and humanity is plagued with a nearsighted tunnel vision. We sharply separate harmony and conflict, defining harmony as soft and good, and conflict as harsh and evil; with each person standing in the center of his or her own private universe, we decide what is fair from the limited perspective of one individual participating in his or her own space at his or her own immediate timing. We do not comprehend the all-encompassing harmony of nature, nor truly understand the exquisite justice of the Creator's universal laws. Harmony does not mean that there are no conflicts, for the dynamic spiral of existence embraces both extremes. Conflict is the beginning of harmony as death is the beginning of life. Filled with conflict, the flow of nature remains flexible enough to adapt and change, bringing all of creation back into balance.

Nature's balance is process, the process of recycling. The word *infinite* has captured the poetic imagination of man, yet more and more we are beginning to understand that it cannot describe the earth, its resources, or even the universe. Only the creative vibration of God is infinite. We live in a finite world of cycles as carbon, nitrogen, oxygen, elements that blessed the earth from the nuclear fires of ancient stars, pass in an instant of universal time through the bodies of living organisms and return to the soil, the water, and the air. The cyclic lives of organisms are systems of energy conversion, the consumers living at the expense of the producers and the decomposers returning the material of the dead to the earth. Even the cycles are so closely woven that there is no clear separation of one from the other.

Dancing prisms of sunlight strike a green leaf laced with morning dew. Much more than a rich and moving visual experience, this phenomenon is the gift of breath and nourishment. It is the process responsible for the utilization and replenishment of carbon (the

The mighty force of harmony, sumi otoshi. *Shigeru Suzuki,* shihan dai, uke.

The effect of a mountain on the flow of air currents around it and shomenuchi kokyunage.

Kevin Choate, uke

The flow of a river and the flow of another kokyunage.

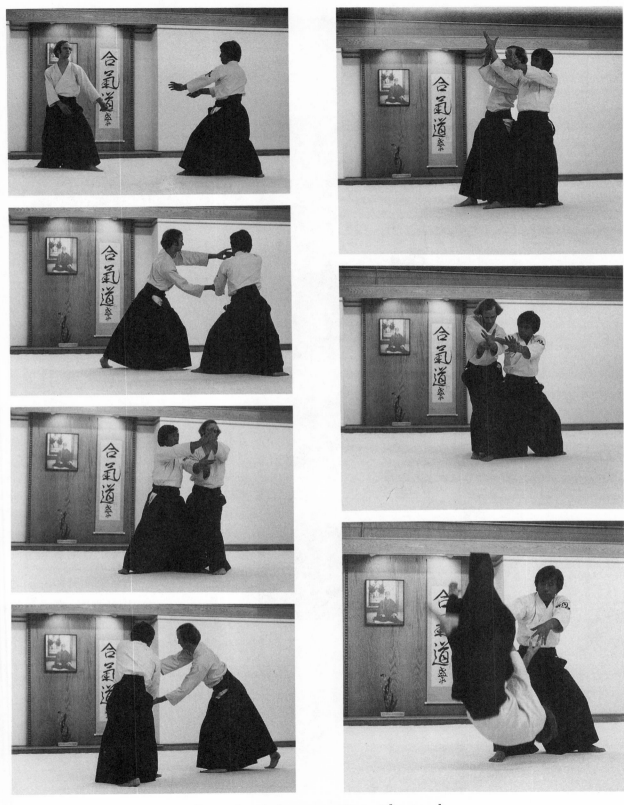

Ryote dori kokyunage. *Kevin Choate*, uke.

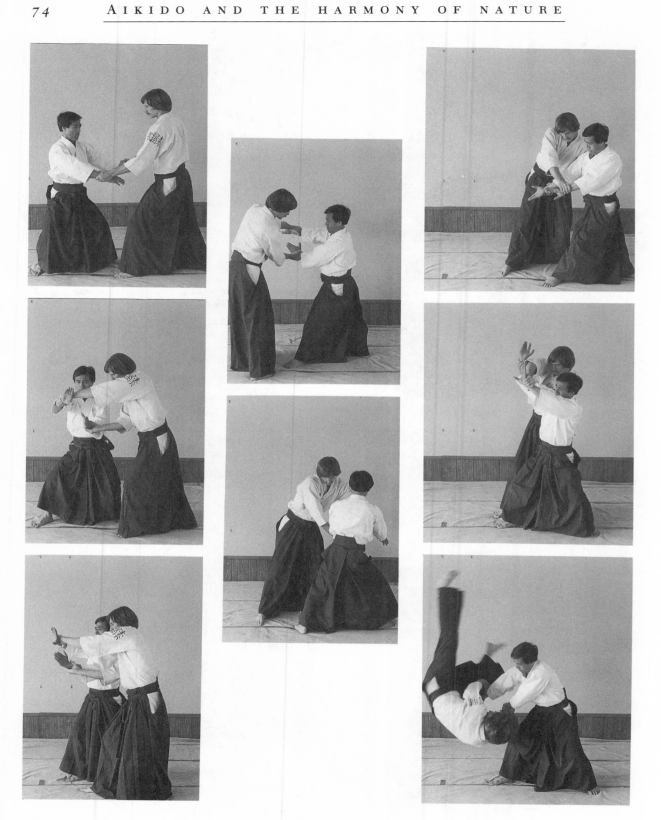

Ryote dori kokyunage. *Bruce Merkle*, uke.

carbon cycle), upon which all life is structured. The green plants, the producers, capture the life-giving energy of the sun and, using the spectrum from red to violet and blue, process carbon dioxide and water, and the chemicals of the earth into living tissue. The byproduct of this elegant process, photosynthesis, is oxygen, giving life forms on earth the fuel for their existence. The consumers, the animal kingdom of which we are a part, then eat the living tissue, inhale the oxygen, and break down the fuel molecules. Releasing the energy back into the atmosphere, they exhale carbon dioxide as they carry out their life processes. But the cycle is not yet complete. The bodies of all living organisms contain great amounts of stored chemical substances. These substances are only borrowed for their time of life and upon the death of the organism must be returned to the earth to be used by other awaiting life forms.

The soil, rich with the remains of former living beings, is the womb of life and the source of its nourishment. With each turn of the seasons, another thin layer of organic material is carefully laid down, forming the natural features of our land. In time it will decay and become transformed into lifegiving soil, rich in the elements necessary for survival. This is the job of the remaining ecological group, the decomposers. Without the bacteria and viruses, the fungi, molds, and mosses, the microorganisms that produce the decay of organic matter, carbon and the other elements in wastes and dead organisms would become locked there forever. The cycle would slow down and eventually come to a complete halt and with it life.

The purpose of soil fertilization is not the direct replenishment of the essential nutrients in the food we grow, but the encouragement of an increase in the soil's microorganisms and the stimulation of their activity. Some utilize hydrogen sulfide, carbon monoxide, and other substances harmful to most animal life. Others take the dead bodies of animals and plants as their source of energy, restoring them to the earth as usable nutrients. Performing the function of *misogi*, they cleanse and purge, enabling the consumers to eventually be of use to their benefactors. It may seem ironic; nature could survive quite well without humanity, but it could not survive without the decomposers. The tremendous significance of photosynthesis should be clear. Animal life as it now exists could not have developed without it. Not only do the plants supply directly or indirectly one hundred percent of our food, but they also produce the oxygen that is essential for its utilization.

> And the Lord God formed man of the dust of the ground, and breathed into his nostrils the breath of life; and man became a living soul. (Genesis 2:7)

To live we must breathe—in Japanese, *kokyu*. We can survive for weeks without food, for days without water, but we cannot stop breathing for more than a few minutes. It is the oxygen that we receive through respiration that gives the brain the energy to conduct all parts of the body in its incredible symphony of existence. Referring to a biology text, you will find that the general equation for respiration is the reverse of the equation for photosynthesis. In a highly efficient process, the same amount of sugar yields many, many times more energy through respiration than through fermentation, the original process for obtaining life energy.

Respiration is not merely the physical inhalation and exhalation by the body, for this is but an auxiliary movement found only in higher animals. The phenomenon of respiration shared by nearly all organisms is a chemical process of renewal that takes place within each cell, the oxidation of organic substances, producing energy. Only a small part of this energy is used immediately; the rest is stored for later use with the aid of a phosphorus compound, adenosine triphosphate (ATP). This extraordinary system of energy storage and retrieval was, after respiration, the next task accomplished by developing life forms.

There is a geochemical side of this complex system that is an important part of the carbon

A waterfall and an entering form of kokyunage

Kevin Choate, uke

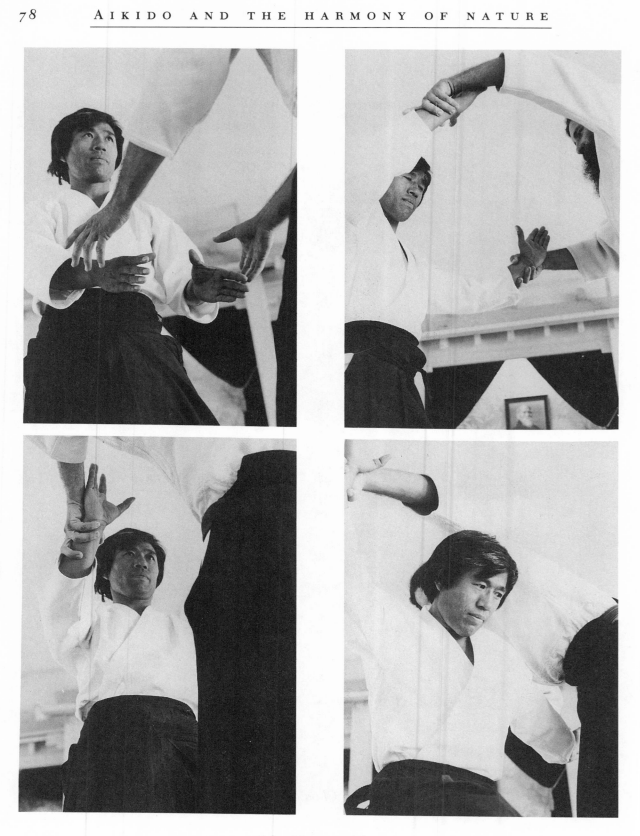

John Messores, uke

cycle. A certain amount of the carbon that is not decomposed stays in the soil to harden and become a part of the material of the earth itself. It is nature's own timing as to when these combustible materials—coal, petroleum, the precious commodities of the living tissue of millions of years ago—should be released in the form of volcano and natural fires to balance the amount of carbon dioxide in the atmosphere. We are destroying this balance with our wasteful burning of carbon products. Already we have raised the carbon dioxide content in the atmosphere by about ten percent. It is estimated that the wanton activities of humanity will raise it by about twenty-five percent before the year 2000. How much extra carbon dioxide can the atmosphere hold before climatic conditions make life unbearable? Could it be that we are reversing one of the miracles that gave life its start? The possible warming of the earth's surface would reduce the masses of the ice at the poles, raising the height of the world's oceans and causing major changes in the climatic conditions in the temperate zones. We are not sure how this will affect the earth, but do we have the time and the option to continue indiscriminately until all the research is completed? As the climate changes, the crops grown in a specific area must adapt and change. The problem is that we have so overspecialized the properties of certain crops for our own convenience that much of that capacity to adapt has been eliminated. Perhaps humanity, too, has become so overspecialized that we can no longer adapt. Instead of exploring the mysteries of this world in order to better understand our heritage and draw closer to the Intelligence that created us, we are insolent children attempting to redesign perfection to better suit the imperfect.

We separate all the environmental conditions essential to life so that we may more easily study and exploit their riches. But, as we have found, the laboratory and reality are two distinctly different worlds. Without a complete knowledge of all the factors that influence a specific condition and a full understanding of its integrated function with all other conditions, we cannot possibly know the final consequences of any action. If we do not have a personal and intuitive sensitivity to the environment in which we live, the very foundation of our lives, it will not matter how many specific measures and countermeasures we adopt. Not only will the basic problem remain unsolved, but new problems will arise. Selfishness and greed have begun a new cycle, one of degeneration and waste.

The spirit of Kannagara sees the rich and growing mountains rising up from the sea, the swollen, poignant greens of mosses, grass, and trees gracing the wet countryside, the delicate living jewels of color at each season, and bows in thanksgiving. All of nature is perceived as God. It is revered and holy, and the thought of intervention by humanity seems absurd. How can mortals tamper with the perfection of the laws that God has set forth?

Clearly the land itself helped shape this attitude, for in contrast to the almost dreamlike beauty of the Japanese islands is their vulnerability to all manner of awesome, unpredictable natural phenomena. Formed by volcanic activity and lying at the intersection of four major crustal plates, the islands and their people are intimately aware of the gripping power of earthquake and volcano, of their helplessness in the face of a thundering wall of ocean wave as it claims their homes and often their lives. Positioned as they are at the convergence of polar and tropical air masses, the same conditions that saturate the air and the vegetation with vital moisture also create the devastating atmospheric release of typhoons and violent storms. With the undisputed knowledge of the limitations of humanity standing naked before the power of God, the consciousness of the Japanese people (at least until the recent move toward modernization and technological growth) has been to remain flexible enough to adapt to all changes brought about by nature. Understood not as concrete, stable entities but as transient and moving, the essence of the living forms and forces of the natural world is change. It is this flexibility

Atomic particles spiraling in the earth's magnetic field, as demonstrated by the sankyo *technique.*

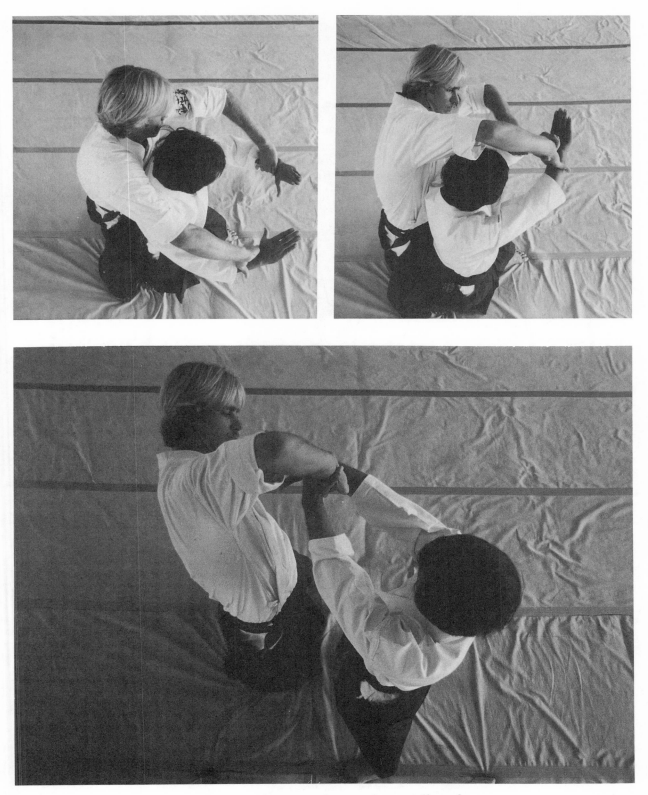

Ushiro tekubi tori sankyo. *Robert Moller*, uke.

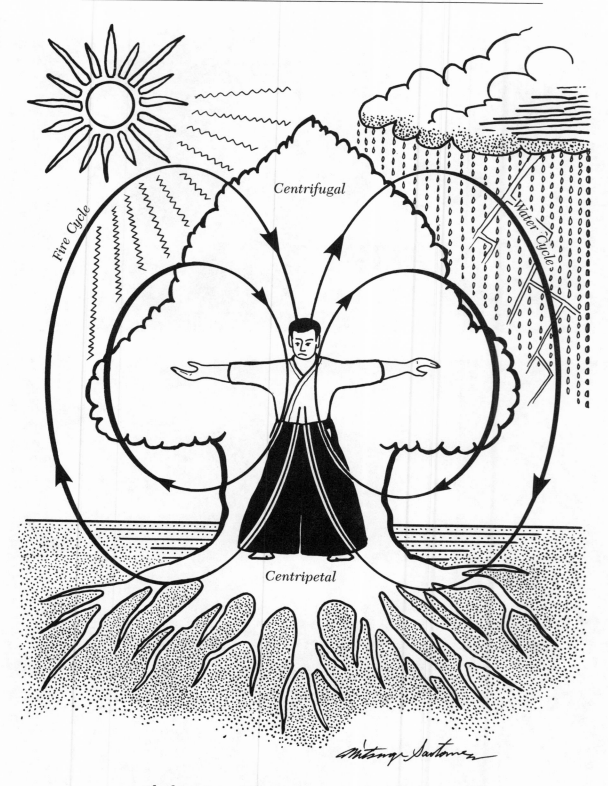

The harmony of opposites support the cycles of life.

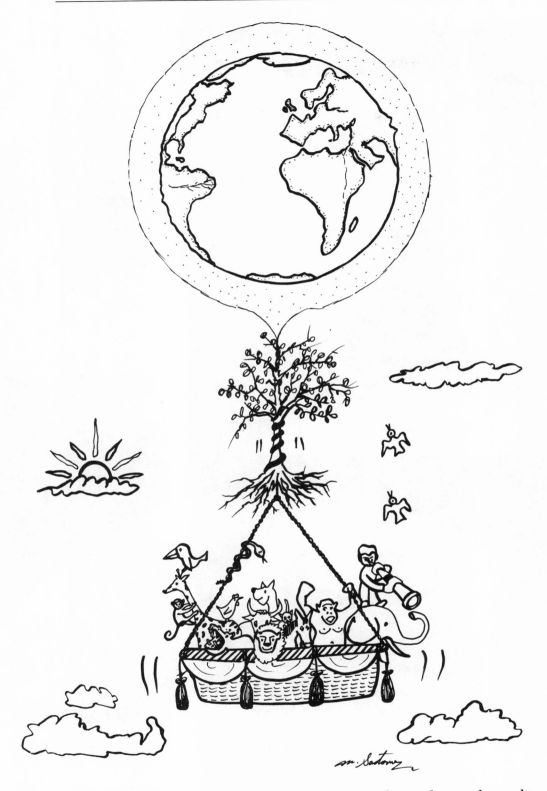

We are all a "planetary family," dependent upon one another and upon the quality of our life support systems.

Positions of attack or defense. John Messores, uke.

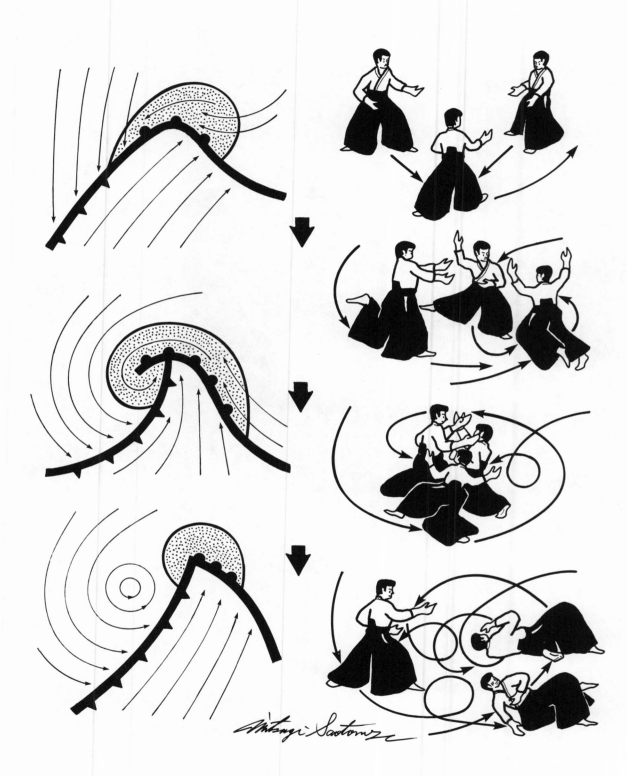

The dynamic movements of adjustment as opposites, warm air and cold air, come together

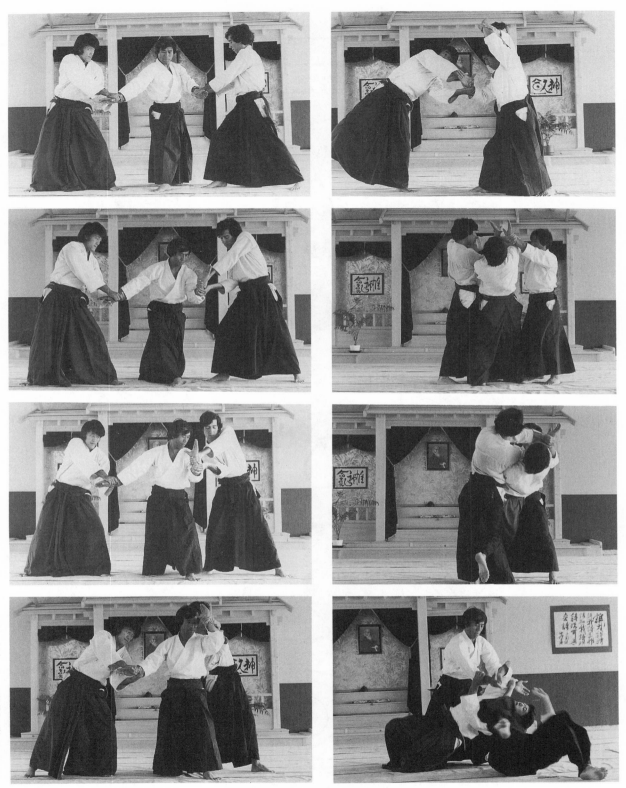

The technique is a little different, but the principles are the same.
Hiroshi Ikeda, shihan, Paul Blackwood, uke.

Fluid dynamics and yokomenuchi kokyunage, tenkan

Kevin Choate, uke

"Aiki has a form and does not have a form." Aikido is an art of communication. You must remain relaxed and open so you can accurately read your partner's reaction. This attack is munetsuki. The initial response to the attack is the same for either technique. In the first sequence, uke continues his forward movement in order to regain his balance, catch up with nage, and strike again. Just as he begins to stand up and renew the attack, this motion is continued and he is thrown with the kotegaeshi technique.

Here we begin with the fourth photograph opposite. In the next step here, instead of continuing his forward movement, uke's response is to pull back and resist. Nage feels this and is flexible enough to follow. The pull is overextended as nage uses this energy to spin uke around and throw him with the kaitennage technique. The secret of Aikido is change. Hiroshi Ikeda Shihan, John Messores, uke.

that has given the living world the strength to continue for these billions of years. Everything owes its existence to change.

This consciousness extends into personal, social, and political relationships. Clearly defined words and judgment for the unpredictable feelings and emotions of others are shunned as are direct confrontation and competition. The final answer is avoided at all cost, for it signals the end of the process. Because of an ever-changing situation, the same process does not always work, and new channels of thought and action are continually opening up. Today's relative truth is incomplete tomorrow. With no strict yes or no—an attitude that may seem illogical or indecisive to the Western mind—a question can be viewed from many perspectives without preconceptions, the lines of communication being left open with the hope of an answer in harmony with all concerned. In order to respond appropriately to the changing reality of every second

and to the changes of the future, one must have a free, responsive mind, undisturbed by prejudice.

Traditional thinking depends on an intuitive grasp of ideas and feelings rather than step-by-step analysis. The Japanese word *kan* (having the same sound as the *kan* in *Kannagara*, but written with a different character) is the expression of this instinctive grasp or sixth sense. When one is armed with this sensitivity, it is possible to catch the situation of a changing environment or the essence of a personality at first meeting without any analytical preparation. It helps to prepare for the unforeseeable future by "expecting the unexpected" and by developing an open mind so that response to the unexpected is without hesitation. The uncertainty of the future makes this spontaneity necessary and a rigid lifestyle obsolete.

Spontaneous response and respect for the natural flow of a situation are the foundation of

O Sensei's teaching. His method of education had two opposite but complementary poles. First was the study of basic technique, learning the movement to a high degree of technical precision until its execution became instinctive. But equally important was the second opposite: spontaneity and flexibility of technique, mind and body, to escape getting caught in the mold of a mechanical precision that is not alive. When the enemy strikes, there are no absolute ways to deal with the situation. Because of the uncertainty of that action and of the next action, there is no time to consider or analyze. Only intuition and insight can decide the appropriate reaction to an ever-changing situation.

Morihei Ueshiba said, "Aiki has a form, and does not have a form. Aiki is a life which has a form and still flows with change; it expresses itself by changing itself. A form without a form is a word in a poem that expresses the universe limitlessly." This is the form of fire and water. Words cannot express their ever-changing shapes, but we feel their power and understand them intuitively. Steam, flowing water, and solid ice are all composed of the same material. This is nature, one God and many gods. The creative nature surrounding us is still being created, an indefinite present progressive.

" 'The Way' is a struggle to perfection that never pauses," said the Founder. "The realization of this 'Way' in one's own mind is the flexibility." Perfection can only be understood by the Creator, yet we must continue to strive for harmony with this perfection. We must struggle to become closer to God, for as our understanding grows, we shall continually receive new insights into His perfection.

> When water is scooped in the hands, the moon is reflected in them; when the flowers are handled, the scent soaks into the robe.

Whether we regard the phenomenon of life as the evolution of energy circuits that connect the universe, life, and humanity or as the many manifestations of Cosmic Intelligence, it is clear that our perspective of this relationship is narrow, self-centered, and precarious. The Founder of Aikido told us that if we forget the way the universe works, we cannot exist for an instant. The practice of Aikido is a path that leads to the supreme vibrations of harmony at the center of creation, and the earth and our lives upon it are manifestations of that great love, a direct flow from God.

Tenri Shizen No Ki *is the power of natural law.*

6

The
JUSTICE
of
NATURE'S HARMONY

Life is one karma, an ecology of cause and effect, and nature's balance operates to maintain a rich quality of life for all. Life is diverse. Each life group and each member within the group has its own indispensable function; all share different responsibilities. Selfishness is not allowed in the highly developed feedback system of communication. It is a most elegant system of checks and balances, which nothing in the biosphere escapes. The law is absolute; the harmony of the system must not be threatened.

The conditions from which life spontaneously burst into existence have been washed from the earth by the very beings that those conditions created. Life can only come from life, so the original force of creative energy evolved into the creative expression of refinement. Its function is to produce optimal life forms that are adaptable to their environment and capable of maintaining a dynamic balance to the other forms with which they must coexist.

Every community of living matter has its own limited area and function, its ecological niche in the balance of the global ecosystem. Each individual life form has its own time, place, and significance within the community. No form of life is independent of the need for the functions of the others; therefore the limited supply of space and energy can not be monopolized, but must be shared for the benefit of all concerned. Living space is divided and shared in a multidimensional arrangement. In a community of plant life there are towering trees that stretch to the sky, shorter trees with spreading branches, bushes, grasses, moss, and many layers of root depth beneath the surface of the land. Sources of energy are also multidimensional. There are birds that eat seeds from the ground and those that eat the seeds and berries before they fall. There are small birds that eat insects and large birds that hunt prey, birds that feed from the waters and birds that clean up debris. All live together in harmonious balance.

I repeat, harmony is not synonymous with weakness, and balance is not another word for stagnation. The way of life is growth and change. This is Aiki. And nature's way of pro-

Terry Dobson and Ken Nissen, uke. Photo by Carl Shiraishi.

ducing life from life is based on a geometric progression so that growth and change are possible. Yet nothing can grow or expand forever; everything is limited. Understanding the limitations is also Aiki. Growth and decay, expansion and contraction, can only take place within those limitations. When expansion attains a certain preordained degree, it must then retreat. A life form cannot live forever. It will grow for a certain time and then begin to decay. The universe cannot expand forever. It must contract again when expansion reaches its maximum. This is the rhythm of nature, *shizen tota*, natural adjustment. It is clear that if the increase in reproduction were to go unchecked, the number of species would soon be much greater than the available food and space. The relationship between space and numbers is crucial and must be strictly controlled; and so it is by the absolute truth of a life-and-death struggle for existence. Preserving the characteristics for the success of the species and of the system, destroying the weak, the imperfect, and the unadaptable, nature carefully selects and refines the recycled materials of life. Heredity is the messenger and life itself is the executioner.

Nature's sword is sharp with a multi-edged blade. It has instilled life with an instinct for aggression, the self-defense of the species, and the resulting struggle for existence occurs in many different forms. The territorial fights of an animal with its own kind ensure that the environmental resources are so divided that all of the individuals of a species can maintain a rich level of existence in the community and remain strong. The rival fights for sexual supremacy ensure for succeeding generations that the strongest, best-adjusted characteristics will be passed on and that the young will be nurtured and protected by the most efficient and successfully adapted parents. Never have these natural forms of aggression within a species been aimed at the extermination of its fellow members.

Maintaining a dynamic balance between a population's available significant resources and the activity of other life forms in the environment, the natural enemy helps to fine-tune the existence of itself and its prey. Given the tools with which to defend its life through natural selection, the hunted continually refines its means of detection and escape. At the same time, through the same process, the hunter refines the abilities to capture and kill. It is a race that, fortunately for the continuity of both, neither can hope to win, and equilibrium is always maintained between them.

In the true sense of the word, the hunting enemy is not the enemy. When the wolf attacks and kills the deer, there is no hostility or anger. The wolf is simply hungry and must kill for the energy to sustain his life. To cause the extinction of the species upon which survival depends is suicide. The hunted supports the hunter by giving him nourishment. In return the hunter supports his prey. Aiding in the refinement of the species, he cleanses it of the weak, the sick, and the social outcast, so that its members may grow strong and multiply. This is *misogi*. The mutual dependence is clear. The ultimate survival of the one is absolutely necessary to the survival of the other.

In the system of natural selection, life forms must struggle against the environment, against their own kind and against their natural enemy. All of these are necessary to the development of a healthy and adaptable life form, and vital for the proper response of the self-governing system with which life regulates its aggressions. Without the natural enemy and the balancing effect of environmental struggles, the deeply ingrained defense mechanisms of aggression will find their only outlet in aggression within the social group. When this is the only influence on selective breeding, the self-governing mechanism is distorted, and the form and behavior patterns of the species often become exaggerated, having a negative effect on its survival potential. Humanity, in its newly acquired sophistication, is quickly approaching this limit.

Life has continued through innumerable changes in the natural world because of its own ability to change. The essence of heredity, the materialization of evolution, is the convey-

Heredity is the messenger, and life itself is the executioner.

ance of successful changes to subsequent generations. Through the spiral strands of DNA, the changing secrets of existence, of form and function, are recorded and passed from generation to generation. The individual members of a species are not independent or separate; they come into being as a part of the group and diversify as a part of the group through this transmission. Humanity appeared on this earth and continues to exist as an expression of the enduring knowledge gained from the experience of all forms of life. It is a living flow of love that surpasses time and space, the ever-present now reaching from the past into the future. This love, neither weak nor sentimental, is supremely fair and completely unprejudiced. The strong will succeed and flourish. The weak, with characteristics that could threaten the existence of the group, will perish, and the group will be cleansed of those flaws. The individual is important first in relation to the group, for if the group is lost, the individual is doomed. And so it is with the species. When a life form becomes perverted and nonadaptive to the harmony of the whole, nature is cleansed of its insolence.

Although the same as the other forms of life, humanity is also different. We have been given the gift of compassion. We protect our weak, for the weak are often our greatest strength. We respect and revere the spirit of God within each individual. We do not blindly follow, for we have been given intellect and have developed morality. We search for truth and try to move closer to the Universal Consciousness. Although above the other animals, we are still very much like them, for we have the same basic instincts for survival. Yet within the mind of humankind, those instincts too often manifest as hatred and prejudice. The behavior patterns of the individual selfish ego are endangering our species and the earth. We are refusing to adapt. It is not individuality that must be overcome for the good of the group. It is hatred and selfishness that must be overcome. Our aggressive patterns must be redirected, and we must realize that our very survival depends on the survival of our earth and each other.

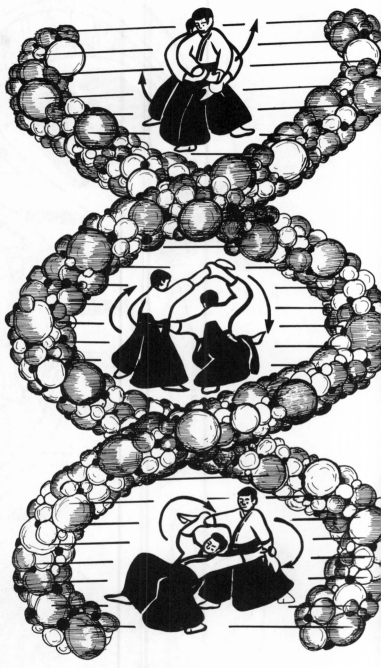

Through the spiral strands of DNA, the changing secrets of existence, of form and function, are recorded and passed from generation to generation.

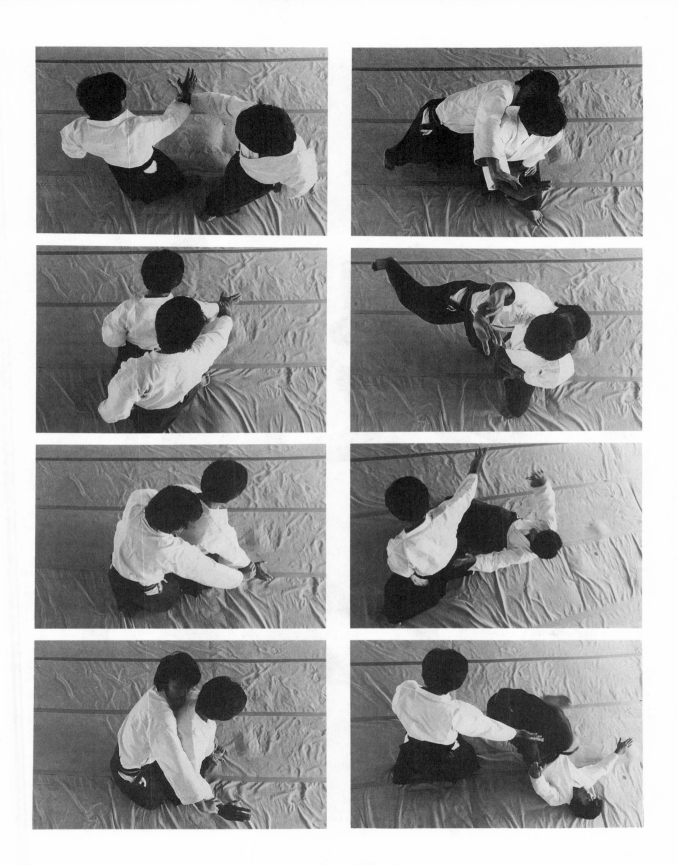

Ushiro waza. *Hiroshi Ikeda*, shihan, uke.

Bujutsu tanren *is the training of martial technique.*

7

AGGRESSION
and the
EVOLUTION
of BUJUTSU

The process of life on earth and the evolution of humanity began with the birth of the sun, but the true emergence of the being as human arose when we began to walk upright, leaving our hands free for the creation and use of tools. With hands performing the tasks of catching and carrying, the mouth was left unburdened to develop the more sophisticated function of communication, the exchange of ideas; and our knowledge and our stature grew. But is this evolution simply the result of the laws of natural selection caused by environmental changes, ecological pressures, and timing? It is almost certain that the ancestors of modern human populations first evolved near the equator in the savannah country of Africa. Discoveries in the Afar depression in Ethiopia show that our direct predecessors were fully adapted to upright posture and bipedal locomotion as much as three million years ago. The continuing skeletal changes evidenced between the fossils of our beginnings two million years ago and the individual of today are remarkable. The two-million-year-old fossilized remains found of

the other animals of that same region and the skeletal structure of those animals that still exist today are just as remarkably unchanged. Not just another animal, not merely a product of evolutionary change, in a very special way the human spirit was touched by the hand of the Divine. Half beast, half god, the human being is depicted with great insight in the early drawings and art forms of the ancient civilizations.

The process of evolution toward technological growth has been an ever-increasing spiral of dramatic change and progress. Branches and thorns bit into our flesh and we clothed our nakedness. Battered and worn by the wind, chilled by the rains, and parched by the glare of a midday sun, we constructed shelters. Vulnerable and alone, hunted by wild animals, we needed companionship and the protection of numbers, so we developed a complex social organization. We shared our food and helped each other. In doing so, we helped ourselves.

Combining knowledge and skills for the enrichment of the group, the society of ancient humanity pulled itself above the other animals and began to fashion its own destiny. But the link with the past and our heritage was strong. As intellect became more sophisticated and the balancing effect of environmental hazards and natural enemies were no longer factors influencing our development, those valuable instincts of aggression to which we owed our existence began to develop in bizarre and distorted ways. Still deeply intact, older and more demanding than the newly acquired intellect, those basic instincts had to find expression.

In the first part of this book, I have introduced the concept of the harmony of Aikido. Its spiral roots, which wind throughout the processes of natural phenomena, have been followed from the very beginning of physical creation to our own appearance on earth as an integral part of the process. Yet we have found in our search for harmony that conflict is its creator, a natural state necessary for the continuity of the process.

Whether we believe that humanity is locked into its behavioral patterns, the product of natural drives and instincts, or that we can aspire to a higher consciousness and escape our never-ending battles, the truth of the path we have chosen thus far lies in our gory history.

It is now time to examine Aikido from its roots in conflict, its seed sown deep in the rich spawning ground of Japanese soil and nourished with the blood of the warrior. The study of the classical arts of war and of the classical warrior is the study of Aikido's process. A two-thousand-year process of refinement set the course for the development of an amazing educational system. Many *bujutsu* masters spent their entire lives in search of the ultimate connection with the power of truth. Hundreds of thousands of warriors died in a continuing martial contest of natural selection. It is an evolution etched in blood.

There are many parallels between feudal Japan and feudal Western societies. For both the samurai and the knight a code of ethics was held as the ideal. This chivalrous way was based on loyalty and honor, selflessness and

Butoku: *chivalry*

duty, and an attitude very close to worship for the glistening steel of death. Yet in feudal Japan these ideals were refined to a depth that affects the consciousness of the nation still. From the time of the eighth century until the nineteenth century, when the feudal era was formally declared closed, the changes in the consciousness of the people and the evolution of the *bujutsu* (the techniques, the practical arts of war) have been written in the rise and fall of military power. But the search for conquest was mainly confined within this isolated group of islands and not pursued on foreign shores. Perhaps this, along with the greatly extended time of civil war, was the central reason that such a strict and unique code of ethics and ritualized warrior conduct was allowed to develop.

As in most societies it was the farmer who left his fields and took up the sword to defend his own existence by defending the existence of his society. The control of the government, confined to the capital in Kyoto, was ineffective. In the outlying agricultural regions, war and the struggle against invading marauders had become an inevitable fact of daily life. Survival of the individual depended upon survival of the clan; and the survival of the clan depended more and more upon the self-reliance and skills of the warrior farmers. At the end of the twelfth century, in an effort to stamp out the lawlessness that threatened the nation, a great warrior and strategist, Minamoto Yoritomo, gathered the provincial landowners and their volunteer armies together under one

Chusei: *loyalty*

banner. He demanded absolute loyalty, a quality that came naturally to those clans who had shared the hardship of constant war. Loyalty, honor, and martial virtue were rewarded above all other considerations. From those men who banded together to protect their homes, a new power emerged. A professional warrior class began to devote their lives to the refinement of the arts of war. Assuming the title of shogun, Minamoto Yoritomo set up the first truly military form of government, *bakufu*, in Kamakura, far removed from the emperor's court. (The shogun was general-in-chief of the emperor's armies; with Yoritomo's rule the title came to denote the military dictator who ruled in the name of the emperor.) He did not want his *bushi* (warriors) influenced by the soft, effete culture of the *kuge* (court nobles), for the strength of the warrior culture was founded on a simple life of severe discipline and constant devotion to training.

The code of Bushido, which was not actually given a name and recorded until the seven-

Bushido

teenth century, experienced an atmosphere ideal for its growth under Yoritomo's rule. Developed within the philosophies of Shintoism, Buddhism, Confucianism, and the Chinese philosophy of yin and yang, the military way was enriched with spiritual and ethical qualities. Two great Shinto shrines, the Katori Shrine and its companion, the Kashima Shrine, were the spiritual centers for the development of the most illustrious schools of swordsmanship and some of the greatest swordsmen known to Japan.

The philosophy of the Shinto priests, an outgrowth of Kannagara, held that action is the natural consequence of prayer. Their responsibility to God was to protect society, and in a society at war, words alone were an empty substitute. Erected in the eighteenth year of the first Sovereign Jimmu's reign, the Katori Shrine is dedicated to Futsu-nushi-no-mikoto. This mythological deity pacified the ancient land of Yamato (Japan), bringing it under the rule of the grandson of the Sun Goddess (Amaterasu-o-mi-kami), ancestor of the Imperial family. Futsu-nushi-no-mikoto, the guardian deity of martial valor, is also the guardian deity of government, of security of state and social welfare.

It was during this time of the Kamakura bakufu (1185–1333) that the philosophy of Zen began to make its influence strongly evident in the arts of the warrior. Promoted by Yoritomo because of its emphasis on a spartan way of life and its philosophy of a mind with no attachment and no ego, the training, which relied on spontaneity and intuition, held a great appeal for his *bushi*. The Zen temples sponsored many styles of *bujutsu*, devoting much time to their conceptual development, and the art of swordsmanship and Zen grew together, illuminating each other. Together the ways of the spirit and the ways of war formed the structure and the culture of the samurai society.

During the time of military domination, the role of the emperor took on a different quality. Westerners are sometimes mistakenly led to believe that his position was totally stripped of its power by the military governments. Although often manipulated, the royal family was never unseated, and no Japanese military or political leader ever attempted to take for himself the title of emperor. This bears witness to the spiritual power that the unbroken lineage of centuries held over the people. It was a spiritual leadership that was founded with the Japanese nation itself, descended from the deities that gave birth to the islands and their surrounding seas. Although the emperor's function underwent many changes, no shogun would dare to rule without paying allegiance to the emperor and making the journey to his capital to seek his support.

After Yoritomo's death, the post of shogun lost much of its power in the absence of a central figure who could match his integrity and martial skill. But the ideals he had insisted upon were embedded even more deeply into the subconscious heart of the nation because of his rule. Once again the country was thrown into the chaos of power struggles. The *bushi* rallied under the separate banners of the powerful landowners, the *daimyo,* their loyalty once again centered on the protection of the clan.

But of course, ideals are only ideals, and human beings have never attained perfection. The high ideals of loyalty and honor were often overruled by the baser instincts, and history was rife with intrigue, betrayal, and ruthlessness. The *bujutsu* that had developed for protection were distorted by many leaders into a way to gain power by appealing to the sense of honor and duty of the *bushi.* They were all bound by a vicious escalating cycle from which the dishonor of surrender or the honor of death was the only escape.

I will touch only lightly on the history of Japan, fascinating though it is, for it is available from many sources. What we are concerned with here are the attitudes, beliefs, and ideals of the individual warrior that allowed him to live his life under the omnipresent shadow of death and to use the tools of warfare in his quest for spiritual refinement.

The spirit of the samurai was the spirit of self-sacrifice, his virtues being those necessary to an effective warrior. Believing that his individual being was nothing compared with the continuity and success of his clan and his line, he pledged in blood and with his whole being total allegiance to his duty and absolute loyalty and unquestioning obedience to his superior. The idea of sacrifice was natural to him, and if the loss of his own life could lead to the salvation of many, he would abandon it without hesitation. He lived a frugal and spartan life, fearing that excess of any kind would make him unfit for battle and hesitant to die.

In time of war, thoughts always turn to death. But in the special culture that evolved in feudal Japan, the greatest emphasis was placed on the way in which one met his death. His first duty was on the battlefield, and with this attitude toward the inevitable, the samurai was the most dangerous of warriors, a fanatic with no regard for his own life. Having pledged to fight until victory or death, he considered being defeated or captured in battle the deepest of shames. Rather than live with this dishonor, a true samurai would take his own life in a highly ritualized display of courage.

The choice of disembowelment, *seppuku,* an excruciatingly painful form of suicide, has its basis deep in the Japanese culture. The

切腹

Seppuku

lower abdomen, the *hara,* in addition to being the place of courage, is considered to be the seat of earthly consciousness, of one's mind and spirit. It is the place in the body where physical and spiritual energy originate and join together. Those who speak English speak of reading someone's mind in order to understand his or her feelings, but the Japanese say *hito no hara wo yomu,* to read another's *hara,* or abdomen. When someone is described as black-hearted, we say he has a black abdomen, *hara ga kuroi.* So ripping open his own *hara* not only proved the warrior's courage and determination to die by his own hand, but also showed his sincerity and the pure state of his mind and heart. Having been trained in the ritual since the age of fifteen, the samurai would often spontaneously create a farewell poem to show his composure at the moment of death.

Not only did the samurai willingly die in battle, but by the wisdom and honor of his own hand and his own sword, he died when he failed in an important mission or when he committed a crime that could bring disgrace upon his clan or his name. He was a warrior, and the warrior's function was to protect the honor and continuity of his group. His responsibility and his duty were his pride, and death was preferred to living with dishonor.

This attitude toward suicide probably illustrates more clearly than any other one of the major differences in the spiritual beliefs of Japanese and Western cultures. The Western conscience views suicide as a mortal sin, believing that life is a precious God-given gift, and it is not within the province of man to interfere. Japanese culture also looks upon life as a precious gift, but if one brings shame upon that life, it is his responsibility to atone for his transgressions and apologize to God by his own hand. The inability to carry out his own punishment would be an insult to God, an insult to his clan, and an insult to all his family, past, present, and future. To die by the hand of another would cause greater shame; for someone else to pronounce him guilty would be an unpardonable invasion of his life and spirit. Judgment of self was the samurai's responsibility. To redeem his honor and show that his heart was pure, regardless of his deeds, the samurai became his own judge and executioner. This final act of purification left the memory of his life and his name cleansed

and pure. Entrusted to him by his ancestors and carried on by his children, he must protect the honor of that name and keep it worthy for future generations.

As confident in his spiritual beliefs as he was in his abilities of war, the samurai knew that death was not an end to his spirit or even his earthly existence. In his mind there was neither fair nor unfair, only the immutable laws of cause and effect. Life came again and again, and he, like the ceaseless ocean waves, washed over the earth, each time leaving a small part of his spirit to influence the path of the future. Reincarnation was another chance to refine his spirit and move closer to the perfection that is God; each life is a different training ground for the ultimate union with the spirit of universal power. The samurai held deep within his heart the knowledge that every second not only contained the present but was filled with the richness of the past and the promise of tomorrow. Faced as he was with the constant reality of war, defeat was certain if it was his habit to dwell on past deeds and worry about future situations. Just by living correctly in each moment, as though it were the only moment, he was cleansing his past and preparing for the future.

Even in the smallest details of daily life, the warrior lived as though each day were his last.

Hokori: *pride*

When he arose each morning, he would bathe and rub perfume on his shaved crown and in his hair. He cut and polished his nails and with the greatest of care cleaned and polished his long and short swords. This personal attention was not motivated by an effete taste for elegance but reflected the acknowledgment that he might this day fall in battle. If he fell, unkempt, before his enemy, it would reveal by his physical appearance a neglectful and sloppy spirit, and his enemy would despise him. Before a battle he would apply rouge so that even in death his face would glow with the color of health. The consciousness of the true samurai took the form of the enemy himself, and he was constant in his determination to maintain an attitude of pride and respect before him.

Often on the battlefield, realizing that defeat was imminent, the samurai would retreat to a nearby place of serenity and, a little apart from the horrors of war, take his own life. The enemy would not pursue but with sincere reverence would allow him to carry out his final and supreme act of loyalty. If it happened that the suicide had no second, a notable swordsman from among the opposition would join the ceremony and with one clean, merciful stroke of his sword end the prolonged agony by cutting off the suicide's head. This function was performed with deep respect for his enemy's pride and courage. The samurai wanted only a great enemy, one of skill and honor. The enemy was his inspiration. The enemy caused him to fine-tune and perfect his responses in the same way a natural enemy polishes and refines its prey. Victory or defeat did not matter. If his enemy was a strong and noble enemy, he was a great warrior. If his enemy was of small skill and honor, victory was empty and defeat the cause of lasting shame. As two warriors closed in to do battle, each would in turn announce his name, his lineage, and his *ryu* (school of swordsmanship), praise the maker of his blade, and boldly declare his expertise and intent to emerge the victor. The enemy was not dehumanized by hatred and fear into a nameless shape without a soul. The enemy was glorified, and hatred and love became one.

The outcome of any combat between such fierce and dedicated warriors did not depend on mere physical strength. The determining factors—timing, intuition, an instinctive, spontaneous response, and confidence of spirit—were the result of intense training and discipline, and the constant reality of battle.

Fighting techniques that held in their balance the delicate thread of life were studied, perfected, and tested over and over. And it happened that on rare occasions, after years of disciplined training, after facing death time and time again in combat, a great warrior would undergo a spiritual transformation. Receiving a spark of illumination, of inspiration and understanding, he would begin to see deeply into the essence of strategy. Attributing this insight to the benevolence of a buddha or one of the Shinto deities, he would center his study and teaching around a temple or a shrine in gratitude. These enlightened men were the grand masters, the founders of the martial *ryu*.

For the warrior the teachings and specialized techniques of the *ryu* held the balance of life and death. It gave him confidence, for he was privileged to practice techniques and strategies that had already been tested and proven effective in battle. Given a practical training method that had been handed down by the masters of the school, he devoted his time to continuous, severe training. He perfected his reflexes, seeking the freedom of a liberated body that could meet any situation spontaneously, without the binding chains of ego and thought. The *ryu* was not only the study of fighting techniques. It was an educational process in the martial virtues of self-sacrifice and courtesy, confidence and courage, discipline and patience. The warrior sought to refine his spirit by practicing the martial virtues as set forth by the founder of the *ryu*, for the master was believed to have been given divine insight into the ways of life and death. Daily training was *shugyo*, helping to purify and cleanse body, mind, and spirit.

Within each *ryu* there were closely guarded secret strategies, techniques, and teachings that were passed on only to a few of the most trusted and honorable warriors. For those secrets to fall into the hands of the enemy could mean almost certain defeat. The ultimate teachings were only hinted at to most, and few who witnessed that elegant power in battle lived to describe it. Many legends developed around those who were said to have attained this mysterious power.

Loyalty, courtesy, and valor, these were lofty, noble ideals, yet they were centered around the field of battle, and the samurai were most highly rewarded for their skill in combat. The concentrated study of the *bujutsu* served to refine the spirit, but it was refined so that death could be faced without fear and the enemy destroyed. What had begun as a way to protect life and family from lawlessness had evolved and become distorted by incessant wars into a way to attain power, a method to elevate the position of one group at the expense and suffering of another, creating a social ladder with rungs formed by the corpses of thousands. Always during times of war and hardship, great people and truly inspiring leaders arise. This period of Japanese history was alive with people of honor and integrity, those who believed that there is in life something much more important than their own individual ego. But it was also alive with treachery and people who used the principles to enhance their own power and prestige.

At this time in history the Chinese character *bu* was too often associated only with war. But the ancient and more accurate translation is that of governing and protecting the people, thereby developing a strong society. This is evident in the function of the ancient deity of the Katori Shrine, Futsu-nushi-no-mikoto. The guardian deity of war and of martial valor, his most important function was as guardian of public security and industrial and agricultural development. The title of the *bushi*, samurai, comes from the verb *samuru*, which means to serve and protect. The samurai was first of all a man of the sword, an aristocrat born, bred, and trained to fight, for war was his daily reality. But the military class was also the ruling class, and it was his obligation to perform civil duties as well. At his best, his sense of honor echoed strongly in the performance of those functions. At his worst, he was arrogant and all too quick to draw his sword at an imagined insult. Power so often breeds insolence, and as the samurai class rose higher in the social or-

der, they were often feared and mistrusted by the common people.

Takeda Shingen, a great *daimyo,* an incomparable warrior, and a brilliant strategist of the mid-sixteenth century, was a great example of devotion to the public cause. Many believed that had Lord Takeda been unhampered by the many mountains and great distance that lay between his rural province and the capital of the imperial court, he could easily have become shogun. He felt that war with weapons and bloodshed was the most primitive way to resolve a conflict and educated his warriors in diplomacy and political strategy. Living deep within the mountains, he refused to build a castle. He cherished the thought that "people are my castle; loyalty and devotion are stronger than walls of stone." He enriched the lives of those he governed. Takeda Shingen introduced innovative procedures for the construction of dams, canals, and irrigation systems. He taught the people to protect the riverbanks from erosion by lining them with bamboo nets filled with stone.

Lord Takeda understood that no matter how great and powerful an individual, he was never separated from the need of the skills and help of others. A man of benevolence and foresight, Lord Takeda was also very strict. He abhorred violence. Personal duels among his officers were looked upon as a petty display of ego and a waste of highly trained and capable warriors. Realizing that this type of violence would eventually infect his whole society, he outlawed it. The victor was judged guilty and, not allowed the honorable choice of *seppuku,* condemned to crucifixion. Although a man of peace, he was left without choice in an age of war, and Takeda Shingen led his warriors in many battles. In 1573 he died of a gunshot wound, for guns had arrived with the first Europeans thirty years earlier.

In that time of war and power struggles, guns were at first quickly adopted, but soon the *bushi,* who revered honor and bravery in battle above all else, came to believe that to kill with a gun required neither. With the sword, a man's fate depended upon his skill,

Kumi iai *technique using* shoto (*short sword*). *Kevin Choate,* uke.

his intuition, and the spiritual progress of his training. The conflicts within a battle were personal: he met the enemy face to face and was inspired by his spirit. Within this framework, stories of great pathos and heroism abounded.

The sword itself, symbol of the samurai class, was a highly refined and beautiful work of art. An excellent sword by a fine artist and

Katana: *long sword*

craftsman was the most highly prized of all personal possessions. The only physical symbol of his pride and honor, the two swords the samurai wore at his side also embodied his spirit. They were truly believed to be the "soul of the samurai."

Before the process of making each blade, the master swordmaker cleansed his body, mind, and spirit and his surroundings in an ancient Shinto ceremony of *misogi*. The steel was purified by fire and water as it was folded and pounded and folded and pounded again and again until all the impurities were refined away. Each blade was an individual with a different face and a unique personality. The steel was not cold but alive and glowing with the fire that had forged it. The sword, one of the three spiritual symbols of the Japanese nation, mirrors within its steel wisdom and honesty. Noble, sharp, and strong, yet flexible and clear—these were the qualities to which the warrior aspired.

When the sword is used properly and efficiently, the movements of the body must naturally conform to the artistic rules of economy of line and movement and the balanced use of space. Grounded in the philosophies of the Way of Kannagara, the samurai did not separate the physical and the spiritual worlds. If

his body moved in a refined and elegant way, it bespoke a refined and elegant spirit. As he trained to refine and perfect his physical technique, it was exerting a great influence on the refinement and perfection of his spirit. It was one of the most noble attempts of humanity in a feudal society to transcend and control its own aggressive drive by directing it into a pattern for the enrichment of the human spirit. While recognizing the effectiveness of the gun, most samurai left it to the ranks of the farmers and *ji-samurai* (low-ranking foot soldiers, not members of the samurai class) and, with their elegance and pride still intact, charged into battle wearing their two swords. (For anyone who is interested in a more in-depth study of this unprecedented phenomenon, which could have an important application to the world today, I highly recommend Noel Perrin's excellent book, *Giving Up the Gun*.)

It was also during this period that three great leaders emerged and, in a series of wars and political intrigues, fought to unify Japan and bring the war-torn nation under one strong central rule. Begun by Oda Nobunaga and carried on by Toyotomi Hideyoshi, this goal was finalized and made reality by the iron grip of Tokugawa Ieyasu. Although the people were bound under an exacting and inescapable set of laws and customs that left them with little social freedom and no chance to move out of the social class to which they had been born, their lives were ordered and enriched with a peace and prosperity unknown since the Kamakura bakufu.

A man of great insight into the ways of human nature and political strategy, the shogun Tokugawa Ieyasu instituted many reforms. He sought to control the ambitious *daimyo* and ensure the succession of the Tokygawa shogunate, which in turn would ensure the continued peace of the nation. He kept the powerful warrior families busy developing their cities instead of fortifying their castles for defense. The money that they would have spent on armament now provided good salaries for the common people. The population prospered and enjoyed a freedom within their class that was much greater than that of the samurai, whose lives were more structured. Ieyasu began a strict program of gun control whose success owed as much to the samurai's distaste for the weapon as to the Tokugawa power.

Japan, however, had been diseased and weakened from so much conflict, and the people were weary. The *daimyo*'s lust for power was insatiable, and their battles had resulted in a seemingly endless cycle of destruction of property and human life. Watching the destruction of their farmlands and their homes over and over, the people could find no security or peace. An invasion by the Europeans at that time would have been disastrous. Military and political leaders had observed European aggression in Asia, and a dramatic course of action was required. So beginning with the second Tokugawa shogun, Hidetada, Japan sealed herself away from Western influence for a period of two hundred and sixty-three years and fourteen Tokugawa shoguns.

Tokugawa Ieyasu, like Minamoto Yoritomo before him, understood the importance of the *bushi*'s pride in the spirit of the past and in their own martial skills and virtues. He knew that to promote martial excellence and martial virtue was to promote loyalty to his rule. Ieyasu clearly perceived that the ways of war were so deeply embedded into the consciousness of the samurai that they must be allowed a way to express their fighting instinct while refining it into more constructive and socially responsible patterns of education and public welfare. To accomplish this he bound the lives of the military class with rigid customs and burdensome official obligations. With so much of their time spent in fulfilling various duties at the shogun's court, competing for his favor, and pursuing the obligatory study and refinement of *bujutsu*, literature, tea, and the other traditional art forms, there was little time and opportunity remaining for rebellion or preparations for war. Without constant warfare, there was now the time and the necessity to discover and explore abilities other than fight-

ing. Once Tokugawa proclaimed that the brush and the sword are one, the samurai studied the many art forms with the same attitude and philosophy that they had carried into battle.

The *bujutsu* underwent a subtle but profound change. Many of the great masters of the traditional martial *ryu* had witnessed the development of the gun and the new style of warfare and strategy that evolved because of it. Their understanding of war and their insight into human nature led them to believe that the gun was not an end, but the beginning of even more powerful and devastating weaponry. What effect could one man with a sword and spear have against this new wave of power? The masters of the classical *bujutsu* were, above all else, realists. Now the study of *bujutsu*, the techniques of war, must become Bushido, the study of chivalry and protection. The same courage, the same honor and loyalty, and the same strength of body and spirit must be designed to develop a strong warrior of peace, building social morality and a stable social structure. The leaders of the great martial ways became even more adamant that only those of good character, modesty, and samurai breeding could be accepted as students.

The Tokugawa government had maintained strict control over the development of new weapons; however, the rest of the world had not. Therefore, when in July of 1853 Commodore Perry and his naval fleet first steamed into Tokyo Bay, the government at Edo was thrown into a state of shock. Edo lay exposed and defenseless under the powerful cannon mounted on the American warships. A letter was delivered from the president of the United States to the fourteenth Tokugawa shogun demanding the opening of trade relations. Perry promised to return early the next year to receive a reply.

The country was torn by disagreement. The majority, determined to expel the barbarians, had not seen the warships and did not believe in the existence of such power. But those who had witnessed the arrival of the great ships understood that their outmoded form of combat was no match for the fire power now increasingly common in the rest of the world. So Edo, against the advice of the emperor and most of the *daimyo*, succumbed to the demands of the foreign power.

Since the mid-eighteenth century, feelings of nationalism and dissatisfaction for the outdated social structure had been slowly surfacing in the feudal society. At this time of true national crisis, the people began to turn to the emperor for guidance and support. The *fudai daimyo* (hereditary vassals who had been Tokugawa allies in 1600) surrounded Edo. The extended time of peace had centered their lives around literary pursuits and the civil affairs of the shogunate government. Living in luxury and ease, they had never known hardship and had no experience with the reality of war. The majority had become soft and ineffective as military leaders. But the *tozama daimyo* (the families of those who had fought against the Tokugawa in 1600) and their domains were further removed from Edo. Living in a rural environment, their lives were simple, rugged, and disciplined. Although they, too, had no real experience in war, they aspired to the ideals of the classical warrior and continued training daily in the traditional martial ways. Still hungry to avenge their defeat at the hands of Tokugawa more than two hundred years before, they began to see weaknesses in the old feudal armor. They rallied around the emperor and challenged the Tokugawa power with the cry of "revere the emperor and expel the barbarians."

In May of 1863, after adopting the use of guns and cannon, the Choshu samurai drove away an American trading vessel, a Dutch warship and a French warship that were passing through the Straits of Shimonoseki. In retaliation, Shimonoseki was bombarded a year later by a combined fleet of American, British, Dutch, and French warships. Suffering a bitter defeat, the military leaders realized that the movement to expel the barbarians was unrealistic. With the rest of the provincial samurai, they put all their energies into the overthrow

of the obsolete Tokugawa shogunate and the refinement of more powerful weapons.

The British wanted to support the emperor's forces at Satsuma and Choshu, and the French wished to ally with the Tokugawa, but it was a Japanese political problem, which the Japanese had to solve. Both sides, understanding that the use of outside help would leave them obligated and open to outside control and possibly colonization during a time of weakness, refused. They paid for the new weapons they imported and fought their own wars. They had witnessed and understood the experience of China and all of Asia in the face of Western domination. Although in disagreement as to the method, both sides wanted to unify Japan, not split her power and leave her vulnerable to the rest of the world.

During this time of the Meiji Restoration, there were many beautiful stories of honor and bravery on both sides. Tradition does not die easily, and many good samurai died with sword in hand, noble and proud, still refusing to acknowledge the superiority and necessity of the modern weapons. But the eventual outcome of the conflict was the return of Japan to a nation unified in principle and objective under one ruler, the emperor Meiji. Closed as Japan was to the outside world in the seventeenth century, it was now clear to the people that isolationism could no longer work in the new world. The humiliation suffered at the forced opening of the country by the West was a stinging blow to Japanese pride. To redeem their honor and sense of national destiny, the people realized that they would have to study the new ideas and technologies, and meet the rest of the world on an equal footing.

The characteristic adaptability and flexibility of the Japanese culture allowed the change to take place in a breathtakingly short period of time. Although there were many problems inherent in such a rapid change, the people relinquished their grip on the old ways and very quickly joined together to make a strong nation. The old class structures were abolished and a new social order developed. Many samurai held the highest positions of leadership in the government and in the military. But since the obsolete system of hereditary privilege had been abolished in the early modern reforms, the new leaders and educators were chosen, not for their social status, but for their knowledge, ability, and spiritual strength.

At first the nation was so busy digesting the new Western culture and ideas that there was little time for traditional studies, but very soon the people realized that their deepest strengths rested within their own national spirit and identity. Retaining and reinforcing those strengths during the process of modernization was best accomplished through a renewal of the study of Bushido and the traditional art forms of the culture. No longer the property of a select few, the spirit of the samurai became the heritage of the entire population. In Donn Draeger's book *Modern Bujutsu and Budo,* one of the leading exponents of Budo as an educational system for the Meiji society is quoted as saying that Bushido was "an education which aspired to the attainment of stoic heroism, a rustic simplicity and a self-sacrificing spirit unsurpassed in Sparta, and the aesthetic culture and intellectual refinement of Athens. Art, delicacy of sentiment, the higher ideals of morality and of philosophy, as well as the highest types of valor and chivalry—all these we have tried to combine in the man as he ought to be."

One of the finest examples of the strength and flexibility that characterize this period of Meiji of the "man as he ought to be" was Yamaoka Tesshu. A master of the Itto Ryu and founder of the Musu Ryu of *kenjutsu,* he was also a Zen priest and a master of calligraphy. In the beginning of the conflict he was an enemy of the Meiji forces, supporting Tokugawa, but his first loyalty was to the nation. After the new government assumed control, his only thoughts were to help make a strong Japan. A highly renowned and respected master of *kenjutsu,* Yamaoka Tesshu was well known for his integrity and compassion. Welcoming his

help, the government sent him to Choshu and Mito as harmony maker to ease the transition and help soothe the group struggles and conflicts within the newly organizing local governments. Uninterested in personal wealth and ambition, Yamaoka Tesshu and his family lived a very simple life, for he used most of his income to help others.

He was once asked by a captain in the new military force at Choshu, "How can *kenjutsu* be functional against the power of cannon and gun?" Tesshu smiled and replied, "I understand that the style of war is now different, but still I continue to train with the sword. The result of my training is not to fight and defeat the enemy. I'm training myself, my spirit, training my ego. The rifle and the cannon are only tools. People must use the tools. Human quality is most important. You are using a new weapon, but your blood is still *samurai.* It is necessary to train and discover sincerity, loyalty, and honor, to lose attachment to life and death. The new weapons cannot discipline and develop the spirit, for they are not an extension of yourself. By training in *bujutsu* you will discover your own strength of character and will, and will develop spiritual confidence."

The loyalty Tesshu felt for his *sensei* of the Itto Ryu, Yamaoka Seizan, was a responsibility that he carried all his life. (The title *sensei* indicates more than a teacher of technique; a sensei is one who gives guidance along the Way.) The strength of body, mind, and spirit he had developed under his teacher's guidance was a debt that could never be repaid, and through a spiritual bond, unbroken even in death, he carried on Yamaoka Seizan's life in essence and in spirit. Seizan had never married or produced children. So upon his untimely death Tesshu took his younger sister in marriage, changing his own name to Yamaoka so that his *sensei*'s name would continue on this earth.

A short time after his death, there was much gossip among the people of the town that the ghost of Yamaoka Seizan still walked the earth. His elder brother, much disturbed by this, ventured into the cemetery one stormy night to discover the source of the gossip. At length he saw Tesshu making his way by the elusive light of a shadowed moon to talk to his teacher as he had done every night since his death. The wind gathered the clouds more quickly and the tears of Seizan's brother mingled with the icy rain as he watched Tesshu, removing his coat and gently laying it down to protect the grave of his beloved teacher, kneel in prayer.

At the time of his ascension to the throne, the emperor Meiji was in his early teens. His education into the wisdom and spiritual responsibilities of the emperor of Japan (*tei o gaku*, emperor's wisdom) was not yet completed. The country needed a strong emperor, but his position required as its most important quality the spiritual strength and lack of ego that would win the love, admiration, and devotion of the people. It was decided that the most enlightened and capable masters of swordsmanship should become his advisors and councillors. They could direct his education and instill his spirit with the qualities of strength, purity, dignity, justice, and a lack of personal ego and ambition. Yamaoka Tesshu was among those chosen.

The young emperor was fond of parties and would often stay up late drinking. One stormy night, growing weary of this conduct by the man who was to assume the spiritual guidance of the nation, Tesshu hid in one of the alleyways inside the palace grounds and awaited his return. As the emperor approached, Tesshu jumped out from his hiding place, grabbed him, and instantly threw him into the mud. Furious, the emperor demanded, "Stop! I am the emperor! I will have you condemned for this insult!" But Yamaoka Tesshu grabbed him again and with great force returned him to the mud, saying, "My emperor? You lie! How dare you call yourself my emperor. My emperor doesn't creep about, drunken, through the alleyways under the cover of night. You are a thief! I'll teach you a lesson you won't forget."

Attacking the emperor was the greatest of unpardonable crimes, and Yamaoka Tesshu knew that he could be condemned to commit *seppuku* for his conduct. But the young emperor, realizing that Tesshu did not care about the consequences of his actions, knew that his only concern was his responsibility for the emperor's education and the quality of the leadership he would give Japan. The lesson was well learned and the incident never mentioned.

The emperor Meiji, a highly spirited young man, trained vigorously in *sumo* and delighted in showing off his skills by constantly challenging and throwing his advisors and staff. Of course, no one would dare to embarrass the emperor by besting him, and the emperor always won. Perhaps with the previous incident in mind and his ego still a bit bruised, he one day challenged Tesshu. Much to the horror and surprise of everyone who was watching, Tesshu promptly threw him. It was the first time it had ever happened at court. Later Tesshu admonished the emperor, saying, "Physical competition and the display of strength and ego are far beneath your status. This attitude is an embarrassment to the emperor's function. It is the play of children." Yamaoka Tesshu was offered a permanent position of high status and income at the emperor's court, but after serving for ten years, he knew that his job was finished. Not caring for wealth and position, he left the palace and devoted his time to his *dojo*. With the memory of Seizan deep within his heart, he trained his disciples in the ways of chivalry and swordsmanship.

As he matured, the emperor Meiji fully assumed the responsibilities and duties of governing the nation. He became one of the strongest, most devoted, and best-loved emperors Japan had ever known. His character had been molded by the spiritual traditions of loyalty and responsibility, which Yamaoka Tesshu and his many fine teachers had insisted upon. His leadership was characterized by strength, justice, compassion, and love for all his people.

During his reign, Budo was introduced as compulsory education in all the secondary schools, as Tesshu had often suggested. Released from the mistrust and fear of a feudal society, Budo was to become an educational system to build discipline and strength of character in children of all classes. Receiving a breath of renewal, Budo found new strength and purpose in the application to modern life, and the Budo master became an educator and spiritual leader. The education once reserved only for the samurai formed the spirit and consciousness of all the people.

Photo by Ben Rose

Kyo is to teach, iku is to grow. Budo is the Way of chivalry and protection. Budo kyoiku is education in the Way.

8

BUDO:
The
EDUCATION
of INSTINCT

Within the atmosphere created by the enlightened ideals of the emperor Meiji of justice for all and social responsibility, Morihei Ueshiba began his search for the essence of Budo. He studied the many classical styles of *bujutsu:* swordsmanship, the spear, the staff, and the techniques of empty hands. He mastered each technique with amazing speed, reaching into the very heart of each *ryu.* Disciplined, modest, and sincere, he was unrelenting in his dedication. The depth of his understanding and spiritual development was clear, and his teachers educated him in the most profound secret teachings of their art. The Yagyu and Itto schools of swordsmanship and the Hozoin *ryu* of the spear were among the many classical styles he studied. But one of the greatest influences on his development was Sogaku Takeda, a direct descendant of Takeda Shingen and successor to the teachings of this powerful warrior family. Takeda initiated Ueshiba into *otome waza*, the closely guarded secrets of Daito *ryu* and Ueshiba's gratitude knew no bounds. In the midst of his responsibilities for the developing community

of Shirataki, he found the time to devote himself to the severe and demanding life of a disciple and to the care and welfare of his *sensei.*

Otome waza

Having lived a warrior's life, Takeda Sensei was extremely careful in all matters, especially the preparation of his food. He feared the possibility of poison, for he had made many enemies. Only Morihei Ueshiba did Takeda Sensei trust. Every day the *deshi* Ueshiba, although living in a separate house and bearing the responsibility of his own family, would carefully prepare Takeda's food and see that his house was clean and that everything that touched his life was orderly and in good repair. Ueshiba saw from an intimate distance the depth of his *sensei*'s paranoia and unhappiness, for Takeda had killed many times with his bare hands. Unable to trust others around him, he was haunted by the reality of those deaths day and night, his sleep often disturbed with the moans of their memory. This had a profound influence on Morihei Ueshiba's later development. Takeda Sensei's teaching and trust touched Morihei Ueshiba's heart with appreciation, and his loyalty was absolute. The depth of Ueshiba's devotion and the example he set became well known, earning him the respect and admiration of Budo masters throughout Japan.

Still there was a spiritual emptiness with the mastery of each martial Way. The Budo taught deep knowledge and incredible strength of will, but their basic foundation was destruction, and this knowledge seemed somehow incomplete. Developed to protect life and promote the welfare of the people, the original meaning of *bu* was clear, but it had been distorted by human selfishness and aggression. Only promoting the endless escalation of power, the Budo gave no real security or peace of mind. As each new technique was developed, more powerful than the one before, another technique had to surface to counter it. No matter how proficient one became, there would always be someone who was stronger or faster, whose insight was deeper, or whose mind was clearer. The Budo offered only the primitive choice of victory or defeat. Since neither side can find victory in destruction, defeat must be the final answer to the eternal competition.

The personal ego that all the *ryu* tried to conquer still managed to survive, cunningly taking the form of loyalty and honor. In the intense concern with transcending individual ego, there was a failure to recognize the selfishness and overdevelopment of group ego, the righteous ego, and the ego of no-ego.

Looking upon the evolution of *bujutsu* into Budo, O Sensei saw that although a higher consciousness was struggling to evolve, the work was not finished. It had just begun.

There was in the secret teachings of all the *ryu* an essence that was not technique, a perception that hinted at creation instead of destruction, a power that unified rather than separated opposing forces. There was the shadowy promise, unclear and never fully formed, that harmony is the greatest strength. The agony of O Sensei's severe physical training to uncover this secret was small compared with the agony suffered by his spirit. Slowly he began to feel the tug of an elusive idea. He would try to grasp it, but as soon as he concentrated his mind, it slipped away. It was a half-remembered dream shimmering in the shadows, a peripheral vision lost in the focusing.

And he went to the mountain, and he prayed. He searched the essence of God, which was deep within his spirit. In despair he gave up his attachment to the evasive fragments of truth he had been seeking for so long. He trained hard and pushed his body to its very limits and beyond. And as his body, mind, and spirit were emptied and made pure, the blinding light of reality illuminated his soul. He reached out and touched truth. He breathed its perfume and was nourished by its richness. He drank its liquid essence, and it quenched his thirst. His body was cleansed by its golden fire. He heard the song of the birds, and their language was his. Looking into the sky, he perceived the thundering movement of the galaxies, and it echoed through his body. No longer only a man, he was an expression of truth and of the divine power of the universe. As tears of joy and release streamed down his face, he understood. Budo is the protection of all life. It is nothing but this protection and the divine love, and the divine will of God expressed in the movements of the human body, and in the original purity of the human spirit. The spirit of all life is a part of God; the Universal Intelligence is the great unifier of all creation. There can be no enemy; the only enemy is oneself.

Because people have not understood this truth, the evolution of the human animal has been the evolution of violence and power struggles as we destroy ourselves, each other, and the very foundations of our lives. Our self-defense mechanisms have gone awry, and we are rapidly proceeding down the road to self-destruction. Many believe that the violence of humanity is inevitable and expound that we are ruled, without choice, by the instinct of millions of years ago. But to blame the violence of today on animal instinct is a convenient escape from responsibility, denying the very thing that sets us apart from the rest of the animal kingdom. The same Creative Intelligence that instilled all of life with the capacity for survival graced the human form with a creative spirit, compassion, and the unique power to learn and reason.

Unfortunately, the spiritual development of humanity has fallen far behind its intellectual growth. It would seem, looking back through history, that our greatest search for knowledge has been for the knowledge of destruction, and our greatest discoveries the result of an all-consuming drive for power. "Rooted in our genes," the instincts of aggression must have an outlet. But we have the choice of its direction. The gift of freedom and of choice has given us an awesome responsibility, for in the absence of the day-to-day struggle for survival we must create our own challenge.

O Sensei saw the great technological advances, and he marveled. "Maybe in an earlier century the concept of world harmony taught by the great spiritual leaders was thought to be an exercise in logic. People couldn't fully understand that a thousand miles away there was a culture completely different from their own, different customs, different lifestyles, different spiritual focus. They didn't see the problems in communication, or the way the actions on one side of the world politically, ecologically, and economically influence the other. But now, in the twentieth century, people have a different perspective. Through the medium of technology we know the relationship between great bodies of land connected by immense seas, lying under the same sky. We've seen different cultures and studied different languages, and we understand the problems. We cannot step back; we must continue to evolve and find peaceful and healthy solutions to the problems of our rapidly shrinking world."

O Sensei taught: "The concept of world harmony is not logic, it must be reality. Modern technology has given us two choices. With its help we can realize the dream of a great global family, all the people of the earth joined together in a great world community; or we can completely destroy this earth and all of humanity with it. Aggression cannot work in the face of the new weapons. Nationalism cannot work as more and more we understand the depths of the interrelationships around the globe. We must study and understand the saving truth of harmony."

O Sensei believed, according to the Way of Kannagara, that the individual creates his or her own heaven or hell right here on this earth. I am reminded of an old Japanese folktale of an adventurous young man who wanted to know the difference between heaven and hell. He first looked upon hell and saw many people seated at a long table filled with the finest foods. But everyone had gaunt faces with sunken cheeks. They were thin and weak, crying in despair. A closer look revealed that their hands had only two fingers formed into the shape of *hashi*, Japanese chopsticks, four feet long. Although they could pick up the food, their fingers were so long that they could not get it into their mouths. In frustration they were turning their tools into weapons, fighting selfishly among themselves for the food they could not eat. Then he looked upon heaven. He saw the same long table with the same beautifully prepared food and the same long fingers. But everyone was laughing and smiling at the others. Their cheeks were full and glowing with health. There was no fighting, for they picked up the food and, extending it to the other side of the table, fed each other. What is the difference between heaven and hell? Consciousness, compassion, and cooperation.

Painting, sculpture, music, and literature are positive results of the drive for challenge and expression, the aggressive instinct refined and developed creatively. Without this drive there would be no great love; Everest would remain unscaled and the moon untouched by the feet of mankind. Its power is responsible for the great scientific achievements and technologies as we are challenged to uncover the truth of our origins and the origin and function of the universe that surrounds us.

The difference between heaven and hell? Consciousness, compassion, cooperation.

Communications and information-handling systems make it possible to study the many cultures of the world, examine different life habits, and exchange ideas. Through technological advances we eat better, are better sheltered, and live longer. Distances of thousands of miles have been reduced in travel time to hours or even seconds as voice and image flash across a receiver screen. Our lives are rich and varied in experience and knowledge. Technology used for the benefit of humanity is the positive choice: the aggressive drive used creatively.

But when this creative flow is developed in a negative way, the result is destruction and violence. As the tools of early *Homo sapiens* molded our development, the technologies of today have a powerful influence not only on our attitudes and lifestyles, but also on our changing human instincts. At the same time that technology is enriching our lives, its excessive use is destroying human ability and the environment. In our selfishness and haste, we have no time for process. We challenge nature and try to overcome its power. Seduced by the more comfortable life that technological advances have made possible, we seem to forget the power of the individual's body and spirit. The influence of technology can be harsh and brutal.

Seen from space, our earth is a luminous jewel of flowing blues and greens. There are no red lines of separation. Where are the borders? Where is China? Where exactly does Russia end? Is that Italy, or is it France? God has given no person, no organization, no nation, territorial permission. Yet impersonal, nationalistic military technology is an escalating sickness infecting our lives, an expression of fear and mistrust. At the touch of a button millions of people die, whole cities are destroyed, and poisons remain to defile the earth for all of our generations to come. We cannot see or feel the pain of the enemy. Our hands are clean and unstained by their blood, but the invisible stains on our spirit can never be erased. I wonder, is there still time to take a lesson from history, from the samurai of Toku-

gawa Ieyasu, and give up the "gun"? If we must struggle and fight among ourselves, could we return to a less sophisticated time when the battlefield was filled only with the screams of soldiers killing soldiers, a time before whole cities were alive with the horror of the mutilated and burning bodies of the weak and the innocent and the young? War is only a word to much of modern society. Removed by technology, many have never seen the pain in the eyes of a starving child chewing at his dead mother's breast. Frightened at the cold touch of her body, how can he understand why there is no milk, no lullaby? We cannot see the enemy's tears. The enemy is not human. The enemy feels no pain.

The destruction and violence of war, no matter how far we may be removed, is obvious. But within our daily lives there is an insidious violence that, although perhaps not quite as obvious, is just as surely affecting our consciousness and destroying our world. The destructive channels taken by the instincts of aggression are reflected in our modern institutions, the negative symbols of our culture. The complexities of law enforcement agencies and overflowing penal institutions are indicators of fear and hatred. Requirements for hospital beds and mental institutions are indicators of fear and hatred. Requirements for hospital beds and mental institutions are increasing at an alarming rate as our minds succumb to the pressures of the insecurity and stress of modern life. Our bodies weaken from food that is too rich and a physical life that is too soft. Sanitation departments and waste disposal systems are overburdened with waste that cannot be disposed of at all, and we are burying ourselves and our world under a mountain of garbage, an exchange of abundant natural resources for overwhelming waste. Greedy and thinking only of our personal economy and comfort today, we have forgotten the beauty of nature's great economic system of recycling. Humanity has become a global parasite. Robbing the earth of its riches and returning poison, we have created an economic dead end.

Excess and waste are very dangerous forms of violence, for they deeply affect our consciousness. Our society, our economy, our lifestyle is geared to the instant and disposable. We find no satisfaction in the process and no pride in our work or in the community. Our cities are filthy and overcrowded and our waters undrinkable. We are a materialistic society, yet we have no respect for materials. This same attitude toward materials affects our attitude toward ourselves and our lives. Every material has a function; every life has a function. To discard a paper cup seems a very small transgression, but multiplied by a million people, the problem becomes staggering and the act affects the consciousness a little more strongly each time. It becomes a habit, a lifestyle, and extends into larger areas of our lives, even into human relationships. How many people spend the final years of their lives in old folks' homes? Forgotten, filled with loneliness and despair, they hold within their aging bodies a deep understanding of life, experiences to share, and love that cries for expression; thus one of our greatest natural resources remains untapped, the result of a throwaway mentality. We have lost our pride. We have lost our loyalty to each other, and we have lost touch with nature.

Our hands and creative powers were once occupied in fulfilling our daily needs with objects of pride and beauty, simple things that would last a lifetime and beyond: a cup thrown on a potter's wheel, a table of hand-loved wood becoming more beautiful with time and use, a quilt sewn with familiar patterns to be appreciated anew each cold winter's night. Our lives were filled with beloved, personal beauty made by our own hands, the hands of our parents and grandparents, and of our friends. We needed each other. We traded, we bartered, and we shared. Each thing that touched our lives had a story. We struggled together, sweated together, and built a community; our involvement was personal and rewarding. In intimate contact with the life force of nature, we were nourished by the food we grew, free from chemicals and filled with love.

Now the machine has become our slave, but in having a slave the master, too, is enslaved, for he is a part of the process. Robbed of the joys of creation and pride of accomplishment, we run the machines so that we may buy what the machines produce. And the objects we buy are weak and sterile, mass-produced by machines that have no pride and often run by workers with no personal interest in the result. Too many jobs, no longer a source of pride, fulfillment, or the security of a position in the community, have become an impersonal source of money and the false security of material wealth. We have become just one part of the machine, marking time from paycheck to paycheck. Richer in time and material than ever before, people still have not found happiness.

The human body grows weaker as life becomes easier. Elevators, escalators, and the automobile have rendered muscles, once firm and strong from running and climbing, weak and flaccid. Our minds have become dulled from lack of use as we allow calculators and computers to do more and more of the thinking for us. We have at our disposal more free time than ever before, but instead of using it creatively for personal study and inner growth, we lean back in the controlled comfort of our living rooms and demand to be entertained, hypnotized by the endless parade of animated figures on a television screen. Children no longer need to develop their vivid imagination in creating games and play; it's done for them electronically. We are a society of spectators, voyeurs rarely experiencing the peace that comes from physical expression and personal accomplishment. We seek a life of ease and comfort, believing that this is the way to happiness, and then wonder why life has lost its flavor.

Happiness is born of adversity. Without the experience of hardship, all the joys, the beauty, and the blessings of life are taken for granted. If your stomach is always full, food is uninteresting, but after experiencing the gnawing pain of hunger, a bowl of gruel is cause for rejoicing. We do not truly appreciate

(Top left) *Paul Kang, interpreter, with Mitsugi Saotome (at microphone).* (Right) *Shigeru Suzuki,* shihan dai, *Kevin Choate,* uke.

Photographs, 1978, from the second of two demonstrations given by Mitsugi Saotome at Japan House in New York City. This demonstration was part of a presentation of Japanese culture promoted by the United Nations Ambassador from Japan for the delegates to the U.N. and the diplomatic community. The first demonstration, in 1976, promoted by Donald Keyes of Planetary Citizens, was presented to the International Peace Keeping Forces. In both demonstrations the principles of Aikido were presented as a vital approach to world peace.

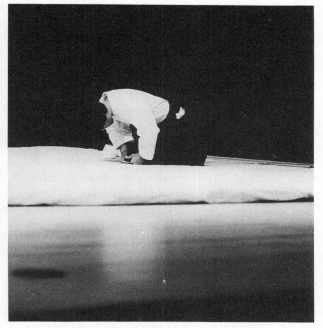

the sight of a tree until we have no eyes, or the song of a bird until we have no ears. And maybe we'll never understand the true meaning of peace and harmony—nature's meaning—until all that remains of our earth is a charred cinder of destruction and death.

Chosen: *challenge*

Kevin Choate, uke.

Happiness is nourished by security. Not material security, but the security of self-trust, confidence, and independence. If life is always easy, there is no chance to know the limitless ability of the human mind and spirit. There is no challenge, no testing, no refinement or growth. Society is becoming richer and more comfortable, but the emptiness of some of our values leads directly to dissatisfaction and violence. In all the great empires throughout history, the people were strong and filled with purpose as they struggled to develop a new society. But as their dreams of power were fulfilled, they found only emptiness. They became decadent, their society began to decay from the inside, and the empires, without exception, collapsed.

We are an educated society, but there is a flaw deep within our system of education. By our example, by the education they receive, and the standards by which they are judged, our children are overloaded with desires for material success. In the drive for material security, we have lost the excitement, the wonder, and the spiritual richness of a close communion with nature. We have lost our soul. Our cities are dry and static and square, for we have forgotten the philosophy and poetry of the dynamic forms of our earth and the universe. Our minds are becoming dry and static and square, for we no longer allow an appreciation and respect for creation to touch our hearts. The values and goals that we have stressed for so long are no longer valid.

People are slowly waking up to the fact that the global resources, the materials of this earth, are limited, and the research being done on environmental problems is of extreme importance. But the entire problem has as its base our mental attitude, humanity's concept of humanity. We have created the pollution by our greed and impatience; we have created the nuclear weapons and the wars by our selfishness and ego. The problems will not change until we change. Life is naturally one karma and nature does not promise infinity. This earth is limited. There are no more empires to build and no more frontiers to conquer. We must redirect our focus in the search for challenge and expression, for the only frontier left is the frontier of the spirit. Our values and the education of our children must be allowed to evolve.

The role of social education through the family and the schools is to establish a foundation on which to build the spiritual and moral attitudes, and to fine-tune and direct the aggressive responses of our children. Yet at school they are too often met with indifference; and at home too often underdisciplined and overprotected, smothered in the name of love. Is this really love, or is it ego? True unselfish love disciplines and gives direction; it challenges and makes fertile for growth. It goes past the intellect, equips the spirit for independence, and then trusts. The function of education is to challenge the spirit and raise the consciousness; it is not the shallow exchange of facts, but the search for truth.

Unfortunately, most education only reaches the mind. Our dimensional scale of thinking is the result of social education. Children know just "myself," but receiving an education should mean that you study "the other" also. Each person has many relationships. I am, but I am not alone. I have the need of others, yet I am not dependent, for I also have a responsibility to others. I am my background; I am the universe.

This is the highest goal of Aikido training. It is not mere psychology training, nor is it a game of logic. It is an education that goes past the intellect. Cutting deep into the core of human consciousness, it touches instinct. Human instinct is the true "center."

Honno: *instinct*

The process of training instinct is not an easy one and must begin on the physical level. All the familiar selfish ego defense mechanisms must be brutally stripped away before the consciousness can be opened and made strong. The fear that blocks out the ability to reason and dissolves higher consciousness into panic must be faced again and again, and we must learn that there is no escape. In order to control and refine the responses of both body and spirit until they become natural and instinctive, stress and panic must be encountered, faced, and overcome. As you study the thin edge between life and death, your senses will expand and sharpen. Your lungs will fill with the incredible sweetness of the breath of challenge, and the intensity of a growing independence and self-knowledge will etch reality with a luminous razor's edge of clarity. This heightened state of awareness can only be achieved by taking the body to the very limits of endurance and beyond.

An intimate knowledge of the limitations of the body and the frustrations produced by this understanding is of vital importance in forcing the application of power past physical strength to the refinement of movement, perception, and intuition and into the realm of the spirit. A hard attack or hard *ukemi* will not in itself help society. But the strong spirit that is developed through hard training can be society's salvation. The study and digestion of the qualities of human uniqueness result in the blossoming of human consciousness. The physical study of reaction centers life around action. If morality and compassion are confined to the intellect and extended only by beautiful words, you can have no effect on social change. But if morality, compassion, and the passionate desire to help society are part of the instinct and deep consciousness, they will be extended through positive action and will help effect powerful change.

During the Russo-Japanese War, Emperor Meiji, even in the bitter cold of winter, wore no coat and ate only a little of the poorest rice. His staff and close advisors were very worried and begged him to eat better food and dress warmly. But the emperor refused, saying, "I want to share the soldiers' situation and create a spiritual bond, keeping them in my heart and in my prayers every minute of every day. Why are people not thinking of their struggle and suffering?" His actions added truth to his understanding and sincerity and power to his compassion. Upon hearing this, many people were ashamed and followed his example. When news of these actions reached the soldiers, their hearts were deeply touched and tears of pride and respect for their emperor flowed with renewed dedication.

To make compassion and morality a part of the instinct and consciousness, we must learn to perceive the pain of others. Sharing the same hard experience, the same stress and frustration, an essential part of Aikido education, penetrates ego, forms a strong bond of respect and concern, and develops a sensitivity and awareness of another's situation. If we could sincerely feel each other's pain, there would be fewer wars and less loneliness and hunger. People are passively awaiting a miracle, but *Homo sapiens* is a miracle, the miracle of billions of years of universal evolution and the miracle of the spirit of God. Now it is our responsibility to make another miracle and become a strong society of action. All throughout history, the truly great social and spiritual leaders were shaped and formed by adversity. None lived a life of ease, for only the stimulus of hard experience can make great action. At this time in our evolution we desperately need heroes, leaders of action and spiritual power. This responsibility falls upon each individual.

The universe is even now in a state of change, creative and creating, continuing a step-by-step refinement, and humanity is a process of the universe. Our evolution is not completed but is simply at one small stage in the growing process. We still have a future and the choice of its direction. The universe is attuned to one creative direction of dynamic improvement to the final level of perfection. If we do not reflect upon our past and proceed to the next step in our evolution, spiritual growth, the laws of the universe will give us no choice. Nature has a very strict love, and the universe and natural law will continue. Only through the education of instinct and the refinement of human qualities can humanity continue.

合氣道主
植芝吉祥丸

Aiki by Doshu Kisshomaru Ueshiba

9

AIKIDO: The TRANSMISSION of TRUTH

The greatest challenge for the enlightened masters of Budo has been to define and explain their understanding of the secrets of the forces of energy, of power. They used the spiritual world as metaphor, the natural world as metaphor. They used simple ideas and complex ideas, striving to give voice to the nameless. They tried to demonstrate their understanding through the medium of technique, but the connection in movement was as obscure as their words. At last, Morihei Ueshiba, through the development of Aikido, organized a technical and spiritual movement that clearly expresses the true principles of power, the supreme power found in universal phenomena.

Each technique is a graphic display of the circulation of energy that moves throughout the cosmos in the same way that it moves within our bodies. With practice and study, the truths of the spirit and the truths of science fuse together and become one understanding of insight and intuition, which cannot be expressed in words. From the gentle comfort of the valley, you cannot see the top of the mountain. Without the experience of challenging its heights, clouds obscure even the imagination. Experience is true knowledge. It changes concepts and expands spirit. The universe, life, and human relationships all hold the same truths, and love is the guiding power of all. This is the meaning of Aikido. You must see and feel, taste and digest Aikido movement before its secrets are revealed.

Often those with only shallow experience criticize Aikido upon first observation, saying the movement is too soft and too weak, or that it is only a dance. Their world is very narrow, for they are grasping their own image of the martial Way and their minds are stopped by the old concepts of struggle and conflict. Understanding power only through impact, they comprehend its most limited form. Does the moon impact with the earth? Does the earth challenge Mars or Jupiter? Their stubborn preconceptions block the acceptance of truth. Their hostility blocks the development of true power.

People from many different styles of *bujutsu* and Budo came to O Sensei, seeking his teachings. To them he ordered, "You must have *shoshin*, a beginner's mind, a mind of pure white paper on which to see the moving images of Aikido's secrets. You must try emptiness. A mind that is filled with opinion and prejudice has no room for the truths of the universe. If a cup is always full, the water becomes stale and spoils. To be refreshed, it must first be emptied. If your ears are always filled with the sound of your own voice, you cannot hear the rich harmonies of God."

Shoshinsha: *beginner*

Before the Second World War, O Sensei strictly controlled the acceptance of all students into Aikido. Acquiring power, any power, can affect the personality in many different ways. This is perhaps even more relevant to the study of Budo and the martial arts. On the one hand, it can build modesty and respect for others, reinforcing social consciousness. It can open your eyes to your own strengths and weaknesses. It can promote spiritual confidence and inspire positive action. But on the other hand, if the mind is closed and the personality is self-centered and seriously flawed by a deep attachment to selfish ego, training in the martial arts may provoke a fanatical search for power until the obsession magnifies negative ego and creates an anachronism, a social outcast who lives in a comic-book world of violence and dreams.

When a teacher accepts a student to continue his teachings and philosophy, his responsibility for that student is not only a personal one. The student continues not just the teacher's technical skill, but his spirit as well. Passing on the knowledge of power, the teacher is responsible for the reactions and social influence of that knowledge, be it good or bad. The student is the raw material, the clay, the wood, the stone. If there is a serious flaw in the personality or spiritual attitude that cannot be corrected, no matter how strong or good the technique, the finished creation will be weak and flawed. For this reason, even before considering a student, O Sensei required

Shinrai: *trust*

letters of recommendation from two persons of good character. Then, watching him closely, he carefully checked the student's character during a period of waiting, and finally held a personal interview before the decision was made. Initial acceptance was no guarantee, for O Sensei continually tested his students in many ways, checking their character and development. If at any time a student failed to measure up to the highest standards, he would no longer receive O Sensei's teachings. Technique was not a commodity that could be bought and sold. The price that O Sensei placed on his teachings was an open mind and the sincerity, dedication, and integrity of the student.

After the war O Sensei recognized the need for the teachings of harmony and a peaceful coexistence through the example of Aikido to be spread throughout the world, and he swung wide the gate. That Aikido could not be confined to any one nation was evident, for the teachings were universal truths. And Budo evolved to its highest form. Emerging from the rusting chains of nationalism, it became a gift of strength and spiritual power to all the world. But at the same time, O Sensei recognized the necessity for the teachings to be passed on in the correct manner. He continued the traditional style of apprenticeship and the high standards for his personal students, his *uchi deshi*, remained. The final teachings were reserved for only the few whom he considered qualified to pass on the essence with honor and integrity for the benefit of humanity. Succession is most important, for it is the continuation of the spiritual stream. This is Kannagara; this is the Tao.

It is the same in a Zen temple. There are teachings for the masses, valuable teachings to help them live a better life and develop a better society. But only the very few initiates who are open to truth will understand the teachings and be shown the secrets of enlightenment. "Many are called, but few will be chosen." So often a little knowledge, like a little power, is a very dangerous thing. People read and study and believe that they understand, but this understanding is easily infused with their own ego and personal opinions. They parrot beautiful phrases without the foundation of true knowledge and become insolent, reveling in the sound of their own voice. True understanding does not pressure others. It does not insist "my way is the only right way." Beware of arrogance and self-righteousness.

For true study and eventual understanding, you must give up attachment to your own opinions and ego. One of the greatest barriers to study is the concept of equality and its misinterpretation. Life is diverse. Everyone is equal in the respect that we are all the children of God, each life a part of the universal essence and a part of each other life. But we all have different knowledge and experience, different abilities. Ability, intelligence, and strength of character are not confined to a particular race, nationality, or religious group. They are not the product of social status or wealth. There is no difference between a master musician who understands his instrument

and the mathematics and harmonies of music and the farmer who grows the finest vegetables and understands the rhythms of nature, or the mixer of concrete who understands the exact timing, proportions, and properties of his material. Each has a special talent, refined through experience and intuition. They are equal, but they are not. If you need to lay a concrete foundation on which to build a house, you do not consult the musician. If you want to study music, you don't ask the farmer to teach you.

If you and the teacher are equal, study is unnecessary. If you have no respect for the teacher's guidance and experience, you cannot learn. If one hundred inexperienced people misjudge one fine teacher because they are not yet ready to understand his teachings, the rules of democracy would say that they are right. With this attitude study is impossible, for you must trust. There is no democracy on the mat. Everyone you practice with has either more or less experience than you. Either you learn from that person or you help and support his or her study.

Particularly in the study of a martial art, it is most important to strictly follow the teacher's guidance. The possibility of mishap and injury is always present, but through years of experience an intuitive teacher will direct the study so that this possibility is kept to a minimum. He will quickly see when ego is getting out of control and will take measures to correct it. In one second even a small misunderstanding in the execution of a technique can result in a broken arm or a fractured shoulder. O Sensei created the Aikido educational system to be a natural system that moves with the natural flow of the body rather than against it. *Jujutsu* has many of the same techniques— such as *kotegaeshi*, *shihonage*, and *nikyo*—but the result is different. The techniques of *jujutsu* are designed to destroy. The techniques of Aikido are designed to continue the process and redirect it into the creative path of harmony. When one understands the body and understands the Aikido educational system, the incidence of injury will be very small.

Aikido was developed for communication, not competition. It shares the truth of natural principle to discover the movements of harmony. In this way people of entirely different physical abilities, the very strong with the very weak, often the child and the adult, can practice together, learn from each other, and develop their abilities to adjust and harmonize with any situation. But the paradox of attack and defense, studying conflict to understand harmony, is difficult for most people to understand. The student can very easily become misdirected and follow the wrong path in the search for power and strength. The ego wants proof and cries for expression through competition.

The samurai did not allow himself the egotistical display of emotion, for it betrayed weakness. Even if he had no money and nothing to eat, he would smile contentedly and chew on a toothpick as though he had just partaken of a great feast. He maintained his pride at all times, for his problems were personal, not to be displayed before others. Only his social function was important. If his weaknesses were common knowledge, he would be ineffective and unable to carry out his duty. In the same respect, he did not trust the egotistical display of power and strength in others. Accustomed to exaggerated displays, people of today associate a grimacing face, tightened and inflexible muscles, and a loud, insistent voice with strength. But these displays are merely the signs of insecurity, a distorted psychological defense mechanism. This strategy relies on ego. Ego makes us blind to reality and causes many mistakes. If someone talks too much, or promises too much, or insists too much, I cannot trust their words. Too often words are not an honest form of communication. Actions do not lie. Daily lifestyle does not lie. You must learn to look past the mask to see the true heart through intuition and perception. People are only making small entertainment with their wild emotional displays. They are actors who have forgotten their true reality.

Teaching a competitive martial way is not the teaching of truth. Competition can be a constructive and positive outlet for our aggressions. It can shake us from our complacency and push us to do things we never would have tried, make us go a little farther or run just a little faster. This is the desired result of games and sport. But Budo is not a game. Budo is a Way of life, a life attitude. The reason behind the supreme effort must be different. When competition becomes excessive and becomes the driving force in daily life as it has in much of modern society, it breeds more frustration, distorting the personality and destroying human relationships. We continually challenge the ability, intelligence, self-image, and ideology of others, from the petty fight for a parking space to the meaningless display of wit as we seek, not the exchange of ideas, but to have the last clever word. The ego rears its ugly head and says, "I'm better than you. I want you to know it, and I'm going to prove it." And competition, no longer an outlet for aggression, becomes an act of aggression. We feel constantly threatened and clothe our insecurity with great displays of arrogance as we compete for the center of attention. Everybody wants to be a "star." Constantly at war with each other, we are afraid to trust. We become jealous, selfish, and violent, defending ourselves by attacking others. Life becomes a race to be won, to be finished, and we forget to appreciate the process of being alive.

With so much attachment to victory, most of the modern styles of the martial arts that promote competition have lost their essence. This is evident from watching some of the martial sports competitions. What has happened to fine technique and principle? They have been destroyed by aggression and the fear of defeat. Inside the ropes, after the style of boxing and wrestling, they have become poor imitations of these sports, the elegance and philosophy taught by the grand masters of the many styles forgotten. The application of the arts has narrowed. Concerned only with victory and defeat, they have become an ex-

Where is the enemy?

travaganza for the strutting display of childish ego. In this context harmony cannot be understood. Budo is not a sport.

The sports-oriented martial arts concentrate on aggression, on the negative aspects of defeating the enemy. You cannot control the reactions of another through aggression, for aggression only draws more resistance. If you push, you create a situation in which the other can resist your power, and it becomes a struggle decided by physical strength. But if the other pushes, and you are flexible enough to turn without hesitation rather than resist, the other will be drawn into the vacuum you have created and be within your sphere of control. This cannot be accomplished only with the physical body; it must be directed by spiritual attitude.

The goal of Budo training, of Aikido training, is not to magnify aggressive response but to control and refine it. We must learn to appreciate the process that leads to the true wisdom of harmony. Sports championship is only small entertainment. The way of Bu teaches us to throw away private ambition and greed and to become empty. This is a true Budo master's education to his students: education in the power of gravity, the power of a vacuum. He trains the spirit, for through hard training he has come to understand the limitations of the body.

We must understand that human life is limited and must develop the modesty that comes from that understanding. Behavior is universal. It is the same for all forms of life. All life has ego, for the function of life is to continue and refine its existence. The Creation is God's ego, a giving, loving ego. If there is no ego, there is no love. But attachment to selfish ego creates a weak, sentimental, and narrow love. Teaching is ego. If there is no ego, communication is not important, education is not important. Jesus Christ had ego. The Buddha had ego. They wanted everyone to understand God's love and to realize that we are all the children of God. They were empty, and the spirit of God directed their path.

This is Universal Ego. The truth of I AM is that I am the other. I am a part of God. I am a part of the cosmos. I am a part of the earth. I am part of you. I AM is true God Consciousness, Universal Ego. But people have forgotten. We are arrogant and do not wish to acknowledge our own limitations. Instead of embodying God's mission, it appears that we are invading God's function as we selfishly destroy our limited global resources and each other. Understanding that our physical power is limited by engaging in hard training will help us to deeply understand the limitations of all life. We must truly acknowledge that life and the universe are one system, not just with the mind, but intuitively, with the heart, the body, and the spirit. This is reality, not just ideology. Don't say, "I know!" Get past "I know" and truly seek to understand and believe.

Not until you understand through experience that the body is limited can you hear the voice of the body's natural feedback system of adjustment. If you are unbalanced, the body will naturally try to adjust and correct the imbalance. If your body is unbalanced inside, it will be corrected by pain, fever, and discharge. The feedback system is the Way of correction. If it is silenced by a fearful and aggressive ego, the body will be weak and unable to adjust. The martial Way will be weak and the abilities for self-defense lost. Correct training in Aikido will silence the ego and allow you to discover the natural defenses of

Misogi

your body and mind. You will understand good balance, developing perception and a stable attitude, with all parts adjusting according to the laws of natural phenomena. This is the system of *misogi*: purification and adjustment.

For strong martial movement, dynamic martial reaction, you must have good physical balance. The study of movement is the study of dynamic balance and will help you to develop balanced ideas and spiritual stability. If there is disharmony in your physical situation, if you are not flexible enough to adjust, if you are stubborn, you cannot execute dynamic movement. The ego is greedy and calculates results. This calculation and strategy are the foundation of competition. But in reality, if the enemy attacks and you hesitate, taking the time to calculate and decide, you will die beneath his blade. This is also *misogi*.

God's law is *misogi harai*, the universal feedback system that protects all of Creation from disorder. The wind breaks a dead branch and blows away the dead leaf. Rains cleanse the rock and wash away the dust from the leaves and grasses so they can breathe; the seas wash the shore, and the natural enemy cleanses the earth of the weak. A life form reaches nature's breaking point, and then its function is exchanged. The dead leaf, the dead tree, the dead animal help to make another life. This breath of renewal is the concept of reincarnation, one more chance in a different form. Before creation there must be destruction. Before the final breaking point, there must be intensification. All of Creation is balance. Sometimes hard training builds up the ego, but strength and ego cannot work to produce final Aikido movement and technique. Before the refinement of Aikido can be expressed, the movement must be purified and aggressive reaction exhausted by proving over and over that competition does not work. This exhaustion is the ego's breaking point. This is *misogi* and only the beginning of severe training.

Hard training is not just muscle training; it is not only discovering the redirection of force through strong resistance. It is more than fast throws and hard *ukemi*. These trainings are important, but the hard training that builds strong spirit and develops spiritual confidence is the training of a hard situation. It is easy to train vigorously every day if you have plenty of good nourishing food and lots of rest. Try fasting for one week and still continue to train regularly. Or try not sleeping for three or four days but continue to train. As the body reaches its limits, the spirit takes over and begins to grow. Obviously this kind of training may be dangerous. It should never be undertaken without the supervision of a qualified teacher.

In the *dojo* of Yamaoka Tesshu, there was a special training for silencing the ego and developing a strong and confident spirit. It was the training of defense against one thousand attacks. Over an extended period of time—weeks, months, or, in one case, a year—the student would, every day, face one hundred training partners who would attack with all their power ten times each in any style they chose. On the final day of this training, the student received no rest and only one small cup of soup for nourishment. Legs turned to jelly from the weight of the *kendo* armor, arms quivered with the pain of the effort to wield the *shinai*. The physical body soon became exhausted, and it was at this point that the student gave up attachment to physical strength and good technique, and met his spirit. Though he was knocked down again and again by the blows of fresh attackers, the student's spiritual power did not stop and his concentration intensified. He continued to fight and attempted with all of his spiritual might to defend against each attack. Many times, by the end of the training, the student was completely unconscious, yet still standing in *kamae* (a posture or stance of readiness), his *shi-*

Kamae: *stance of readiness*

nai held in the posture of defense. This is not narrow physical strength. This is the true essence of strength.

Yamaoka Tesshu knew the day on which he was to die, so he called his family and his students together to prepare them. Seated formally, he asked them to please not be surprised or sad. After thanking them for all their help and devotion, he passed away. Even in death he remained seated in *seiza* (formal kneeling/sitting posture), in perfect form. The body passes away, but the spirit continues.

A very long time ago, one man stood alone in front of his teacher to protect him from the arrows of many attackers. Arrow after arrow penetrated the man's body, but he continued to stand, still protecting his master. The attackers, seeing this, became very afraid and ran away. They understood that his power was no longer of this physical world.

Once in Ayabe, when O Sensei was perhaps fifty years of age, he was visited by a very accomplished *kendo* master. Anxious to test himself and to prove a point, the *kendo* master challenged O Sensei. They walked into the garden together, the *kendo* master carrying his *katana* (sword), O Sensei empty-handed. The sun flashed off the brightly polished steel as the *kendo* master moved into his *kamae*, O Sensei standing quietly before him. And they stood. Sweat began to break on the *kendo* master's forehead, rolling down his cheeks like tears. It fell like a thousand prisms from the strained and glistening muscles of his powerfully developed forearms. And still they stood. O Sensei, calm and detached, aware but not

In the kamae *in the top photograph, the weapon is held in the* gedan *position. In the bottom photo it is in* jodan.

waiting, only reflected the image of the man and the glittering steel before him. Five, seven, maybe ten minutes passed. Exhausted from the struggle of attempting to attack the universe, the *kendo* man surrendered. He had been unable to move. His acute sensitivity and perception had revealed no openings in O Sensei's defense.

Many people misunderstand the reality behind this encounter, wishing to believe that O Sensei hypnotized his opponent by calling upon a mysterious secret technique of ancient Oriental origin. In fact, O Sensei's technique was spiritual confidence and strong spiritual concentration. Harboring no thoughts of fighting or competition, devoid of the fear and greed that create an opening, he tied up the spirit of his opponent so intensely that the swordsman's power escaped and rushed into the vacuum created by O Sensei's purity. The enemy could not attack, for O Sensei's spirit was without conflict and his mind revealed only harmony. The enemy's spirit was mirrored within O Sensei's eyes. He could not attack, for there was no one to attack but himself.

The mind of conflict and challenge is a mind that thirsts for the enemy's blood. Though your hands never close about the enemy's throat, though your hands are never soiled with another's blood, if your heart is filled with hatred or the desire to win over another, to watch the other's suffering, these thoughts will lie like death, decaying within your spirit, and you will never understand spiritual power. The true martial Way, Budo, is the Way of adjustment, not destruction. It is social *misogi*. It seeks to correct a problem, not to judge or destroy a life.

True power is found in the spiritual world, and true self-defense is the protection of the enemy's karma. The movement of defense is not a game; it is a very serious reality. When the enemy tries to kill you, the only choice is life or death. If you are weak, you cannot defend your own karma or the enemy's. Weakness is an excuse, an easy way out. If you cannot defend yourself and fall beneath the enemy's attack, the enemy is guilty and be-

comes a murderer. But you too have sinned because of your weakness, for you've made a murderer. And the karma of the enemy and yourself is the same.

If the enemy attacks and you kill the enemy, then you are the murderer. The result is the same: a life has been destroyed. The karma is the same. It does not matter who was right and who was wrong, for the enemy is your shadow. You and the enemy are one life. If you kill the enemy, you are committing suicide. There are no excuses. The Way is very strict. You must defend yourself, and you must defend the enemy. This is your responsibility.

"True victory is not defeating an enemy. True victory gives love and changes the enemy's heart." O Sensei's great *satori* was the realization that love is true power, the application of the wisdom of God, not the narrow application of human strength. The great spiritual teachers have always taught that you must love your enemy; this is the highest love. If there is love and respect, there is no enemy. When you are no longer blinded by hatred and ego, the enemy becomes a part of yourself. The enemy becomes a teacher to help refine your concepts and your technique, the necessary counterbalance that sharpens your senses. Unclouded by hatred, you can accurately reflect the other's position and movement, and understand the other's life and weaknesses. The most important point of Budo training is to understand the enemy. If you understand, you cannot hate. Only in this way can you discover the true path of harmony. This is not the weakness of sentimental love, but the strict power of universal love. Love must never be weak, for often the function of love is to discipline and give pain. Sometimes there is no other choice but to destroy a sickness.

In Japan we say, "*Hotoke no kau mo sando.*" Loosely translated, this is the answer to a prayer for another chance. But it warns that if there is no reflection and a second mistake is made, there will be no chance to make a third.

As the Buddha was watching a spider spin its web, he was reminded of a man, a murderer and a thief, who had been condemned to hell. This man had once shown a spark of compassion and mercy in his short and evil life. While he was walking from one town to the next, a spider crossed his path. Without thinking, he tried to step on it and kill it, as was his natural inclination, but the spider escaped. The man laughed as he watched the spider scurry away. "Even you, who are so small and insignificant, value your life as much as I do mine. I'll let you live."

So the Buddha decided to test the man, to give him a chance to escape the horrors of his situation and find salvation. He wove a silken cord of spider's thread extending from paradise into hell, past the mountain of needles and into the river of blood. The thief saw the cord and, grasping it with all his might, began to climb. Soon all who were imprisoned in the river of blood were frantically swimming after

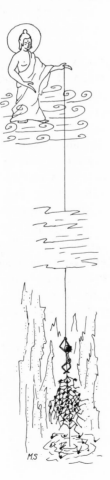

the silken cord. In the hope of finding salvation, they began swarming up the cord after him. Fearing the delicate threads would break from the weight of so many, he kicked them away, cursing them and screaming, "I saw it first. This is my salvation. You will not endanger my chance of escape!" The Buddha, seeing this, was deeply shamed and severed the cord with the weight of his tears. This man was too selfish to enter paradise. He did not deserve salvation.

"San Goku Shi" is a famous Chinese story of the territorial conflict between the great empires of Shiyoku and Gi. The prime minister of Shiyoku, Shokatsu Kome, entrusted the protection of Gaitei, a most important strategic position, and the command of his armies to Bashoku, a young general of great military genius whom he had personally trained. Kome discussed in detail his plan for protecting Gaitei with Bashoku and sent him off with much confidence and love. But General Bashoku was guided by his ego. Believing more in his own precociousness than Kome's wisdom, he disobeyed the prime minister and used his own strategy for the protection of the territory. He lost the war, he lost his armies, and he lost the important territory of Gaitei. After the war there was a court martial, and Bashoku was found guilty. Although Kome loved him as though he were his own son, he realized that such ego and disregard for authority could infect the whole army. Bashoku was executed. Selfish ego is a communicable disease that spreads rapidly. One person inflicted with this violence can transmit the disease to an entire community. The community can infect the nation, and the nation the whole world.

Love of the enemy is a very strict love. Sometimes, for the protection of others, that love means destruction. This is not an excuse for wrongdoing. To take the responsibility for destruction, nature's cleansing system must be fully understood. The object of the destruction must truly be a danger to social welfare. A dairy cow drinks the pure water from a stream and gives nourishing milk, but a poisonous snake drinking the same water from the same stream can only make poison. The same is true of education. Given the same teachings, one person will make a good member of society, while the other will make only poison. Society must be protected. The rights of the individual and of individuality must be protected. The weak and the children must be protected. But personal ego cannot be involved. Group or national ego cannot be involved. Greed or prejudice must not be involved. It must be an act of purification, of true *misogi*. Right or wrong, the destruction becomes your karma, and you must accept the spiritual consequences for the action. If you must kill the enemy, then first you must die. This is the only way. To truly destroy the enemy is first to destroy the self. This is pure. If you are worried about your own life, selfishly thinking of yourself while trying to kill the enemy, this is a lie. You must sacrifice your selfish ego. If there is attachment to selfish de-

Jikogisei: *sacrifice*

sires, there is no objectivity, and the health and harmony of society will be destroyed.

Disharmony always comes from attachment and the defense of selfish ego, greed, fear of lost territory or lost power, and fear of a different opinion or a different way. It is easy to see and understand personal ego but much more difficult to recognize group ego. Humanity's misunderstanding of loyalty to God has caused more suffering than any other form of self-righteous ego. The loyalty of genocide, the

loyalty of the gas chambers, the loyalty of the human torch—does God order this kind of loyalty? Can we really call out God's name to absolve us of this kind of guilt? Blind loyalty is most dangerous, for it is all too easy to twist the ideas of loyalty and righteousness with the lever of human greed and selfish ego. A selfish ego has no respect for differences. It orders, "Everybody think like me, everybody look like me." How would you really feel if every face were only your image, if every mind affirmed your thoughts? People talk of harmony but have no respect for a different idea or a different way. The study of harmony means learning to respect the differences and studying the unity found within those different points.

Organizations, first developed to serve their members and help them to reach a common goal, set down basic rules to protect their interests. While they are small and growing, they maintain an open line of communications between the leaders and the members and between the organization itself and others of like purpose. In this way a healthy feedback system is established, and the organization functions properly and is refined for the good of the membership.

But many times, as the organization grows and begins to taste success, the leaders begin to impose their own ideas and personal ego on the goals of the organization. Rather than helping the members, they seek to control the members by appealing to their sense of loyalty to the cause. The individuals for whom the organization was formed become merely a collection of numbers and dollar signs. Jealously protecting its sphere of influence and economic stability, the organization becomes a closed society, and the feedback system is destroyed. Greed escalates into a power struggle of organizations fighting for control, and the organization ego shouts, "This organization is the only true organization. Our way is the only right way!"

Many groups, whether social, spiritual, or educational, speak of love and harmony, so it is difficult to understand why there are so many political conflicts. They speak of being open, but why are there so many closed and narrow minds? The groups and organizations fulfill the human need for companionship on a chosen path. But everyone's needs are different. Everyone's path must necessarily take just a little different direction. If a group is not flexible enough to accommodate those differences, it will perish. Personal opinions of the wrong way or the right way, or of which organization is the true organization, have no meaning. The many paths were not developed for organizations; they were developed for people. Everyone should be training to understand the same basic principles, to refine the spirit, and to discover the path of harmony. True harmony must take many different directions, for harmony is, by its own definition, flexible. If it is not flexible, how can there be harmony? This is not to say that ideals and principles must be compromised, only that *selfish* ideals and principles must be compromised. The path of harmony is not an easy one.

Organizations also need to discover *shoshin*, beginner's mind. Always, after the death of the founder of a Way or of a spiritual or political leader, the group struggles begin. Most believe that their way of succession is right and that all others are wrong. They forget the spiritual essence of the teachings and lose the qualities of modesty and respect for others. The big pie of territory is sliced up and the witch hunts begin.

Every day the universe is fresh. Every day there is revival on earth, as the sun rises, sets, and rises again. The dynamic energy forces of life never stay the same. Organizations need this same freshness, not only expansion, but expansion and contraction. They must make the necessary application to "now" without losing the essence of the past. Please heed this warning, for our responsibility in Aikido is great. O Sensei's dream is for the world to truly be one family, without hatred, without prejudice. Through Aikido we must set an example by our actions. If we allow ourselves to become controlled by power struggles and political conflicts, it will choke O Sensei's true

spirit. The gate that he opened will be closed by fear, selfish ego, and blind loyalty.

Weakness needs to follow blindly. It needs the attachment to loyalty whether right or wrong, for weakness fears the freedom of emptiness. Weakness fears responsibility. If you are selfishly attached to one righteousness, you cannot be free. If you grab righteousness, your fist tightly enclosed around it, your knuckles pale with the effort, you cannot extend your hand to another in friendship. O Sensei once told me, "You must learn the freedom of no desires. If you grab water or air, the essence will escape. If you want to drink, you must cup your hands lightly. If you want to breathe, you must first open your mouth to exhaust the old air. If I give you gold and you grasp it as tightly as you can, fearing its escape, you cannot touch the diamond that I offer."

Many of a master's students understand the teachings in a different way, and each one has a different explanation. No one person has the complete answer. For that reason, the student of art, philosophy, science, or Budo must have one teacher as a guidance, as a reference point, but that student must also have the stimulation of other explanations and other points of view. Boundaries must never exist that the student may not cross. A student must have loyalty to a teacher, but it must be a loyalty of freedom and choice. The most important function of the personal students of O

Sensei is the transmission of his teachings, not the business of developing organizations. The study of Aikido is training in the philosophy and spirit through action. Technique is not just technique, but the physical manifestation of the concept and understanding of the art. If there is a split between technique and philosophy and human relationships in daily life, the Way is not true. The most important quality of a leader is emptiness, the quality of no ego. We must study deeply, realize the spirit of the samurai, and reinforce control, not over others, but over ourselves.

Why is it so difficult to control the ego? You cannot touch the ego, you cannot see it. It has no concrete form. You cannot control the ego because the ego is an illusion. Your actions are your ego. Your life is not your life. We have nothing; we own nothing; we are nothing but a part of God. Did you make your body or control the color of the eyes you were born with? Did you choose your own timing? Everything belongs to God. The ego is not reality, for the ego cannot see the truth of a miracle.

O Sensei lived a simple life of quiet strength, only striving to move closer to the reality of God. He never demanded authority, he never demanded loyalty, yet these things came to him naturally. He could not be controlled by politics or people or money, for he possessed no greed. He did not care about others' opinions of him, he did not worry about the number of students he had, he did not care for territory or wealth. His only strategy was honesty, for he had no weaknesses to hide. He was a completely free spirit, and he had the grace and freedom to laugh at life and

at himself. In technique or personality his intuition sharply cut through the veil of deceitful and cunning strategy, for he was a mirror. If you stand in front of a mirror and try to deceive the image, it does not matter how cunning or how clever you are, the mirror will always catch and reflect your true image.

Shinjutsu: *truth*

Deceitful and cunning strategy depends on the nebulous shadows of greed and weakness for its effectiveness. If you study this kind of strategy, you will never see the clarity of true wisdom and strength. Tricks and subterfuge may work for a very short time, but their power is soon exhausted. If you plant a seed in shallow soil, at first it grows very quickly. But not having the depth to sustain its growth, it soon dies. The patience and courage of honesty will live forever. You must learn to be open and discover the wisdom, the courage, and the power of truth.

A LECTURE BY THE FOUNDER

Throughout the ages, innumerable religious teachers and philosophers have carried the message of truth and spoken of the ultimate power of harmony. Yet why is it that those who opposed truth and fought using the destructive power of Budo arose victorious? Very few of the teachers and philosophers could actually embody truth and express it with their whole being. Their teachings, only expressed in words, could only train the mind. Truth is not logic.

To discover truth and attain the ultimate power of the universe, there are three forms of training that must be undertaken simultaneously. You must train your mind to harmonize with the movement of the universe; you must train your body to harmonize with the movement of the universe; you must train your *ki*, the power of spirit that unites the mind and body, to harmonize with the movement of the universe.

If your mind is to be in harmony with the universe, your words must also be in harmony with the universe. Your words must be one with Kami. Then the movements of the physical body, your actions, must be in harmony with those words. This is the secret taught to me by Budo. When I grasped the essence of the universe through Budo training, I realized that first the physical body and the mind must be united by *ki*, and then as one they must join with the universal movement.

It is through the miraculous function of *ki* that you will unify your mind and body and make that union one with the powers of the universe. Through the correct training you will naturally come to understand universal truth, your mind will brighten, and your body will glow with health. You will find it possible to resolve all conflict and transform this world into a place of great peace. But if the miraculous function of *ki* is misused, the mind and body will fall into disorder and the universe will become chaotic. It is essential that we bring mind, body, and *ki* into correct harmony with the rhythms of universal movement.

Aikido is the path of truth. Aikido training is training to express the essence of truth through our daily life. It is this expression that gives rise to the power of Kami. It is useless to theorize; we must put this into practice. The power of truth will expand within our body and mind only if we actually train ourselves, and Aikido shall unite body and mind through *ki* with the universe itself.

K_I
and
$KOKYU$

What is *ki*? This is perhaps one of the most difficult questions to answer, and yet it is very simple. If I were to give you an onion, saying, "This is *ki*," you would take off the skin, examine it, and think, "This isn't *ki*." Then you might begin to peel it slowly, layer by layer, until nothing was left. No, you wouldn't find it, but without *ki* that onion would not exist.

Many Aikido students search for a special kind of magical energy streaming from the end of their extended hands, believing that their progress depends on its mystical development. But since ancient times, the term *ki* (*ch'i* in Chinese) has represented something that extends into the most ordinary aspects of daily life. It is the activity of life, the essence of spirit. *Ki* is vibration as light and sound are vibration. Sunlight is *ki*; thunder is *ki*; the wind is *ki*. It is tinier than an atom and more awesome than the galaxies. It is the vital essence of the universe, the creative energy of God. *Ki* fills the universe and all it contains from its beginning to eternity.

The word *ki* can indicate a flow of energy, a vibration, an atmosphere. It can describe a state of mind, a state of health, the activity of life, the existence of spirit, or the pulsating movement of the soul. *Ki* is affected by light, by sound, by time and space. Density, pressure, and direction of force will cause it to change its form and application. Countless expressions in the Japanese language contain the word *ki*. The weather is *tenki* or heaven's *ki*; the air is *kuuki*, the *ki* of the sky or the void. Heat is *hi no ki*, the *ki* of fire; the soil is *tsuchi no ki*, the *ki* of the earth. If you are impatient, you have *tanki*, short *ki*; if you are ill, your *ki* is sick, *byoki*. If you are *kichigai*, you are crazy, your *ki* is incomplete. And the laws of nature are *tenri shizen no ki*.

I've heard people say, "I have no *ki*." This is nonsense. If you have no *ki*, you cannot say, "I have no *ki*." If you have no *ki*, you have no life. Perhaps you do not understand *ki*, but you perceive *ki*. Why are you uncomfortable in the presence of one person and joyful at meeting another? When you see someone smile, why are you happy? When you see someone cry, why do you feel pain? How can you understand love or hatred?

Ki

When you see an object, you understand its weight and density without measurement. You know whether it is hard or soft without touching it. You understand heat and cold without a thermometer. *Ki* is perception.

O Sensei used the word *ki* in many different ways. He would refer to an aura as *ki*, and con- centration was *ki*. Sometimes it was confi- dence, sometimes vitality, and sometimes strength. He used it to describe the universal energy force and many times to describe the function of God. So there is no complete an- swer to the question of what is *ki*. Just know reality and you will know *ki*.

Kokyu

Ki is the cosmic essence of life. We know intellectually that water is H_2O, but when you drink from a cold mountain stream you are not thinking of hydrogen and oxygen. It is water that quenches your thirst. We breathe, touch, taste, see, and hear reality every second of our lives, but still we search for a philosophical explanation. The universe gives no philosophical explanations, only experience. You must acknowledge the truth and reality of now.

Your mind and your ideas control your physical situation. This is one kind of energy process. But the true power of *ki* is not to be found in the mind. From the limited perspective of the rational mind, you can never understand the essence of power. Concentration on intellectual knowledge will cloud the spiritual vibrations, and you will develop only strategy. This is the greatest barrier to true understanding. Logic, ideas, and psychological attitude are not necessarily truth. But the spirit is truth. *Ki* and the spirit are one.

I once asked O Sensei, "How can you see God?" He pointed at himself and then at me. "My God perceives your God." The human body is the movement and the essence of the universe, condensed in one form. This is the shape of God. The entire body and the spiritual space that surrounds it is one brain; every nerve, every cell, inside and out, every microunit of space in the spiritual aura, a receiver for the exchange of the essence of *ki*, God's spirit.

There are four elements of *ki* that hold the secrets of the absorption and resolution of the life-sustaining energy that moves within our spiritual and physical body. The *ki* of the earth, of the soil, *tsuchi no ki*, generates the flow of energy through the elements of nutri-

Mizu No Ki

powerful *ki* of water is the energy of the lungs and the heart.

Hi no ki, the *ki* of fire, is the flow of spiritual energy coming into the mind. It controls the power of intuition, of insight and perception. Also controlling the powers of thought, reason, and concentration, it is the *ki* of the subconscious and the conscious mind. *Kuu no ki* is the *ki* of emptiness, the spiritual space through which the energies of the universe ebb and flow. It is the spiritual communion,

Tsuchi No Ki

Hi No Ki   Kuu No Ki

tion. The essence of sunlight and water come together with the components of the earth from which our bodies were formed, and the digestive system resolves their energy into the movements of life. *Mizu no ki*, the *ki* of water, is the power of breath, the resolution of spiritual energy into a physical form. Responsible for the exchange of energy through respiration and the cleansing circulation of the blood, the

the exchange with God through the spiritual aura. The body is a machine controlled by the mind. But it is *ki* that energizes the batteries of the body and mind, uniting them with the essence of spirit, the guiding energy of all.

Vitalized by the charge of energy, we are then purged and emptied by the cleansing process of *misogi*. Fresh energy is constantly flowing throughout the body by the yang and

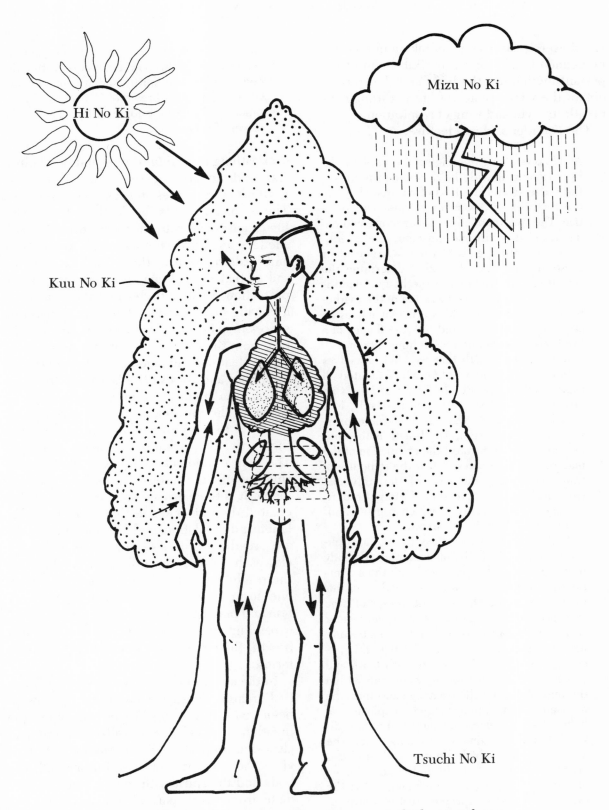

Hi No Ki

Mizu No Ki

Kuu No Ki

Tsuchi No Ki

Our skin and lungs function in the same way as the leaves of a tree,
our digestive system as its roots. All are a part of the same process.

yin of exercise and sleep, of taking in nourishment and eliminating waste. But the most important method for the body and the spirit to obtain the vital essence of life is through the breath, the yin and yang of respiration.

The Founder said in a lecture:

> Aikido is realizing the original power of life, ki, by harmonizing with the throbbing rhythms of the universe and the laws of nature. They are the textbook of Aikido techniques and practice. The laws that define the structure and dynamics of the universe must become an intimate and intuitive part of our awareness, for these are the same laws that determine the structure and dynamics of the body. Aikido is the intuitive physical expression of the mathematician's formulae. The spirit that moves an atom, waves the sea, and lifts the flames of a fire is also circulating in each human being.
>
> It is by the breath that we align ourselves with the wonderful art of ki, which created all things. When this wonderful art of ki—ki no myo yo—is expressed through the body, it is called Takemusu Aiki and is truly the expression of universal truth. The breath is the connection of fire and water, the circulation of the materials of the universe. It is the structure of time and space, the laws of the universal rhythm. It is the expression of eternal pulsating energy, the reality in which spirit, mind, and matter cannot be separated.
>
> As this universal awareness grows, the application of the laws in the movement of the body must be vigorously exchanged with the universal laws. Takemusu Aiki is the freedom of this awareness as you stand in the center of time and space, the living essence of fire and water rushing into your spirit and your body, becoming one and giving birth. Through this exchange the laws will resonate with truth and will be the same within the body and within the universe. First the exchange and then the resonance. The nuclear force, explosion of light, of ki; the electromagnetic vibration, diversity, and excitement of change; and the force of gravity, which empties and produces order—all are created and united, and the art of Kami, of life, comes into being. Ki is the nuclear force, the supreme creative power at the center of all things. But it is the yin and yang of respiration that diversifies and cleanses all things with the exchange, the separation and reunion, of this power. Creation within the body, within the spirit, and within the universe is the living breath of God's love. Respiration is the driving force of life. This is the power of kokyu.

Breathing is musubi, the resolution of physical and spiritual essence into one, the rhythms of the cycles and relationships of life. The exchange of life for death and death for life cleanses and refreshes our world. The oak shelters and gives nourishment to squirrels and birds. In return, their deaths enrich the soil so that the oak may grow and give more protection. Small ants clean up the remains of a praying mantis and in their turn nourish its successors. The power of the sun draws moisture from the earth so that it may be released again, cleansed and made pure, to cool the atmosphere and refresh the lakes and the seas. Kokyu is an open-ended process that joins the galaxy to the universe, the sun to the galaxy, the earth to the sun, and humanity and life to the earth. The evolution of energy is kokyu. The reincarnation of energy is kokyu. It is the rhythms of the seasons, the oceans, and the moon. It is the expansion and contraction that created the universe and the earth, the inhalation and exhalation of global phenomena. All are breathing processes of an inseparable cycle, each helping the other; all combine for the resolution and refinement of energy from one form to the next, refreshing the system and making new life. This is the universe, expanding and contracting with the same breath, the circulation of one energy in many forms.

In the study of the martial arts and in spiritual training, a strong emphasis has always been given to the practice of controlling the breath to most effectively realize its power and cleansing properties. Breathing not only provides the body with oxygen, but also fills the body and the spirit with the energies that radiate from every part of the vast universal spaces, rich living radiation charged with the pulse of God's love.

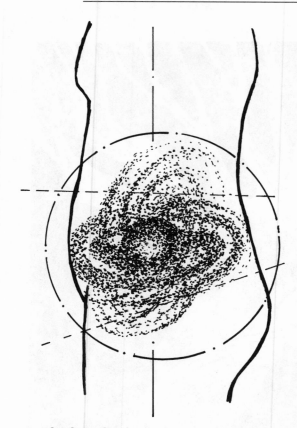

By the breath, the space inside the body is equalized and unified with the space outside the body. Stale air, depleted of energy and carrying accumulated poisons, is exchanged for air that is fresh and charged with the many universal essences, the electricity of the universal spaces. This cosmic energy that fills the air must penetrate each individual cell of the body.

Normally we take about sixteen breaths each minute, but by sitting quietly in *seiza*, formal seated position, relaxed and breathing deeply from the *hara* in the *tanden* method, the number of breaths is easily reduced to two or even one each minute. Drawn in slowly and powerfully, the air is forced deeply into the *hara*. As the *hara* expands, the air begins to fill the lungs and the chest expands. As the cavities are filled, inhalation continues and all the cells of the body are infused, inch by inch, with the electric pulse of life. Although held momentarily within the body, the air is not static. Continually moving and expanding with the fever, it forces the vibrations of life into

every tissue. Then, starting again with the *hara*, the air is expelled even more slowly. The body is completely emptied, and a vacuum is created within each cell. Fresh air rushes in with expanded energy to fill the awaiting vacuum as the next breath is seized by every cell in the body.

As the breathing slows, becoming more complete, the volume of air greatly increases. The heart slows down; its rhythm echoes with power as it forces the blood to surge mightily through the veins, quickly purging waste and dead materials from the body. The brain is stimulated and sharpened by the increase in electrical current. The signals transmitted by the central nervous system are transported more rapidly, the body's defense mechanisms are stronger, and all parts of the body glow with the vitality of improved circulation. The delicate membranes at the tip of the nerves are bathed and coated with a fluid that calms and refreshes the body and the mind.

Heat expands and makes flexible. It relaxes and quickens reaction. The fever produced by the power of deep breathing encourages the flexibility of all the organs, muscles, and tissue in the body. It excites the movement of the atomic structures, causing a more vital reaction and charging the entire body with the physical and spiritual fires of creation.

During meditation, the openness and flexibility created within the mind and within the spiritual aura are essential for transcending the ego. The vacuum of the physical space is echoed in the spiritual aura, and as the ego is dissolved by fever, the electric pulses produce a spark of inspiration in the emptiness to illuminate the true knowledge of intuition and perception. *Satori* comes from *ki*, the energy of the cosmic spaces flowing through the universal mind. Transmitted by the breath, the pulse of God must fill the physical and spiritual body for we are both, and both are one.

Many times O Sensei began the practice of Aikido with the meditation/deep breathing practice *funatori furutama*. Students usually looked upon this practice as only an exercise, missing its true significance. *Funatori* is an ex-

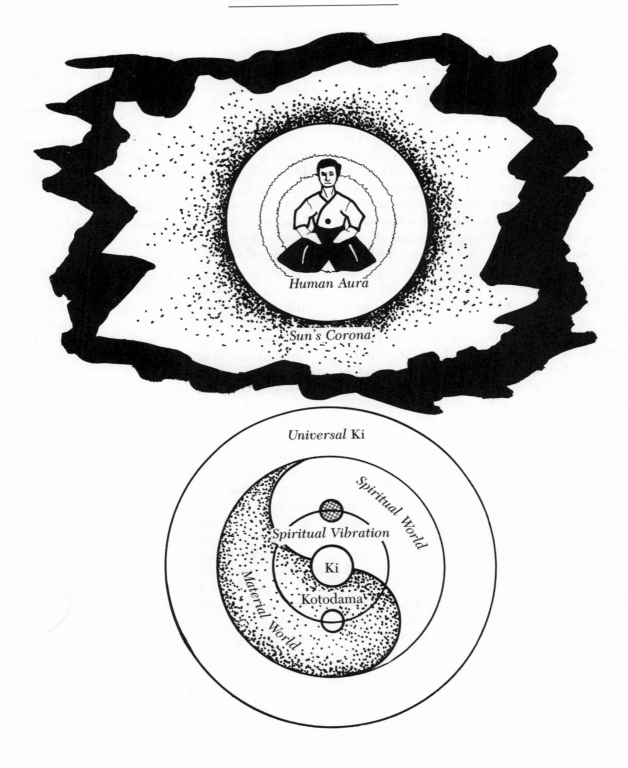

Human Aura

Sun's Corona

Universal Ki

Spiritual World

Spiritual Vibration

Ki

Kotodama

Material World

ercise familiar to Aikido students everywhere. Its movement from the hips is the classic motion of fishermen as they row their boats to their daily work, or of the samurai as they rowed their warships into battle. It is accompanied by a powerful *kotodama* from deep within the *hara*, so that voice and body set up the vibrations of the ebb and flow of life. Students become as one, each individual's power absorbed and magnified by the power of others until it becomes impossible to separate one's own voice and vibration from the union. Bodies and spirits, through the breath, become one with nature, become one with the rhythms of the universe, become one with the wind and the sea. The self becomes an ocean wave, endlessly moving, and the constraints of time dissolve into space.

The movement of the body ceases as the vibrations of the last sound roll out into the farthest reaches of space. Feet, released from the *hanmi* of *funatori* practice, move into the relaxed shoulder-width stance of *furutama* meditation, with knees slightly bent and spine erect. A deep, slow breath is drawn in through the nostrils. The hands are joined, left over right, lightly enclosing a small emptiness between the palms. They are lifted overhead as if one were stretching the entire body to the heavens and are then brought down to a position just below the *hara*. As the hands fall, a pressure in the *hara* forces the breath deeper and compresses it within the body. The eyes are half closed, and time becomes nothing as the breath is slowly but powerfully released through the mouth. The joined hands begin a smooth, steady vibration that resounds throughout the body, causing it to shake from head to toe.

The rhythm is set up and the vibration on each breath brings fresh energy more deeply into all parts of the body, into the *hara*, the brain, the fingertips, the toes. The breath is released naturally by the rhythm of the vibration, and all the air is expelled from the body. The vacuum is allowed to increase and intensify before the next breath is taken. The pause between the yin and the yang, and the yang and the yin, allows the cycle to reach its fullness before the exchange. Throughout the process, the rhythm is allowed to continue and develop, steadily, unforced, without conscious thought. The body resonates with the vibration and expands into the spiritual aura. The spiritual body resonates with the vibration and expands and joins the universe. As one, the body and the spirit become empty and melt into the surrounding space.

As with sonar, the vibrations that are extended return. Fever is produced. It calms and it cleanses. It scrapes the dust from the mind, and purifies and transcends aggressive ego. As you experience the oneness of all around you, you may begin to discover the peace of the universal mind. The body, mind, and spirit are charged with energy and adjusted to receive and generate power. You are now ready for the vigorous meditation and rhythms of Aikido movement.

Funatori furutama can also be practiced as an individual training for the advanced student, but the guidance of a knowledgeable teacher is most important. The exercise should not be attempted by the beginner. The body must be strong and well conditioned, and the practice must be approached cautiously, little by little. Alternating between the two forms, you gradually build up to an hour of sustained *misogi*. You will sweat profusely and become dizzy and sometimes nauseated as poisons are flushed from the deepest recesses of the body and the mind. As you pass through this point of intense physical cleansing, you may see light explode within, and your mind will sparkle with a new clarity. Strange images may come, but do not try to hold them. Nor should you fight them. Allow them to continue in the ebb and flow of the space that is within you and within the universe. And perhaps for a small stroke of eternity, as the illusions of the ego die away, you will truly experience the reality of now and become one with the spirit of God. But do not search for *satori*. Only become empty, transparent, and melt into space. In time this training will help to purify and enrich the function

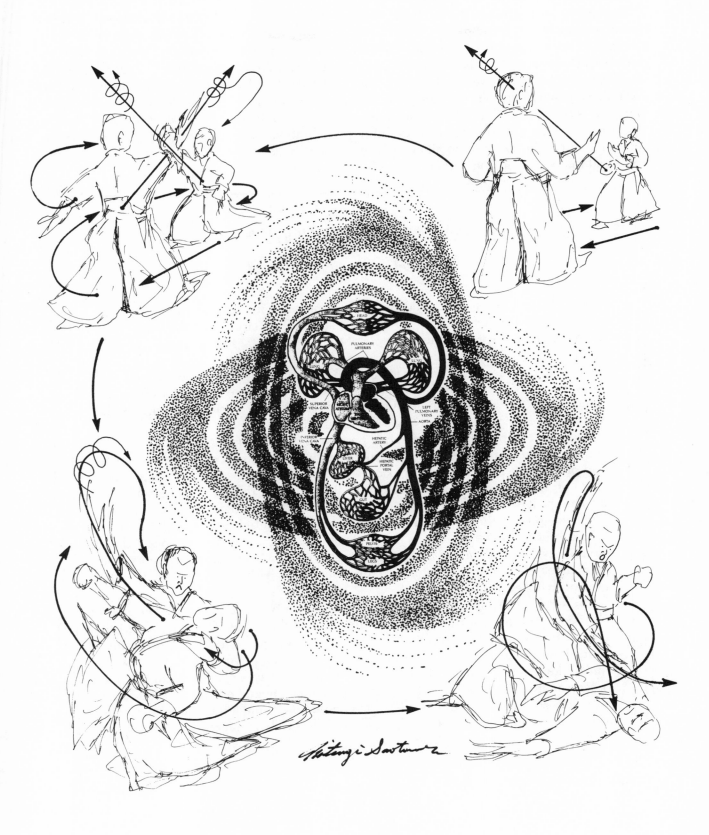

of your *ki*, your own life energy force.

Training to develop strong *ki* is not the training of the Way. The judgment of strong *ki* or weak *ki* has no meaning, for strong can be evil, as weak can be good. The important quality of *ki* that you must strive for, the only quality that you must consider, is the quality of purity. It is the purity of emptiness that allows space for the power of the universe to enter into your spirit; the mirror that allows you to reflect all that is around you without the judgment of ego. This is Aiki. Only if you are open to the changes of power and empty of judgment will you be sensitive enough to react freely. In Aikido training, a clean, spontaneous energy force, unsullied by calculation, is strong *ki*. This kind of reaction is exactly one with the movement of the universe. Negative *ki* can only make a discordant and unclean vibration. It is the positive *ki* and reaction that make a chivalrous, noble, and awesome vibration.

THE FUNDAMENTAL PRINCIPLE of the CIRCLE
A Lecture by the Founder

Aikido technique is structured on circular movement, for harmony is brought about and all conflict resolved through the spirit of the circle. The response of the body, mind, and spirit to the principle of the circle is vital to the creation of technique.

A circle encloses space, and it is from the perfect freedom of this emptiness that *ki* is born. From the center of this birthplace, the creative processes of life are joined with the infinite, immeasurable universe by the spirit. The spirit is the Creator, the eternal parent giving birth to all things.

Through this principle, the creative process of the spirit is without limit. Within the circle, the *ki* of the universe is guided in the processes of creation, evolution, and protection. The movement of karma in this world is the circle of balance. The Budo of Aikido is the circle of protection. The circle of the spirit is the source of *ki*. The spirit of the circle joins spirit, mind, and matter through Aiki and nourishes life. The spirit of the circle contains and creates unlimited technique for it holds all the *ki* of the universe. This is the circle of the spirit in Aikido. Without it there is no glory, no wisdom, no integrity, no truth, no possibility of uniting spirit and substance. Without it the restorative functions of the body cease to exist. It is the ever-evolving cycle of *kokyu*.

The circle of the spirit begins and ends in the unity of the universe. The Budo of Aikido springs from the mastery of the spirit of the circle. The essence of this Budo is to embrace the complementary action of cause and effect and to draw into yourself all things as if they were held within the palm of your hand. You have a spirit, therefore you must realize that each person has a spirit. When the life processes are connected with the spirit and the fundamental principle of the circle is given birth in Aiki, all things are led to completion through the circle. All things are freely created by the circle. The secret of the circle is to create technique by piercing the very center of space.

Piercing the very center of space

Tada ima, *"only now."* *There is only this moment.*

11

MARUBASHI: *The* ELEMENTS *of* REALITY

This is the Takemusu Aiki of Ueshiba. With one swing of my *bokken*, I gather all the life essences, all the vitality of the universal *ki*. This is the sword of past, present, and future.

As I grasp this sword, it absorbs the energy of the universe and condenses it into this one moment. I am holding the past, I am holding the future, for I am holding infinity, now. There exists no time and no space.

With the origin of the universe, my life began as all of life began. My whole life, its essence, its vitality, is contained within this sword. My life from the early part of this century to this moment, from the beginning of creation to this moment, is the dynamic reaction of infinity. This is the sword of infinite life.

O Sensei's voice thundered as his *bokken* shattered the transfixed breath of those watching. I was his *uke* for the demonstration, and, preparing for the long lecture that I knew was to follow, I relaxed my *kamae* to *gedan*, lower position. I was behind him. He could not see me, nor did I make a sound as the posture of my body shifted. But he had

sensed a subtle change in my vibration, an ever-so-slight lowering of intensity, and he perceived the most minute separation of my spirit from his.

My heart leapt and lodged in my throat as he suddenly whirled about. All I could see were his piercing eyes, angry and exploding with fire behind the *bokken*, which had stopped within a fraction of being driven into my throat.

"You must never lessen your concentration!" he screamed as he spun. "You must never relax your guard!" And he continued:

The universal *ki* is never separated from space. Your spirit must never be separated from the enemy. The eye of Aiki is not a physical eye. Whether it be light or dark, no matter the timing or direction, the vibration will be detected and met with the spiritual eye. The spiritual eye transcends selfish ego. The opening of the spiritual eye is the echo of the expanding universe. It is the eye of emptiness. It is the eye that mirrors the light of truth.

Only immature technicians use the physical

"This is the sword of infinite life."

eye. This is the eye of strategy and of clever tricks. They cannot cut with their spirit; they can only chop with their ego. For the physical eye, technique is a game. The physical eye is in a hurry; it can only enjoy victory. Why can't people understand that the meaning of victory is no conflict? The meaning of no conflict is no separation. The physical eye cannot see the truth of *satori*.

Training in Budo is the study of reality, of life and death, and the pursuit of the spiritual strength with which to face this reality. The truth of reality cannot be experienced by a heart that is filled with questions of victory and defeat. When the objective of training is to win, a sports consciousness is developed. It becomes a game, not reality. There must be rules to protect the contestants, and the out-

Kan No Mei

come decides nothing. The only questions asked in competition are: Who is the strongest according to the rules? Whose technique is the fastest according to the rules? You will never know your true self through competition, for you will never know your true reaction, only your strategy. As you stand on the edge of absolute punishment when the only answer is life or death, the reaction, therefore the result is completely different. Unhampered by rules, where the only consideration is survival, the very weak can become very strong, and the very strong may lose their power in fear.

When life is not at stake, it is too easy to forget that physical strength and technical expertise have limits. The ego wants to forget these limitations and seizes the opportunity to grow to unrealistic proportions. Truth is lost and training becomes distorted. The *misogi* of Budo training is lost. The spiritual strengths of Budo training are lost, because the question of life or death is no longer relevant. If you are attached to winning, how can you give up attachment to life and death? How can you give up attachment to ego and enter into the enemy's mind and spirit? The value of training is to experience the essence of reality, to break down the barriers of judgment and desire, which separate us from communication, and to achieve spiritual confidence.

Morihei Ueshiba said: "A mind to serve for the peace of all the peoples of the world is needed in Aikido, and not the mind of one who practices only to be strong and conquer an opponent. Therefore, to compete in techniques, winning or losing, is not true Budo. True Budo knows no defeat. Never defeated means never fighting."

I once told O Sensei, "In Budo training and also in Zen training, one hears the phrase 'Life and death are one,' but I don't understand its meaning."

O Sensei laughed. "It's all right. Go ahead, die."

"But Sensei, I don't understand. If I die, then I can't ask you about life and death. It won't matter."

O Sensei replied, "Ryokan Zenji said, 'If it is the right time to die, then go ahead and die. If you encounter great suffering, then you must endure. . . .' This attitude can be developed only by giving up your desires and your preconceptions, by giving up your very existence to the course of nature.

"I know you have read Ryokan Zenji's teachings, but literature will not teach you about life and death. If it could, we would all be saints by now, and the world freed from misery.

"You just returned from your farming chores. How many steps did you take to get here?"

Surprised, I stammered, "Perhaps fifty, maybe sixty, I'm not exactly sure. Maybe I—"

Shaking his finger at me, O Sensei said sharply, "How many years have you trained in Aikido? Why are you so stupid? Why don't you understand my question?"

Unable to understand why O Sensei was yelling at me, I just bowed my head in apology, and he continued: "The journey of a thousand miles begins with one step. Our life is the continuum of this movement in time. It does not matter if your life is for a thousand years; you can only live in the present moment. Not the past, not the future, but now is the time of life. A time that is past is forever lost. A time in the future will never come. Light contains shadow, and in the shadows there is light. So, too, within life we find death, and in death there is life. Life and death are inseparable."

Sei Shi Ichi Ryo: *Life and death are one.*

"Is this similar to the idea of Kannagara, reincarnation within the continuous spiritual flow of creation?" I asked.

"Very much. Life is reborn every moment with the purpose of contributing something of value to the process. When you eat a grain of rice, it is transformed into the energy that will sustain your life. If there were no life in that grain, it would be of no value. If there is no life in the air, it will not give you breath. The many essences of the universe are constantly being reborn and transformed into a part of your life. The food that nourishes life comes from Mother Earth. When living beings die, they return to her womb. Thus, all things recycle themselves, eternally coexisting and sustaining the creative processes of nature. This is the meaning of 'life and death are one.'

"You must remember, no life, not even the tiniest bacterium, can perish from this universe. One who pursues Aikido must grasp this truth well. In our life, which is called the Universe, death as an end does not exist. The relationship of yin and yang is the ebb and flow of *ki*; the ebb and flow of *ki* is the process of life and death. Can we truly call this phenomenon a process? Both elements are one and never two. Death is but a time of transition in the evolving metamorphosis of eternal existence."

"Sensei, most people worry about death, about the world they will enter after death. What happens to the spirit? What determines whether one goes to heaven or hell?"

"Obviously, I cannot know what will happen to your spirit after death, and I cannot predict your next life. It is known only by the Omniscient Creator. If anyone claims to be able to predict someone's life or situation after death, it is blasphemy. Those who are too concerned with life after death cannot be aware of the immortality of life. When good is done with the intention of gaining admittance into heaven or with the hope of a more prosperous situation in the next life, it is hypocrisy. Truth is not made, it is given. Our duty is to live this life to the fullest with appreciation and respect for all of the manifestations of God's love."

Then I asked, "But what does it mean to heighten one's spiritual awareness through *misogi* training?"

"The objective of *misogi* training is to become aware of the expression of God's love within you and to embody the purity of His spirit. If the crystal of your spirit is clouded, His truth cannot be seen. Thus, Takemusu Aiki means to become one with this truth, the truth which knows no past nor future, the truth of now.

"In this very moment of truth there is only emptiness. There is no death. There is only eternal spirit. It is in this realm that one finds wisdom and the uncountable variety of Aiki *waza*. Therefore, do not escape into the past and do not dream of the future. Live for this moment, and therein find your true self."

During many of his demonstrations and seminars, O Sensei would say, "No external force or conflict can threaten me. I remain calm no matter how or when the enemy attacks. Why? Because I am empty. I have no attachment to life or death. I leave all things to the wisdom of God. Have no attachment to life or death and leave everything to Him, not only when you face the enemy, but also in your daily life."

To give up attachment to life does not mean to die rather than fight for truth. To give up attachment to death does not mean escape and run from conflict. Both of these reactions are the manifestation of fear and weakness of spirit. Giving up attachment to life and death is the refusal to be controlled by fear, the refusal to be controlled by the selfish ego, which clouds the spiritual eye. With no thought of escape, whether the threat is pain, discomfort, or death, you must continue in the Way with all of your might, not with the purposes of ego in your heart, but leaving your fate in the hands of God. This is the mind of no conflict.

Now is now. Yesterday is a memory, tomorrow a hope, but now is reality. There is no separation between past, present, and future, for all are contained in this moment, this reality, the decisive moment for reaction without hesitation.

Marubashi, translated as "the bridge of life," is a technique of the Yagyu School of swordsmanship. As the enemy attacks, cutting with his sword, movement is neither to the left nor to the right, but directly into the path

Marubashi

of the attack, cutting in one timing through his sword and through his spirit. It is a technique of entering and choosing death.

The philosophy that underlies this technique perceives life as a narrow log bridge spanning a torrential river. As one comes face to face with the enemy in the middle of the bridge, there is no escape. To retreat or even to hesitate is to be followed and cut down by the sword. To escape to the right or the left is to plunge into the turbulent waters. Choosing life is death. The only path is the enemy's path. There must be no separation, but an exchange of time and space with the spirit of moving into the very heart of the enemy. This is the spirit of *irimi* (entering). When you extend your spirit into the future, the present is neutralized. Negative becomes positive; positive becomes negative. Past becomes future, and future becomes now. Only by abandoning attachment to time and space, attachment to life, will you attain the true freedom of choosing death. The bridge and life are the same. Heaven and hell are now, infinity is now. Choosing death is life. This must be practiced and become instinctive.

Ma-ai, space or distance, can be compared to the past. *De-ai*, the timing of the meeting, is the now of each encounter. *Zanshin* is the continuation of energy and awareness, the future. While practicing Aikido, many students think much about the technical aspects but seem to forget these three vital elements. Their coordinated execution is, in fact, tech-

nique. Without it no technique can exist. Because of it the movements of Aikido go beyond the artistic beauty of dance and become the powerful movements of the warrior. By controlling these three elements—time, space, and energy—one can control those whose physical powers are vastly superior.

Ma-ai is the distance in time and space between forces and their relative position. *Ma* can be translated as "space" or "interval," *ai* as "joining" or "confluence." *Ma-ai* is the joining of space, the harmony of the emptiness. The universe itself exists as a principle of *ma-ai* expressed in the distances and positioning of the galaxies, the stars, and the planets. It is the same in the world of nuclear structure. For the forces to function, there must be a shared emptiness between them, and the distances and positions must be exact. The structure of our bodies is based on *ma-ai* in the spacing of the eyes, the ears, and the vital organs within to maintain a harmonious balance of life.

Ma-ai

In the technical world of Aikido, to say that one is a good technician implies that one can effectively control space with the physical body. It is rare indeed to find two people who are exactly matched. Everyone's physical situation is different; each person has a different physical handicap. But in space and in time, all individuals are equal. A true martial artist understands this and relies not so much on his physical power but on the use of space control and timing.

In a battle the arrows may have a range of perhaps one hundred yards, but the enemy

Cutting in one continuous timing through his sword and his spirit. Kevin Choate, uke.

understands this distance, and if he stays just outside their range, he will not be struck. In warfare and in personal combat, the same principles apply. When the enemy strikes, no matter how strong the attack, if you are outside the range of the attack, you will not be harmed. If you change your position, the strike may pass without touching you. *Kami shitoe* is a Japanese expression often used to illustrate this principle, the space within the thickness of one piece of paper. On one side of the paper is the character for *death*, but on the other side is written *life*. In the control of space, very small distances have very big meanings, and in the thickness of one piece of paper lies the secret of *irimi*.

Kami Shitoe

A great artist is a master of *ma-ai*, for through the balance and control of space, whether on canvas, in clay, or on film, the artist creates to grab the spirit and force an emotional response. His true mastery is not expressed in the space that is filled; rather, it is within the negative space that he may capture your soul. The same is true in the art of war. A great general will create a design through the movement of his troops, strategic positioning, the use of space. He strives to create an illusion in hopes of forcing an emotional response based on fear or overconfidence, based on ego or hatred.

The most important study in advanced martial training is not the study of the technical system, but the discovery of this spiritual world of *ma-ai*. The movement of the mind, the stream of spirit and their direction, as well as physical distance, determines the balanced and proper use of space.

When two masters of swordsmanship face each other to do battle, they do not immediately begin the attack with the hopes of an advantage, for there are no physical openings. They wait. Their bodies remain apart while their spirit and their will close in and lock in combat. They must remain completely calm, completely open and balanced, with no attachment to life or death.

Standing on the edge of life and death, you cannot make a lie. Standing on the edge of life and death, your physical and your spiritual vibration can only speak the truth, and your deepest self will appear. A master understands this and he awaits an imbalance, an opening in the other's defense. He surrounds the emptiness, the negative space in which to catch the enemy's spirit and vibration, with his presence.

If the enemy catches a vibration of anger, or a vibration of uncertainty, or a vibration of ego, the imbalance is clear. As the spiritual space is filled by that vibration, an opening is created, and in the instant of that opening he will strike. If the enemy perceives the slightest loss of concentration, the slightest separation of spirit, he will seize the moment of weakness. An opening has been created and he will move into the opening. You must contact and control the spiritual space before the enemy's reaction. This is Aiki—no time, no space.

When you discover the spiritual world of *ma-ai*, your training will begin to advance into the realm of perception, intuition, and insight, for spiritual *ma-ai* is the emptiness, the electrically charged negative space that conducts the echoes of vibration. You will begin to develop true communication with all life. When you are completely open to that communication, you will understand the enemy's spirit before the physical reaction. To know the enemy is the first rule of war. You must understand his character, his psychology, to under-

An exchange of time and space with the spirit of moving into the very heart of the enemy.

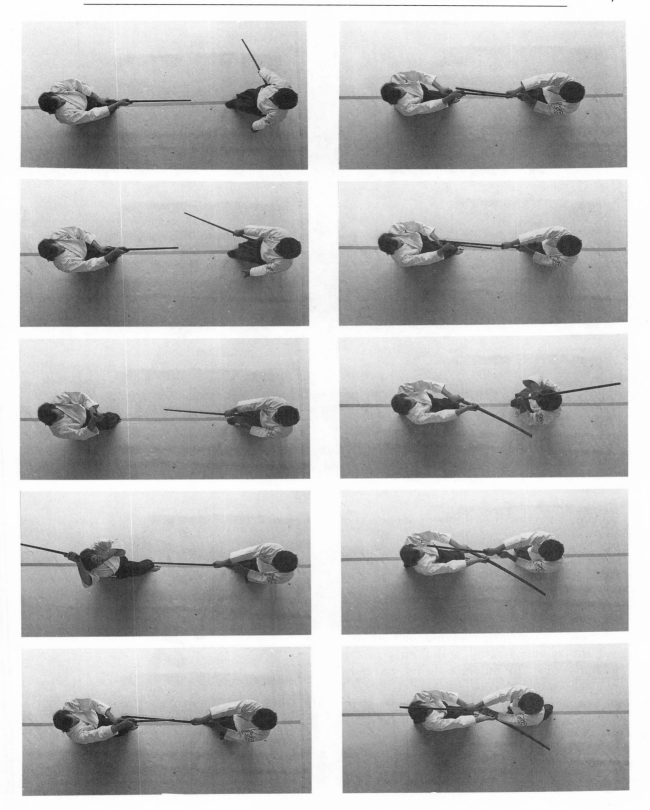

Kevin Choate, uke

You must control the emptiness and surround it with your presence. Within the negative space you may capture the enemy's spirit and vibration, and move into his opening. John Messores, uke.

stand his reaction. It is the body language of the spirit.

People often talk of psychology training for Aikido students, but this is a very shallow form of study. The deepest understanding comes within the natural context of serious training. You learn to read the enemy's body movement and then you can read his mind. You learn to read the enemy's mind and then you can touch his spirit. To understand this, you must practice. No matter how many words I use, I can but reveal the abstract philosophy. The true secrets of Aikido are only revealed through constant training.

De-ai is the timing involved in controlling space to create a reaction. It is the meeting of positive and negative, the exchange. *De-ai* is the moment of truth. In science, *de-ai* is a process of timing that results in the creation of

De-ai

energy through nuclear reaction. In our society, the meeting of East and West, two diametrically opposed cultures, is a form of *de-ai*. The same principle is witnessed in nature through the seasonal changes, which transform our environment. Training to improve *de-ai* becomes critically important in Aikido practice. Only by understanding correct timing and the geometrics of spatial relationships can one effectively execute the movement. Proper timing is essential to Aikido, for the element of time plays a dominant role in our lives.

The study of timing is the paradoxical melding of intense concentration with relaxed flexibility and perception. Concentrating on a small point such as a hand or a sword or the movement of the feet narrows both physical and spiritual vision. It causes the eyes to strain, the back of the neck and the shoulders to become tense, and the muscles in the legs to tighten. This loss of elasticity blocks perception and makes immediate spontaneous reaction impossible. The timing is lost if reaction begins only after the information reaches physical awareness. It is lost if reaction begins only after the sword moves, or after the hand moves, or after the feet move. An undisturbed spirit that is not attached to one objective, an eye that is not captured by the sword, is vital to the concentration that perceives the spiritual movement.

Effective timing is not necessarily fast timing. The response must be in direct relationship to the other's situation. Timing is process and patience awaiting an advantage. Appropriate timing joins and then creates an opening. To rush the process destroys the timing. It is easy to understand why a timing that is too slow must be avoided. You will be in the line of attack and standing, vulnerable, beneath the sword. But if, while facing the enemy, you begin your movement too soon, before the attack is fully committed, the enemy has the advantage. You have rushed the process. Even though your movement may be flawless in its technical execution, you have given away your position. At this point the direction of the attack can easily be changed, and the enemy will follow and cut you down. Appropriate timing is meeting the enemy so that you are in a position facing the enemy's weakness. It is at the fullness of attack that the enemy is most vulnerable. His full concentration is on attacking; all the power and energy of his body and

spirit is in the attack; his direction is committed, and at this point he cannot change. The mind of attack is weak because the spiritual space is filled with the vibrations of attack, and there is no room for defense. The moment of the greatest strength is the moment of the greatest weakness. You must join this rhythm openly and without fear, with no attachment to life, prepared to die.

After many years of developing your spiritual confidence, when you move into the technique of no technique, it may be possible to seize the moment at its conception. It may be possible to force the enemy into your timing by capturing and controlling his attacking spirit. But your mind must be completely empty and completely pure: no ego, no aggression, no greed, no timing.

In any encounter there is only one chance. *Ichi go ichi e*—one life, one meeting. The same situation will never return. Your mind must always be fresh and receptive to the changing vibrations of each moment, for time does not go backward. In training, when I saw O Sensei standing in the *dojo*, I realized that this may be the last time. Perhaps this is the last chance to receive his guidance in this physical world. Now is now! Tomorrow is maybe. There is no second chance, no "one more time." This is the meaning of *ikkyo*—my whole life is *now*.

Ichi Go Ichi E: *one life, one meeting*

Out of the time of greatest turmoil in Japanese history, a time of constant warfare and bloodshed, the fifteenth century, there arose an art of the most total and intensive search for peace. The tea ceremony is the celebration of *de-ai*, of the present. It is the appreciation and adoration of reality; the simple, the natural, the ordinary, and the vital beauty of the imperfect.

The teahouse itself is built almost entirely of wood, rustic and simple. Infinite care is taken to choose and fit together natural pieces that are twisted and gnarled from the struggle for survival. Left in their natural state, touched with the most delicate sensitivity and respect for their essence, these pieces of wood retain the movements of life and time. The thatched roof, the frailty of the supporting structures, and the apparent casualness in the selection of the ordinary, all serve to heighten the awareness of the transience of material. The ephemeral quality of the teahouse emphasizes and acknowledges the contrasting true reality of the eternal spirit. The bridge is a stream; the river is not a stream.

The tearoom is empty except for what is placed there to emphasize the esthetic mood of the moment. No sound, no color, no shape, no movement must disturb the subtle harmony. The materials are imperfect, the designs are asymmetrical, and something is always left incomplete. The guest becomes a vital part of the total atmosphere, for his or her own imagination must bring it to completion. The joy is in the process through which perfection is sought rather than the unattainable perfection itself.

The mellow glow of age lingers in the atmosphere, and everything about the room suggests refined and dignified poverty. Nothing is new except the bamboo dipper and the snowy white linen napkins. But everything is absolutely clean; not even a speck of dust will be found. The host cleans and prepares for the tea ceremony for hours, alone, in a ritual as important as the serving of the tea itself.

The mood of the tea is first expressed by the garden through which the guest enters the teahouse. The invitation to enter is a delicate scent of incense carried on the breeze. The guest enters without a sound through a door barely three feet high. He must bow low, instilling a feeling of humility and gratitude. Weapons must not enter this hallowed setting, so they are carefully left outside on a rack beneath the eaves. The host enters noiselessly and unassumingly after the guest is seated, and the ceremony begins. The clothes, the poise of the body, the manner of movement of both host and guest are all a study in quiet and natural elegance.

Every movement of the ceremony itself is performed with a natural completeness and a total economy of motion that leaves no openings. The performance is a deep meditation, and the communication between the participants is profound. The host and guest are individuals, but their hearts beat as one; they breathe in the same rhythm. It is an exchange of intuition that leaves spoken communication unnecessary and frivolous. The peace and the silence are absolute. Host and guest share one timing, one space. They share one second of infinity in a cup of tea.

The heavy taste of the tea embraces the moment. They may never meet again; tomorrow one may die. How important is this spiritual communication, accompanied only by the sound of the boiling water, or the sound of a bee against the *shoji* (paper screen) like the distant pounding of a drum. These quiet sounds are powerful echoes in the silence, symbolizing the whole universe.

Host and guest will leave the peace and emptiness of the tea ceremony, pick up their weapons, and go into battle. As they draw their swords, the screams of the wounded and the dying will echo in air that is heavy with the stench of death. They will look upon the twisted face of the enemy, streaked with a mixture of sweat and dirt and blood, and they will face the agony of hell.

In a time of so much suffering, that one shared cup of tea reflects the appreciation that "now I am alive." Its taste is the taste of life, its poignant aroma charged with the celebration of one eternal moment in time. How precious is this brief time of infinite peace, this memory carried like a gift in the warrior's heart. It is a suspended moment in the transparency of life, a moment of true human relationship and communion. It is meeting and it is separation, the joyous and the bittersweet. How long you live is not important. Life is moment by moment, and the measure of your life is the way in which your spirit blossoms each of those moments. *Ichi go ichi e.*

Where, when, and how should one encounter the opposing force? *Ma-ai* is the harmony and control of space. *De-ai* is the harmony and control of the encounter. *Zanshin* is the harmony and the continuation of energy.

Zanshin

Zanshin is the extension of the spirit, the continuation of energy and awareness that prepares for the next action. Each night we die, only to be born anew each morning. *Irmitenkan* (entering-turning) is the same renewal, death and rebirth in one movement. *Kokyu* is the same, the exchange of material and of the essence of energy, death and rebirth, to freshen the spirit. In *furutama misogi* we exchange our breath with the universe to connect with the continuing vibrations of creation. Our vibrations explode into space and continue. The phrase *on kochi shin* means to

Hashi wa nagarete; kawa wa nagarezu: The bridge is a stream; the river is not a stream.

On Kochi Shin

study the process of the past to refine the future. *Zanshin* is the continuity of life, one circulation of energy. This is the Tao; this is *do*.

In the study of Aikido, taking *ukemi* or executing a technique is not the end of the process; it is the beginning of the next action. You must never lose your concentration; you must never allow your guard to slip even for a moment. You must remain constantly alert, aware of your partner in practice, aware of all the movement around you, ready for the next *de-ai*, ready for the unexpected from any direction. Never take your concentration from your partner. Never let your spirit separate from your partner. Aikido is training, and every second on the mat must be filled with the same intensity with which you would face decisions of life and death. *Zanshin* is the future, but *zanshin* is also now. The quality of your *zanshin* is the quality of your Aikido.

Every nerve in your body has *zanshin*. Every action, every touch, is recorded and stored. Locked within forever is the memory of joy, of the correct responses and reactions that were strong and true, as well as the memory of pain, of the responses and reactions that were ineffective and weak. Through the constant repetition of Aikido training, you experience and record within the spirit, within the mind, and within every nerve in your body, the different situations, the different kinds of stress, and the different people of your encounters. *Zanshin* exists as a stage of review. In the emptiness of an open mind and spirit, you can sort out all the experiences intuitively, instantly, in the hope of refining technique and attitude. In the emptiness of an open mind and spirit, you will begin to experience an honest communication with others, a deeper understanding of your relationship to all of humanity and to all of life.

You must not maintain an attachment to your past ideas of righteousness for each situation is different. With a narrow attachment to your own preconceived ideas you cannot create a good application to each new situation. The process of the DNA molecule records each quality of life, continuing the good and eventually erasing the ineffective and unadaptable. This is the meaning of *keiko*: to study the old memory and experience so that the reaction of this moment is fresh, alive, and creative. In daily life, *zanshin* is the spirit of "recycling" in your relationship with others, with the environment, and with God. *Zanshin* is refinement and growth.

O Sensei has given us so much that it seems impossible to understand all of his teachings. But the most important thing to keep in mind is never to give up. You must absorb his teachings through constant practice. You must train and be open to new and deeper understandings, open and receptive to new ideas. It does not matter whether you immediately grasp O Sensei's teachings. It is the spirit of persistent pursuit wherein lies the true meaning of *zanshin*. Each moment contains the residue of the past to influence the future. Life never ends, for energy is infinite.

Is technique born of philosophy or is philosophy born of technique? It does not matter, for technique and philosophy are but one explanation of reality. Each alone is unimportant. Developing a strong spirit and liberating the body by training with the attitude of experiencing the reality of each situation are essential. Every encounter is a choice between life and death.

Every nerve in your body has zanshin. *Every action, every touch is recorded and stored.*
Zanshin *exists as a stage of review.*

Shugyo is the daily training of purification,
the day-to-day struggle, the work of education to refine and purify the quality of life.

12

The
TRAINING
PROCESS

Many years ago I was teaching a class at Hombu Dojo, the technique for practice was *kokyu ho*. Absorbed in explaining the refinements of the technique to some of the *yudansha* (those of black belt rank), I was unaware that in one corner of the mat, two beginners with shoulders hunched, muscles tensed, and arms rigid were locked in competitive struggle. It looked more like sumo wrestling than Aikido training. I was also unaware that O Sensei had come to the *dojo* to look in on the class, as was often his habit, until I heard his voice. "Who's teaching this class!" he thundered, his voice sharp with anger. Then O Sensei saw me and, pointing to the astonished beginners, said, "Saotome, you destroy Aikido principle. I'm developing a system, a training system, an education system. Aikido training is process. You are crushing Aikido meaning!"

This educational process is the study and refinement of *kihon waza* basic technique. *Kihon waza* is the foundation of Aikido practice. It is the essence of Aikido philosophy condensed into a series of basic movements,

each one providing a different illustration of the same underlying principle. So often people study Aikido, but they don't study Aikido. They study *ikkyo* or *shihonage* or *iriminage*, thinking, "This is the correct way to do *ikkyo*; this is the correct *shihonage*." This is nonsense. Instead of separating the techniques for study, we must study to see their similarities, the application of principle and its philosophical result. There is no perfect *ikkyo*, but any *ikkyo* is correct when executed spontaneously, sincerely, and in harmony with a particular situation. Students often try to copy an instruc-

Kihon Waza

tor's exact form, but for the instructor also, *ikkyo* is different each time. The exact form cannot be repeated time and time again. In each situation the degree and direction of force are different; your position is not always the same, body shape and muscular structure differ from partner to partner, and perception and timing change. The application must change accordingly. Technique is, in one second, the creation of form. It is never the same second, never the same form. But the basic principles are always the same.

A sports reporter from one of the large Tokyo newspapers came to the *dojo* to interview O Sensei. O Sensei talked of Aiki principle, philosophy, and purpose. Very much impressed with the things O Sensei had said, the reporter asked him to demonstrate so that they could accompany the article with a photograph of this dynamic philosophy. O Sensei called an *uke* and demonstrated a very powerful *irimi* movement, throwing his *uke* perhaps fifteen feet or more. Very excitedly the photographer said, "Please, Sensei, do that one more time. This picture will be very good!" So O Sensei began to demonstrate many different throws and movements. He stopped and looked at the photographer, but the photographer said, "Sensei, that's wonderful, but could you please do the first one, just once more?" So again O Sensei began to demonstrate, *bam, bam, bam*, never the same throw twice. Then he turned to the photographer and said, "Well, did you get your photograph?"

Obviously frustrated, the photographer replied, "It was all very exciting, but please, couldn't you do that very first throw once more?"

"What? I don't understand. You are a professional photographer and must capture the moment. Aiki has no shape. Each time is a different situation and a different movement is appropriate. The same movement can never be repeated. You must catch the essence. There is no 'one more time.' You must try to capture the image spontaneously. This is Aiki!"

Various groups of people often visited the *dojo* to watch O Sensei demonstrate and listen to his lectures. O Sensei might do *iriminage* each time, but the emphasis and approach would change to relate to the group's specific interests. For a group of dancers, he would emphasize the grace and beauty in the power of his movement. A group of *budoka* would be shown the crisp power and devastating martial application. To a group of artists he would demonstrate the power of creativity and the artistic awareness that develops through practice. The essence of Aikido is spontaneity and change.

The scope of Aikido is as broad as the universe itself. Therefore, each basic technique within the system has many different applications and methods of training to produce different results. With an emphasis on space control, the shape of *ikkyo* will be different from that of an emphasis on technical form. The essence is the same for both muscle training and the training of timing and perception, but *ikkyo* is executed from a different perspective.

O Sensei's teaching changed subtly from day to day and from year to year. Life experience, daily training, and the passage of time expand wisdom. When O Sensei taught *ikkyo* before and then ten years later, it looked the same, but it was completely different. His spirit was different, and his understanding and philosophy were more refined. For O Sensei, training was daily life. He put his whole life energy, experience, vision, prayers, and hope into his training, and he never stopped growing. Those only concerned with form could not see the growth and the change inside.

Students need a special kind of eye with which to interpret an instructor's teachings. They need to see beyond the form to the heart. There is no easy way to understand *kihon waza*, for you must discover truth for yourself. But through the sincere study of the properties and reactions of energy, and the resulting development of your own physical power, you will begin to see more deeply into these principles and prepare the way for spiritual growth. All movement of *kihon waza* is the grand foundation and the catalyst for spiritual revolution.

Until you learn to give a correct and centered attack, you cannot learn to respond to an attack in a correct and centered manner. Until you learn to respond to the technique being executed, you cannot study the reactions and dynamics of energy. When you attack in Aikido practice, you are giving your partner a training opportunity, the chance to react and refine technique. In turn, you are receiving the most valuable learning experience of Aikido training. You are gaining firsthand knowledge, through each nerve of your body, of the result of your partner's movement. You will feel the weaknesses as well as the strengths. As you gain more experience, you will understand, from its direct effect on your body and spirit, why a particular movement was ineffective and how a subtle change made that same movement work. You are learning through your partner's successes and mistakes as well as your own. You must respect this.

During Aikido training, the instructor will demonstrate a technique for study. Everyone will practice that same technique, so everyone understands the movement of defense that is to be used. With this knowledge it is easy for the *uke* (the one who attacks and receives the power of the technique) to anticipate the movement and stop it. Stopping your partner's technique in this manner is dishonest and strictly forbidden. Each technique is designed so that a specific style and direction of force may be experienced and studied. Aikido technique depends on blending with the force of the attack. It is that force which determines the movement. If *uke* holds back the necessary force, there cannot be an exchange of the training experience and that technical application cannot be explored. Each attack must be completely committed, given honestly from your center to your partner's center with a fresh mind and spirit. The attack is given each time with full concentration, as though it were the first time and the only time. Now is now.

Any attack is appropriate in *jiya waza* (free-style technique) as long as it is sincere and committed, for the training emphasis is on spontaneous movement. But *kihon waza* is the foundation of spontaneous movement, and the training process must be strictly followed. Extend your spirit; do not extend your ego.

In advanced training, strong resistance becomes an important part of the study. But it is not a resistance of the ego or of a competitive spirit. It must be given with complete honesty and a pure heart. You must also learn when it is appropriate to resist and when resistance is foolish and dangerous. The saving art of *ukemi* (techniques of falling and protecting oneself from injury) is the first step to the study of Aikido. I have often seen students stop and resist at the most ridiculous times, displaying their weaknesses to their partner. Trying to prove the narrow strength of just one part of their body, they leave themselves completely open and unprotected against a strike to a vital area. I've seen them resist when just a fraction of an increase in pressure from their partner would dislocate a shoulder or an elbow, or break a wrist. This is not self-defense or good training. It is the blind stupidity of stubborn ego. It is your responsibility as *uke* to cover your openings and protect yourself. The smartest way to accomplish this is to follow through with a committed attack and take the *ukemi*, responsive to your partner's reaction, aware of all around you, ready to change, and ready for the next *de-ai*. To learn when it is appropriate to resist, to understand when resistance creates a learning situation, requires much experience. It is a practice for advanced students only. You must learn to walk before you can leap.

The *ukemi* of Aikido practice is designed so that no single part of the body must take up the shock of the fall alone. The force is evenly distributed and dissipated in the form of a roll from shoulder to opposite hip. Instead of landing flat and vulnerable, you end up standing in *hanmi* (triangular stance) and protected. In contrast to the sharp break fall of *judo*, the circular motion does not give undue stress to the

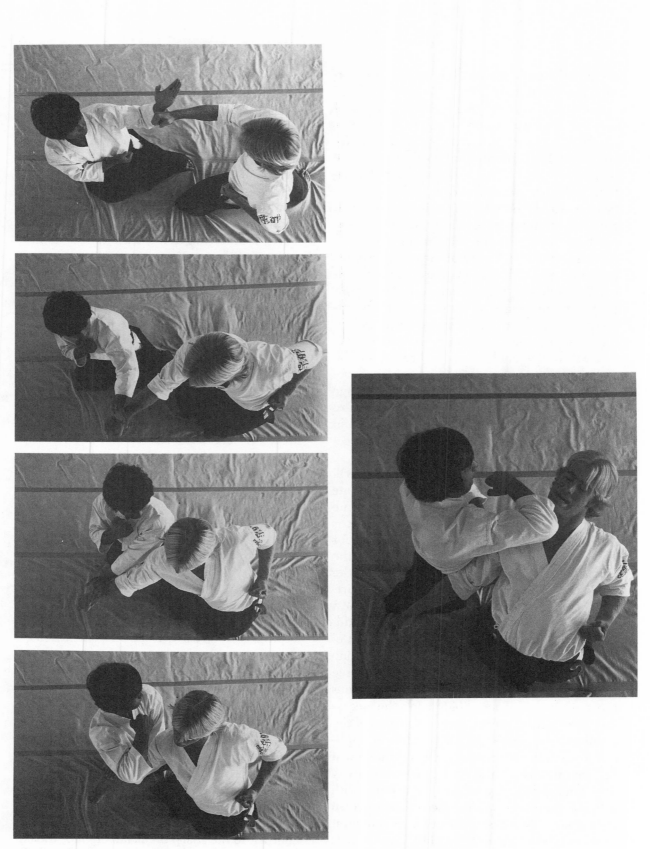

Uke's only chance is often the ability to take a sudden, unplanned fall.

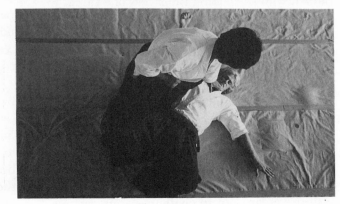

This is the saving art of ukemi. *Robert Moller,* uke.

kidneys and liver. In a sense it massages all the muscles of the shoulders, the back, and the thighs, keeping them strong and flexible. The natural movement in some cases helps to align the spinal column. General circulation is improved by the spinning motion, sending fresh blood and energy to all parts of the body and quickly dislodging and cleansing accumulated wastes from the circulatory system. It is also excellent training in balance perception and stability. Usually the best *ukes* are the best technicians.

Learning to be a good *uke* is, above all, developing a sensitivity to your partner's ability. It is foolish to attack a beginner with all your strength, for in so doing you make that person's response and the study of the technique impossible. It is also foolish to attack in a manner that is stronger than that for which you can take the *ukemi*. A good attack is not necessarily the fastest, strongest attack you can muster. A good attack is a controlled, centered, and sincere attack, taking into account your partner's situation and your own. This is the beginning step in developing perception.

The *nage* is the one who is executing the technique, the one who throws. It is at this time that your responsibility is greatest, the dual responsibility of control and compassion. You must learn to perceive your partner's pain, find compassion, and adjust your movement accordingly. It is at this point that you learn the meaning of Budo training, "to protect the enemy's karma"; to protect the very person who is exerting the stress of a threat to your own well-being. The *uke* is giving you the great gift of trust and the chance to polish your technique, to experiment and grow.

All this you must remember in the midst of the fever and pressure of a martial situation. You must transcend your ego and aggressive energy and discover a positive way to harmony. Each attack and defense is the opportunity for a revolution deep within your spirit. This is the hard training, the struggle within that the inexperienced cannot see. Aikido training means not to challenge your partner, but to challenge yourself. If you are blind to

your partner's feeling, you will never perceive the movement of the universe or its relationship to your own life. Your movement must be an intuitive application of the universal energy force, your spirit melting into the emptiness of that vacuum. You and the universe are one. Realize this! Each time is *katsu*, a spiritual awakening, a figurative slap across the face to awaken the spiritual eye. Your physical eye may be open, but if the spiritual eye is asleep, you cannot make a spontaneous reaction. Now is now! If your whole spirit, your whole life, all of your energy is concentrated into each motion, it will explode within your mind, and each time you will find a small piece of *satori*. A good training partner gives the gift of *satori*. Your partner is your mirror, the grinding stone on which you polish and purify your spirit. As you learn to use your five senses to their fullest, you will begin to discover the sixth and seventh senses of spiritual awareness. As you exhaust your small selfish ego, you will discover the universal mind.

The real purpose of Aikido training is to strengthen the quality of your life. If you are strong, with powerful technique on the mat, but cannot learn to communicate with others in daily life, your training is meaningless. If you always escape from stress, you cannot develop a strong and noble spirit. As you refine your reaction to stress and pressure on the mat, you refine your reaction to the stresses of life in your relationships with others. On the mat you cannot escape from the attacks of your partner. You must learn to face them with confidence and control. Through this training you will find the strength and the confidence to control the conflict that you face everyday.

Sitting in meditation is a valuable training, but the meditation of Aikido practice will teach you to be calm and centered in the midst of danger and threats. It will teach you to remain open, catching the feelings and vibrations of others so that you may receive their aggressions and find a path of harmony. It will teach you to transcend your own aggressive instincts, to refine your reactions so

*As the earth adapts and adjust herself according to the vibrations of the sun,
we must accordingly sense with our body and spirit and process the vibrations we receive
from our partner. This is a vital form of ki training.*

that you may more accurately mirror the spirit of God.

The following semitechnical descriptions of individual technique are by no means complete. They are intended to give those who already practice a reference point, a hint of the direction they should pursue. As for those who have never been on an Aikido mat, I sincerely hope that they may find enough inspiration to begin their search for a good teacher. Aikido cannot be expressed in words. You need the guidance of a qualified teacher and daily practice for the words to have meaning. Aikido is a philosophy of action.

—— HANMI ——

Most martial training systems are concerned with certain stances, postures of defense indicative of their particular style. But the stance of Aikido is not a stance. It is not a posture of defense awaiting an attack. It is a position of reference that allows complete freedom of movement in any direction. All movement begins, moves through, and ends in *hanmi*.

The shape of *hanmi* is the triangle, the natural form of walking through daily life. One foot is placed in front of the other, with knees relaxed and body weight shifting naturally. Students become overly concerned with which foot is forward when their partner attacks, calculating which hand he will use for the strike. This narrows your vision and slows down your response. If the wrong foot is forward to meet the attack in a balanced way, all you need do is take a step, shifting weight and balance within the natural course of movement. Do not make a special *kamae*. Relax and concentrate your spiritual vision to see your partner's movement, his eyes, his feet, his center, the space of his spiritual body. Within the technique allow your feet to move. Never stop and struggle with the energy, allowing your body to overextend past the point of balance. Take a step, keeping your feet beneath your center. Movement is the key to power.

—— SEIZA KOKYU RYOKU TANDEN HO ——
(Sitting Breath-Power Training Process)

Kokyu ho is the power structure of *musubi*, its movement the basis of all Aikido principle. In this practice *uke* grabs both wrists, but through the wrists he must strive to capture his partner's center. This is not a push hands exercise. *Uke* must grab honestly, giving his energy to his partner. Both partners should be seated in *seiza*, knees just short of touching, stabilized with the feeling of pressing into the very center of the earth. There are three basic forms of holding: from the side, which is the most common; from the top; and from the bottom. As the energy flows in a different direction with each form, the movement must be adjusted accordingly.

The *nage* must be completely relaxed and flexible, and a mind of unity must precede the movement. You must strive for emptiness. Never struggle with your partner's mind. Never allow personal conflict to mar the spirit. The spirit reacts first and the physical movement begins at the *hara*. First you must receive your partner's energy, join with it, and make it your own. Absorb it into your *hara*, the two energies making one direction, one flow containing their combined power. Do not try to unbalance your partner with the movement of your arms alone, but extend the power from your *hara*, your whole body redirecting and controlling the energy through the smooth and subtle change of spiral movement. Your concept must not stop with the space occupied by your body, but must extend into the spiritual space of the universe. You are at the center of the galaxy's movement. You are sitting in the center of atomic structure. You and your partner are the living symbol of yin and yang, the circulation of opposite energies making one spiral direction, unified and whole.

Your shoulders must be free of tension, all of your body weight pressing down. Your elbows must be flexible and bent, extending from your *hara* so that the energy flows freely from the center. Following the spiral of your body and the direction of the flow of energy around your wrists, your hands describe a spiral.

Both of your hands must move together, left and right making one spiral movement, helping each other. Your entire body must describe a spiral from your center to your partner's center. As your partner holds tightly and your hands and body draw him into your movement, his elbows will be raised and separated from his center. With this movement his power is split and you only have to extend your energy to unbalance him.

The training system is very strict. The purpose of *kokyu ho* is not to struggle for victory, it is not competition. Especially for beginners, this type of training is taboo. You must train with a flexible attitude as well as a flexible body. Do not practice this movement with the unbendable arm of extend *ki* training, or the driving power of muscle training. Practice with a perception and sensitivity responsive to your partner's movement. When you physically experience the supple power of this movement, either as *nage* or *uke*, your deepest concepts of power must change and expand into multidimensional understandings: strength through flexibility, not resistance; power through harmony, not force. You will begin to understand the all-encompassing power of *musubi*.

All Aikido movement is condensed into the *kokyu ho* exercise. It holds all the technical secrets. Therefore, all other techniques extend from this training.

O Sensei said, "As the dynamics of spiral movement exert a change in your physical situation, you will experience a mental revolution. This change in your mind and heart will create a spiritual revolution. And you will be one with the universal movement."

—— TACHI WAZA KOKYU TANDEN HO ——
(Standing Breath Training Process)

Even though it is stressed in Aikido training not to depend on muscle power, the muscles must be developed and made strong. This must be done in the correct manner and not at the expense of movement and flexibility. The training of two hands very strongly grasping one is an excellent form of muscle development for both *nage* and *uke*. As with most *kihon waza*, the method of execution will differ according to the desired result. But whether the training is static or dynamic movement, the basic principles, the correct attitude, and the proper movement are always of foremost importance. Although the technique when practiced for this particular result is practiced from a static position, muscle training must not be stiff training, or the muscles will develop in a stiff, inflexible manner.

In this training, *uke* grabs one of your wrists very strongly with both of his hands. As in sitting *kokyu ho*, he must grab as though he were trying to immobilize your entire body through that one arm. He must grab your arm as though it were a sword, extending his energy and concentration through his hands to your center. You must not stiffen or let your mind be drawn to the point of the attack. You must direct all of your concentration into your

Kokyu ho *is the power structure of* musubi, *its movement the basis of all Aikido principle.*

Kevin Choate, uke

breath, relaxing body, mind, and spirit. And as always, the spirit moves first. Receive your partner's power and compress all the energy into your *hara*. Your entire body and spirit must contract as the hips are lowered and twisted to direct both energies into one flow. Never struggle with the point of attack, for the center is free and will begin the physical reaction. The point of physical contact moves last, guided by the freedom and power of the rest of the body. Not only the arm that is held, but both arms must be drawn into your center to connect with the energy, elbows down, knees bent, weight dropping, yet back stretched.

To the outside observer it may look like a physical struggle, but inside the mind and spirit a very delicate perception is taking place. Your mind must be silent, an unblemished crystal to catch the vibration. Although the pressure from your partner is intense, you must remain calm, with no ego, no struggle, no thoughts of an enemy. The moment you begin to struggle, your mind will be captured and your movement will be stopped.

By concentrating on the breath, by expressing its power in the breathing action of the physical movement itself, you can begin to understand the breathing of cosmic energy that gave birth to the universe and all of life within. You must train your concentration through the breath, developing stability and expanding the force of your own gravity. The vibrations of the physical world affect the spiritual vibrations. Through the physical development, the spirit will also stabilize, and the greater force of spiritual gravity will be made clear. You must understand the gathering and condensing of energy. The almighty force of gravity compresses the energy until the friction created ignites a tremendous explosion of release. All power, both physical and spiritual, comes to one concentrated point as the arms cross and your body begins to rise. The spiritual essence of water flowing horizontally joins the spiritual essence of fire rising to the heavens. The tension is released from the *hara* in an explosion of united power. The body and the spirit expand into space as the arms open, erupting in the wake of your released hips and returning the power back into your unbalanced partner.

You must train the breath. Concentrate on gathering and compressing energy as you inhale and on the released energy exploding with your exhaled breath. Your movement is the movement of the universe. Your mental image is the beginning of all of Creation, the formation of the stars and the planets, the blossoming of a flower as it perceives the warmth of the summer sunlight, the power of life. Whether your partner is thrown or not thrown is unimportant. To discover your spiritual gravity and transcend your aggressive attitude are the point of all training.

——— SHOMENUCHI IKKYO ———

Shomenuchi is a strike to the head (*men*) directed just above and between the eyes. The old name for this strike is *men no tanren*, "the head's center." It is a difficult strike for the beginning student to execute. Most beginners start the strike with their arms away from the center of their body. The hands must be positioned so that at any time during the process an effective blow can be delivered and so that the center line of your own body is covered.

As you raise your arm, mentally visualize a strike to each of your partner's vital points. You must try to control his space at all times. Your hand must be directed to your partner's center, passing and prepared to strike just above the navel, the solar plexus, the heart, the throat, the bridge of the nose. The strike is finalized and extended between the eyes.

Because of this straight-on direction, depth perception and judging the speed of the attack are much more difficult here than with a strike coming from the side. If you concentrate on the hand when receiving this attack, your body will be unbalanced backward as your eyes try to follow its movement. Your physical posture will be that of escape. Your timing will be captured, and you will be unable to make the instant decision of movement to the right or left. You must see the movement of your partner's center and deal, not with his hand, but with the direction of his force. Your body must be straight and open so that you can move quickly in any direction. Your mind must be open and empty of calculation so that you can perceive the attack accurately. Before contact is made, you should, by your movement and your will, be in control of the attacker's center. You must seize the upper hand, the advantage. Divert and lead his energy so that the advantage is your own.

As your extended arm meets the attack, it is done with the spirit of *kokyu ho*, without conflict, without impact. You must first connect with the attacking arm by joining its direction. Then subtly change that direction with the continuous rolling motion of a spiral, bringing both energies into accord. This is *musubi*. If you do not perceive the spirit behind the attack, if you have no power of communication, you cannot unite your energy with it. If you cannot join with the attack, you cannot control it. You must learn to use all the strength and power of your body and spirit with a delicacy and flexibility that can feel the slightest shift in your partner's body and spirit. You must learn to communicate with every partner on a physical, mental, and spiritual level, intuitively and spontaneously.

Time has no time; speed has no speed. One point in every movement, one point in every strike, is stillness. Your eye will learn to capture it as a camera shutter captures it. There is no fast or slow. An attack that seemed very fast to you as a beginner becomes slower with practice and experience. Your eyes change, and you see differently. If you continue to train, there will eventually come a time when every attack, no matter how fast, will appear

Sei Chu Do Do Chu Sei

to you as a slow-motion film. In true harmony there is no time and no space, for there is no separation. We share the same time, the same space, the same creative vibration, but because we have selfish ego it all seems different and we do not communicate. Harmony is communication. *Ichi go ichi e.*

Ikkyo is the beginning, the first chapter. Concerning the study of technique, O Sensei would say, *"Iriminage, shihonage,* ten years. *Ikkyo* is your whole life."* Your interpretation of the technique will change with experience and time, and your growth and understanding as an individual will manifest itself through the *ikkyo* technique. There is a basic form, but there is no shape. The changes of *ikkyo* are the ever-changing patterns of life. There are no concrete images. Every morning you should awaken with a fresh mind, unclouded by yesterday and open to change. And so too, should you approach *ikkyo,* with a fresh mind every practice.

Many times, as I teach a class, I will emphasize a particular movement or feeling, or a different way of seeing a technique. And many times, as I watch the students practice, it will be the beginners who are really conscious of the point I just demonstrated and trying to practice it. The more advanced students have practiced the technique so many times and are often so filled with preconceptions of the technique that they have forgotten how to see. Their mind is full of yesterday, clouded with memories and their own ideas. They look, but

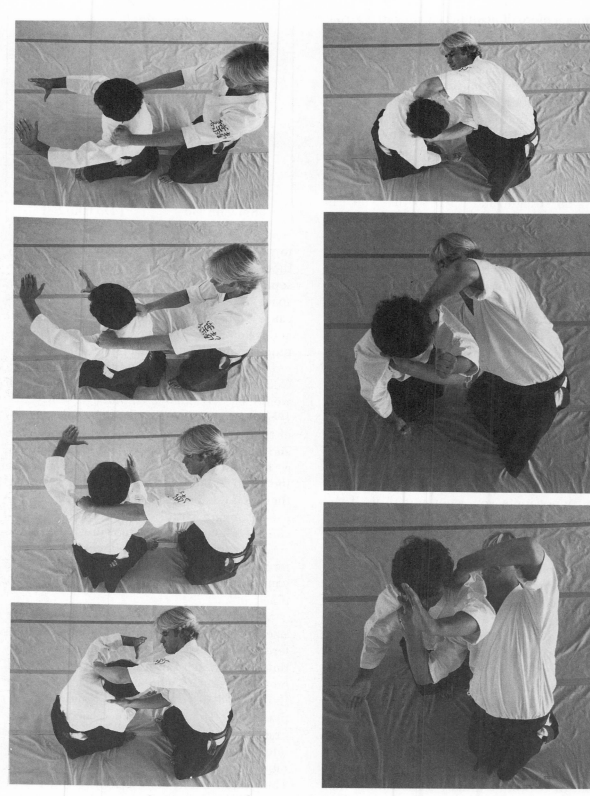

Contraction; gathering and condensing the energy.

*Expansion: the tension released from the hara in an explosion of united energy.
Robert Moller, uke.*

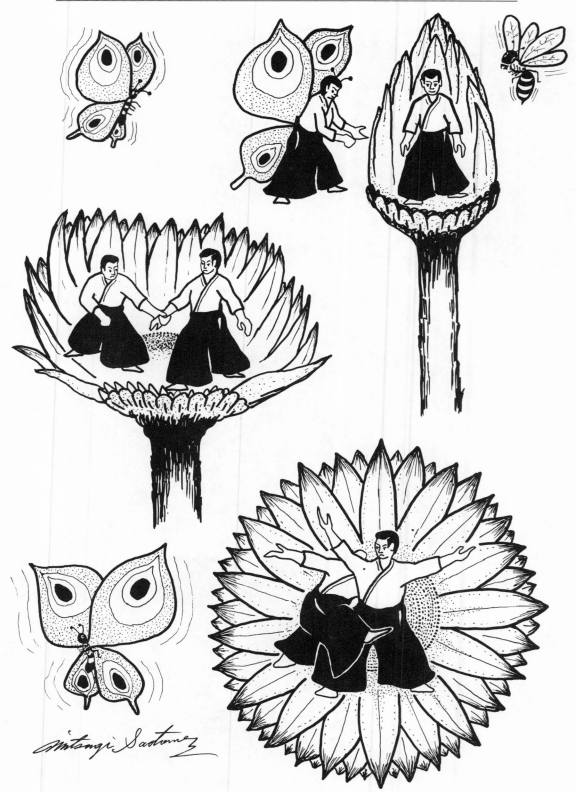

Your movement is the movement of nature,
the blossoming of a flower as it perceives the warmth of the summer sunlight.

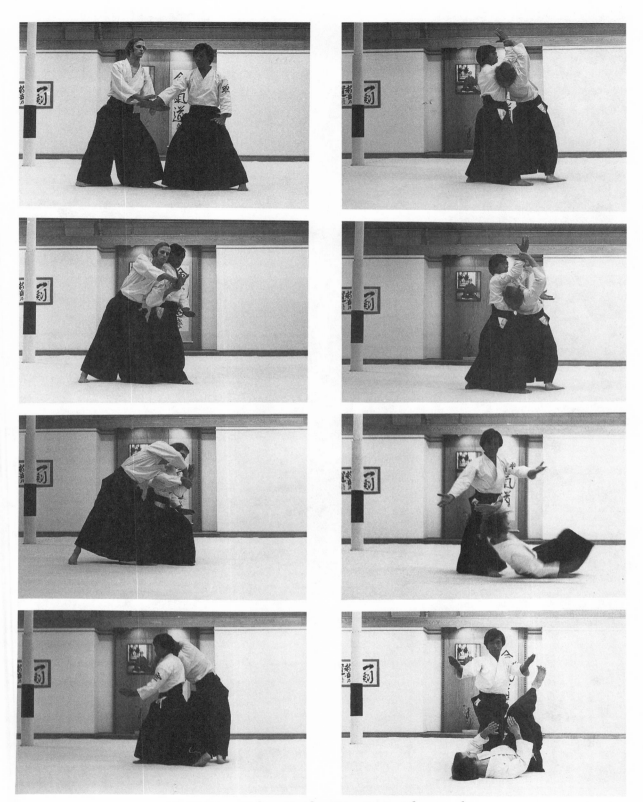

Tachi Waza Kokyu Tanden Ho. *Kevin Choate*, uke.

Embrace and gather the force.

Manen Cho Ho: *always a beginner*

they do not see. They have forgotten the basic principle of life. Now is now!

The study of *ikkyo* reveals itself as light passing through a prism. When you look at an object, you see only one small facet of the light. You perceive only that part of the spectrum which is reflected. But within the light, all colors exist. Each different application of *ikkyo* is only one narrow reflection of an infinite process. You must get past the reflection to experience and perceive the light itself.

As you study the movement of *ikkyo*, you must be aware, not only of your own center and your partner's center, but also of the center that is developed by the relationship between the two of you. The center of the relationship is the *de-ai*, the meeting. Before the physical contact, you must understand this center and control it with your movement. As the attack begins, your movement begins. If your partner is truly attacking and committed, he will follow. It is a lesson in communication. When communication stops, the life of the movement ends. If your position changes after the attack has begun and your partner does not try to follow, he is in effect dead. You will be out of the path of the attack, facing an opening at his time of greatest weakness. The *uke* must follow, he must try to read your movement and connect. It is his only chance.

Create and lead him into a vacuum before the physical contact. Divert and dissipate his force with your gravity. By the acknowledgment of each other on all planes of consciousness, both centers are being drawn into the

de-ai. Control his center by controlling the meeting and the delicate thread that binds you together. If your movement is too quick and too abrupt, the thread will snap. If your movement is too slow, it will slacken. If you divert the energy after the commitment, but before his body sets for the strike, it will be easy to unbalance him. His body will naturally follow the redirected focus of the strike and begin to twist. All you need do is overextend the twisting motion and the lessened power of the attack. The tension of the thread, the communication, is most important.

Lead your partner carefully and exactly, your eyes, your *ki*, your mind, and your extended arms steadily and powerfully drawing his force until you can join it. Arrange the meeting at your own timing and on your own terms. The secret of the movement is the spiritual essence of water. Embrace and envelop the force. Gather it and roll over it like an ocean wave. Don't try to push from beneath your partner's power, or it will overtake and envelop you. First draw it out and turn it around his center.

At the meeting, do not impact with the force. Roll the attacking arm away with the spiral movement of your block. Grasp and extend it, raising his elbow with the manipulation of his wrist. Connecting the elbow from below, continue the spiral and roll it back into your partner's center, and in this way control the entire body. It is at this point that you may deeply explore the principles of human balance. This is the point that determines an *ura* (turning to the back) or *omote* (entering to the front) movement. Examine the coordinated movement of the body and the positioning of its parts, the hips, arms, feet, and head. The principles of balance and geometric structure will become clear. The breaking points of balance will be uncovered as you learn to pressure the diagonals through the center of the opposing force and overextend the energy back upon itself.

The control of the situation is the essence of the movement. To control the situation, you must dominate it with your spiritual gravity.

Magnetic field of interaction between two opposing forces.
To control the situation, you must dominate it with your spiritual gravity.

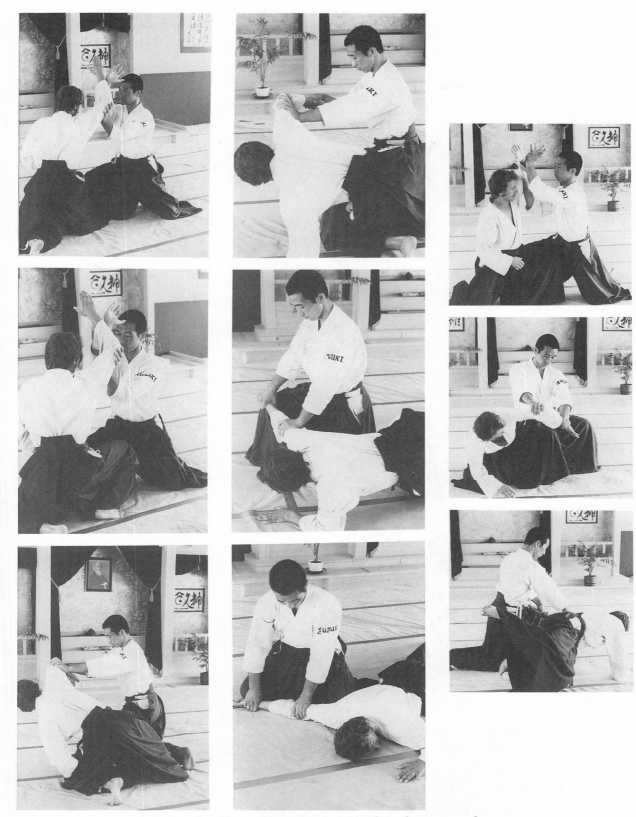

Shomenuchi Ikkyo Suwariwaza, *examples of* omote *and* ura.
Shigeru Suzuki, shihan dai, nage, *Steve McPeck*, uke.

Roll over it like an ocean wave. Shigeru Suzuki, shihan dai, uke.

Ikkyo, *like the mobius strip, folds back*
upon itself and expands into new dimensions of understanding.

Kata Dori Ikkyo Omote. *Bruce Merkle*, uke.

This holds true of all Aiki movement. To dominate the situation, you must communicate with and understand the opposing force. But above all you must control and understand yourself. This can only come with training and time. *Ikkyo* is the first chapter, and it is the last.

SHOMENUCHI IRIMINAGE
(Entering Throw from a Strike to the Head)

Iriminage is also first practiced from the *shomenuchi* attack. The principles and attitude for the execution of the *iriminage* technique are the same as for the *ikkyo* technique, but distance, timing, and structure are different. From the beginning form of *kihon waza* to the exquisite control of time and space and subtle movement of O Sensei's powerful black hole, the technique has thousands of possible variations. Although there are many forms of practice, *iriminage* is always patience. Stand before your partner and reflect his movement. Await the last possible moment before the exchange.

At the moment of attack, create an optical illusion of *ma-ai* by entering into the path of the strike. Enter so that the distance is changed but the extent of your movement is undetected. Give your partner a target; give of yourself. Invite the attack and in a very subtle way initiate the movement. If you try to escape, you will be caught. As the attack becomes more committed, extend your arm and touch the spiritual space of your partner's center. With all your will you must grasp the thread. This extension inside and to the very heart of the attack will cause him to hesitate. At the moment that contact is imminent, you must connect his strike from the outside and, with your extended arm, pressure his center. Do not grab his arm. Roll it away, hand open and elbow relaxed and flexible as you move through your partner's body and spirit. With no thought of escape, join with the energy as you subtly change its direction in an exchange of time and space. This is *marubashi*. As you pass, your arms, your body, and your spirit must open (expansion). Turn and create a vacuum into which he will be drawn. Grasping his neck from behind, drop your weight as you turn his twisting body (contraction).

Iriminage is the interplay of centripetal and centrifugal forces acting together. Your partner's striking hand is controlled by a subtle pressure extending it out as you turn, expansion moving from the center. His head is controlled by drawing it inward, contraction into the center. His energy, his body, and his spirit are split. You are the center of the galaxy controlling his movement. You are the nucleus of atomic structure as he circles around you. Your center must stabilize and push through the strata to become one with the gravity of the earth. The centrifugal hand begins to spiral upward and the body ascends (expansion). All your breath is then released as the energy of the center contracts through both arms, closing and returning the force to the center of your unbalanced partner.

The movement of *iriminage* is the movement of *kokyu*, the breath of expansion and contraction. It is the three-dimensional movement of the combined forces of fire and water. It is circulation, the circulation of the universe, the circulation of the blood, the circulation of the force of life. Your image must be an image of the harmony of energy forces, a graphic display of the universe. This is the training process. Your reaction is your concept. Spiritual attitude, feeling, and movement are never separated but always the same. Forget the struggle with your partner. Only think of concentrating your own spiritual and physical power. Study freedom and transcend your conflict mind. Believe in yourself.

———— KATATEDORI TENKAN HO ————
Wrist-Grab Turning Process)

This is the beginning student's first introduction to Aikido movement. It appears to be a very simple change of position, but it is the heart of Aiki wisdom. *Tenkan* is absolute harmony. Through a complete change in position, you turn to join the direction of your partner. It is the other side of *irimi*. Even as you turn, you must be entering into your partner's center.

It is winter. You are very cold, and you shiver as you look out at the ice and snow. Walk outside and your breath freezes instantly; your toes and your fingers go numb. You are much colder now. This is *irimi*. After a short time you step back inside, and suddenly your perception has changed. The same room at the same temperature is now very, very warm. This is *tenkan*. When you stand under the sword, you are standing on the edge between heaven and hell. The movement of *irimi* is entering hell. But continue the movement and turn, *tenkan*, and you enter into heaven. *Irimi* and *tenkan* are one.

In the basic exercise, *katatedori tenkan ho*, it is *uke*'s responsibility to grab his partner's wrist with one hand while preparing to strike with the other. The attack must be delivered in a controlled and centered manner, with back straight, knees bent. It is not correct for *uke* to rush past his partner anticipating the turn, nor to stand too far away, immobile,

Irimi Tenkan

overextended and unbalanced. Both of these forms are very weak. The approach must be made a little to the side so that *uke* is protected from a possible strike from his partner's free hand. The grab must be firm and alive. If *uke* grabs from a position directly in front of his partner's position, *nage* should strike at his unprotected face. This will cause him to reconsider his position and quickly move to the side, out of the line of attack. When *nage* executes the *tenkan* movement, *uke* must be flexible and react to the movement. His only chance of protection is to follow and continue *zanshin*, centered and responsive. To stand stiff and immovable is to stand open and unprotected.

In one form of practice, *tenkan* is executed at the moment of physical contact. In another, it may be executed a split-second before contact is made. But be very careful, for you must understand the exact moment of commitment. You must not jerk your hand away. Maintaining mental and spiritual contact, offer it as a target and keep it just out of reach as you turn. If the movement begins too soon, *uke* will not follow. You will have given away your position, and your ribs will be open and exposed to his attack. The timing involved is very strict; there is no room for error. *Tenkan* may also be practiced as a form of muscle training. In this practice it is not necessary for *uke* to prepare to deliver a strike with the opposite hand, for it is a much slower form of training. But the movement and position must be chosen with the possibility of the strike in mind. In this case, push with your center against *uke*'s grabbing hand to ensure his commitment, causing him to react and push back. But do not stand and struggle or you will be trapped, inviting his strike. With the feeling of entering into his center through his arm, apply only enough pressure to cause him to give of his energy and push you into the turn.

There are many, many ways of varying de-

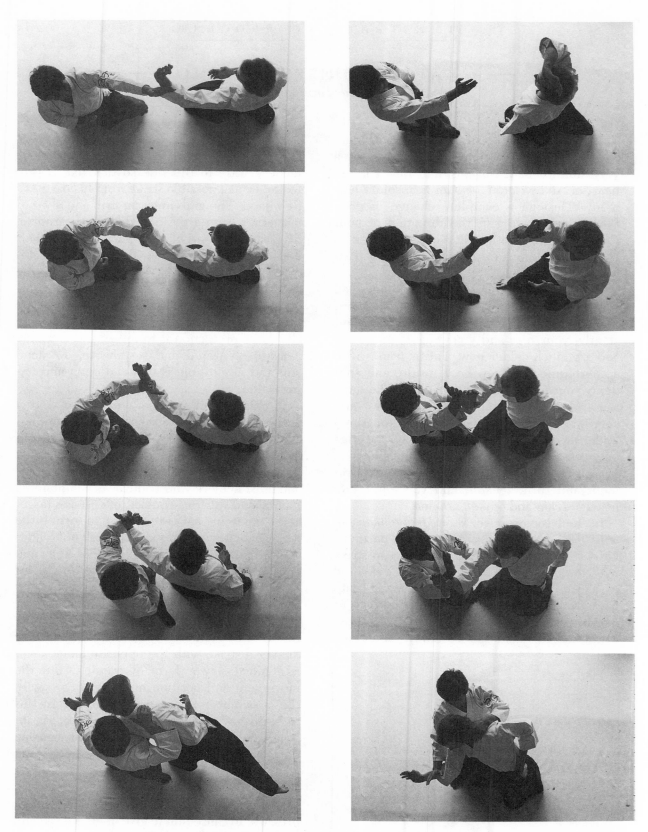

Two examples of irimi *movement from a strike to the head.*
Note carefully the spiral block used to deflect the shomenuchi.

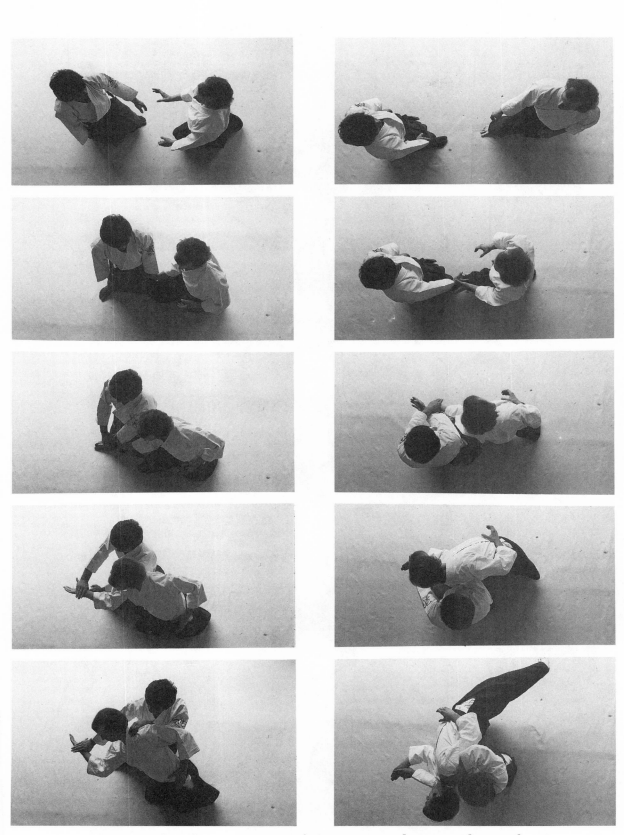

Two examples of irimi *movement from a wrist grab. Kevin Choate, uke.*

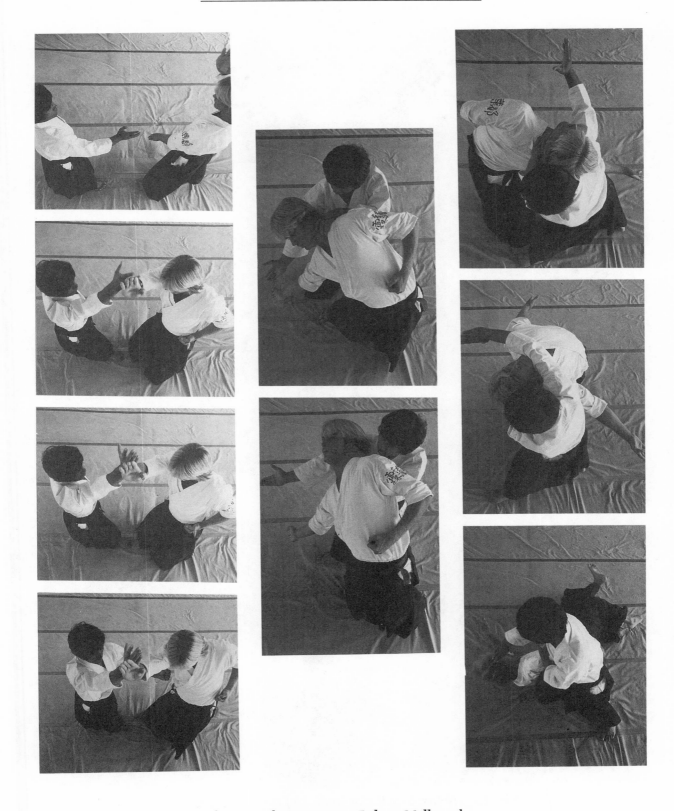

Shomenuchi Iriminage. *Robert Moller*, uke.

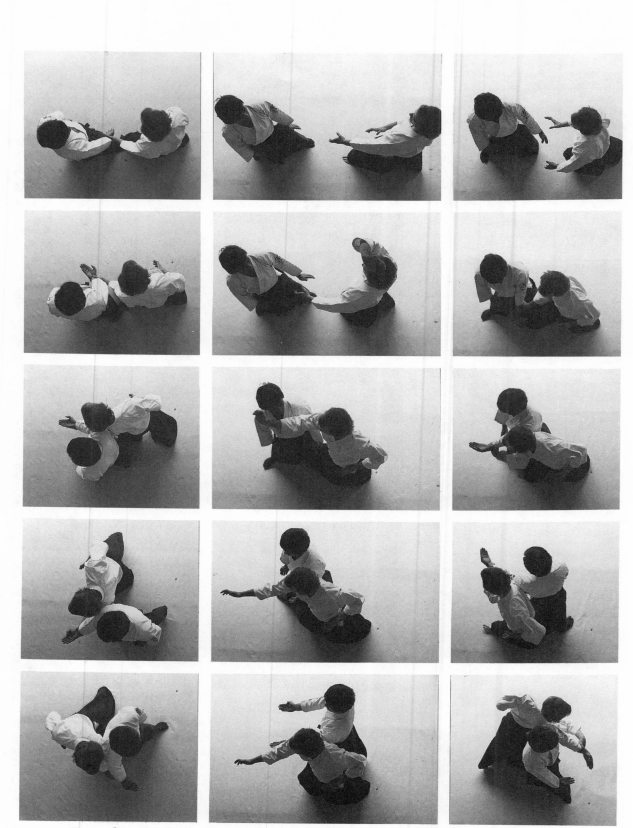

Examples of tenkan. *Notice that the beginning of the* tenkan *movement is* irimi.
Kevin Choate, uke.

grees of intensity to practice this movement and innumerable refinements to discover. But whether static or moving, you must be aware of the next possible action. A grab alone is an incomplete attack. Remember that it is only your arm which is held. Do not become attached to the point of the attack. Do not become stubborn and attached to your own position. You must learn to respect your partner and his position. The rest of your body is free and the final goal is harmony. The secret is change.

The turn itself must be executed from the hips, weight sinking into the earth, knees deeply bent and flexible. *Tenkan* is the study of human balance and reaction in motion. Time in actual contact with force is required to study this reaction, to experiment, and to understand the principles involved in redirecting and controlling it. Practiced by continuing the turn and leading your partner around you many times, *tenkan* will give you this experience. This movement, as with all Aikido movement, is never executed in only one or two dimensions. It is a rhythm of turning, of rising and falling. It completely fills its space with the multidimensional rhythms of fire and water.

As you turn, you must not allow the pressure on your arm to pull you backward or to cause you to retreat. You must move forward, your body aligned and moving as a unit. Do not leave your arm behind you as you turn. Keep it relaxed and in front of your center. If you look back at your partner, your energy will be split. Look where you are going and let your eyes register everything around you. The turn should not be made so quickly that your partner cannot follow, nor so slowly that he recovers his balance and overtakes you. Keep a firm pressure, the thread taut but unbroken.

When you try *tenkan* from a very strong grab, you will at first be unable to move. As you continue to try, your instincts of defense will start to evolve. As you find that aggression does not work, a physical revolution will begin. Continue to train. Grinding, building, refining, polish the negative edges from your reaction until the way of harmony becomes a natural response. Each partner is a little different; each reaction will require a slightly different movement. As you practice with different body types and personalities, your experiences will be recorded into each nerve of your mind and body. They will become a living record from which to draw an appropriate response, both physically and mentally, to many situations. The physical experience will change your consciousness.

—— MUNETSUKI KOTEGAESHI ——

The leaves of autumn trace spirals in the air as they fall from the trees. Just before they touch the ground, they are turned over by the gusting wind. This is the picture brought to mind by the name of a classic *jujutsu* technique, *kono ha gaeshi*. This old *jujutsu* technique was designed to break the wrist and wrench the arm from its shoulder socket. Although it is still a wrist lock technique, in the highest form of Aikido practice it is the rhythm of the movement, not the pain in the wrist, that is responsible for the *kotegaeshi* throw.

This technique is first practiced from a straight punch to the chest or solar plexus. The punch is avoided with an *irimi-tenkan* movement. As you move past your partner, do not attempt to grab his punching hand, for you will surely miss it. In the manner of joining a *shomenuchi* strike, roll your hand along his arm, joining his energy, and drop the weight of your body to unbalance him. Your hand will naturally fall to his wrist. The principles of *tenkan ho* are the same for the *tenkan* movement of the *kotegaeshi* technique, but now you are the one who is holding. If you desire power over your partner, the chance of your

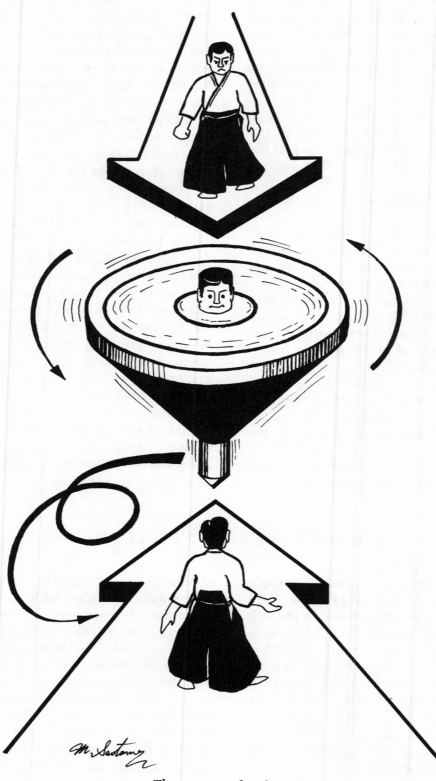

The essence of tenkan.

aggressive tendencies surfacing becomes more acute, and the tension in your body will block the messages of his reaction. As you turn, do not fear that your partner will escape. If you are too aggressive and attempt to lock his arm under yours, your movement will be stopped. You must remain relaxed and flexible. Keep your body upright, your chest open, and your knees bent. Move your partner around you in a descending spiral. Slowing your movement, let him drift. Allow him to begin to recover his balance. Then, at the proper timing, reverse your hips and his wrist together, returning his renewed energy just before he recovers. You will perceive the proper timing only if you are open to his reaction.

Within this movement, the macroworld of the planets orbiting the stars (your partner circling around you) and the microworld of atomic structure (the turning of his wrist) are working together in one movement. Remember as you turn to concentrate on your own movement as a part of the universal power. Do not concentrate on forcing your partner around you. Obey the laws of the universe and it will happen as a natural consequence of your actions. Feel his intention, the direction of his power, and respond to it. If you are filled with aggression, if you only want to make a powerful throw, your shoulders will raise and tighten, your back will bend, and your chest will become constricted. Maintain a posture of pride. Do not retreat back down the evolutionary path to your ancestors. To raise your consciousness above the level of the other animals, you must raise your physical posture above that of the other animals. If your back is straight and your chest open, your heart and mind will be open. Only in this way can you learn to communicate with your partner. Listen to his body and you will hear his spirit.

THE TRAINING OF EMPTY HANDS AND THE TRAINING OF WEAPONS ARE ONE

In an old *jujutsu* technique very similar to the *shihonage* of Aikido, the first movement was a punch to break the ribs. The *jujutsuka* would then pivot under the enemy's arm, barring it across his shoulder. The accompanying twist would separate the shoulder and break the elbow and the wrist. The throw itself would probably crush the enemy's skull as his head was driven into the ground. Very difficult to control and therefore difficult to practice, this technique was developed to kill the enemy.

When O Sensei organized his training process, he saw his technique through enlightened eyes. He saw the possibility of an even greater power through more harmonious movement, and a way to practice the technique safely without restricting its rhythm. With the joints bent in the natural flow of body movement, it need not maim or kill, but would just as effectively control an aggression. O Sensei saw its practice as an opportunity to understand the principles of balance and natural law. And within its movement he saw the elegant rhythms of the sword.

Although people often get the impression that much of Aikido technique is the refinement of old *jujutsu* technique, the rhythm and consciousness of Aikido are based on the movement of the sword, the spear, and the staff. There is no sharp dividing line between *taijutsu* (hand technique) and weapons practice in Aikido, for the philosophy and its physical manifestation in movement are the same. Aikido is a blending of their truths. When you are using the sword, it is an extension of your body and spirit. You must not depend on the sword. When you have no sword, you must move as though you did, extending your body and spirit through the sword.

In feudal times a warrior trained in many different styles of combat. Unless he had some knowledge and experience with a spear, he

The macroworld of the planets orbiting the stars, and the microworld of atomic structure have the same movement. These principles work together to produce the kotegaeshi technique.

Munetsuki Kotegaeshi. Bruce Merkle, uke.

Greater power through harmonious movement. Safety without restricting its rhythms.

Katate Dori Shihonage (*four-corner throw*). *Hiroshi Ikeda*, shihan, uke.

Ushiro Waza Shihonage

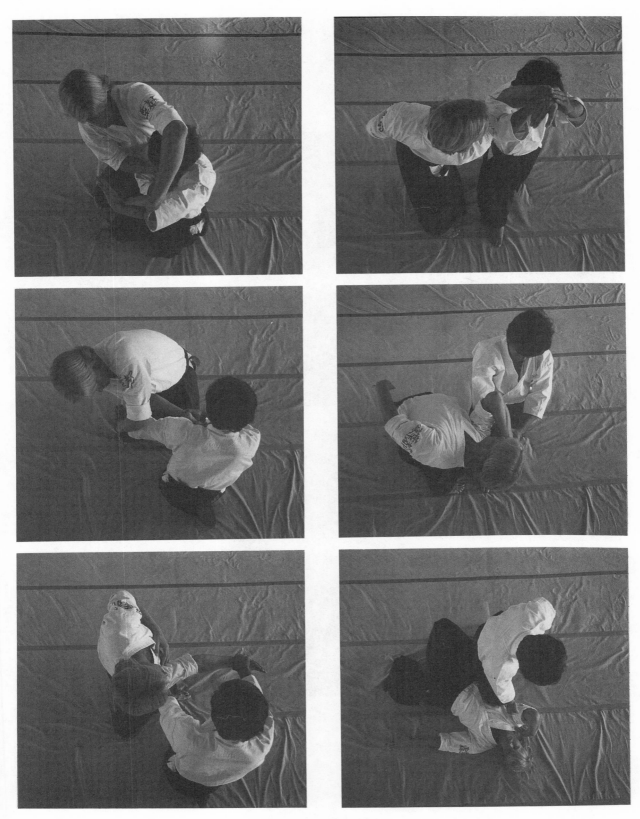

Robert Moller, uke.

Another example of Katate dori shihonage. *Shigeru Suzuki,* shihan dai, uke.

could not fight an enemy with a spear. If he had never touched a sword, he would not understand the way a swordsman moves. He would be ignorant of the enemy's strengths and weaknesses. If he had never trained in *jujutsu* technique, he would be caught off guard and unable to counter. The many weapons and styles of fighting were never separate, and the search for knowledge and experience was endless. It could mean the difference between life and death.

Today it is the same in the martial arts as it is in science, medicine, and almost every other area of modern life. One who studies the sword knows only the sword; the *jujutsuka* knows only *jujutsu*. Much can be gained through specialization, but too much specialization greatly narrows perspective and understanding. One small part cannot be understood out of context. Our universe is a universe of relationships; you cannot separate any part from the others. Your life is the sum of its relationships. It is not the particular art or style that is important, but the spirit that develops from its practice. If you are narrowly attached to one art, your spirit will become enslaved to that art. For a full understanding, you must have a vision that expands enough to encompass all others. Each time the warrior trained with a new weapon or trained in a new style of combat, it broadened his understanding and gave him a new outlook on the principles that are the same in all styles. In this way the warrior was set free. He learned to depend, not on a particular weapon or way of fighting, but on his own perception, awareness, and spiritual confidence.

This spiritual and mental awareness is the basis of Aikido training, but there are times when training only in hand technique brings out a more aggressive, macho attitude. It may easily become a habit for the physically strong student to wait for the moment of *de-ai*, struggle at the point of contact, and depend only on the power of his mucles to execute the technique. This aggressive attitude will confine the student to competitive struggle. He and his partner will descend to the level of two wild

bears wrestling for physical supremacy. Using a weapon is a very unique human quality and must be practiced on a human level. In weapons training you are not grabbing the physical body of your partner. Size is not important. You cannot compare the power of your muscles with his. The stiffness of physical aggression and the narrow vision of a competitive attitude cannot work. You cannot physically feel your partner's reaction, so you must learn to touch his spirit.

All Aikido principle is magnified through the greater extension and distance of weapons training. This practice points out weaknesses in technique, movement, and timing that are more easily overlooked while training empty-handed. It forces you to recognize the increased power and balance of proper form. When you grasp a *jo*, a *bokken*, or a spear with both hands, your arms naturally come together and move from the center of your body. It is easier when holding a weapon to feel the loss of power if your elbows are at odd angles to your body. It is easier to feel the tension in your shoulders if they are raised and tight. Because of the greater distance between you and your partner, it is obvious that your entire body must move. The limitation of extending only your arms and the weapon is clear.

Each small process of hand technique is enlarged at the end of a weapon; every movement is seen as through a telescope. In Aikido training, the most subtle movement of the hand can totally alter a situation. When you experience this movement while holding a weapon, the process becomes much clearer as you watch the change in the angle of a blade, or the larger spiral at the end of a *jo*.

A *shomen* strike with the empty hand becomes many times faster at the end of a three- or four-foot weapon, and because of the greater torque, the power intensifies. Weapons training requires much greater accuracy, a more responsive precision, and the most intensive concentration. You must learn to control your distance, timing, and position exactly. If you make a mistake and are hit during

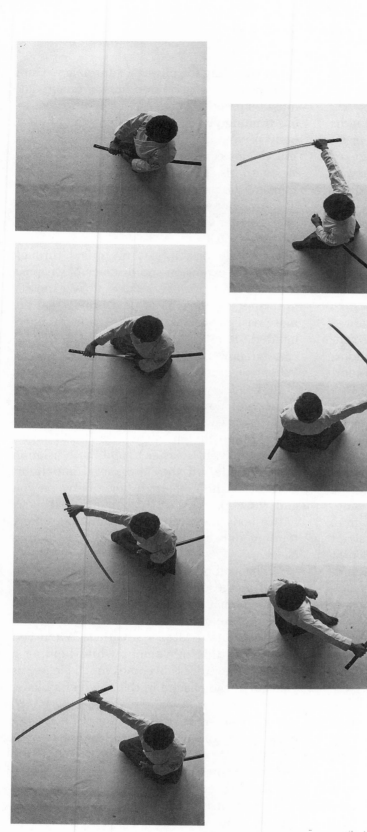

The elegant rhythms of the sword.
Shihogiri (four direction cut) begins with a 360 degree spinning cut.

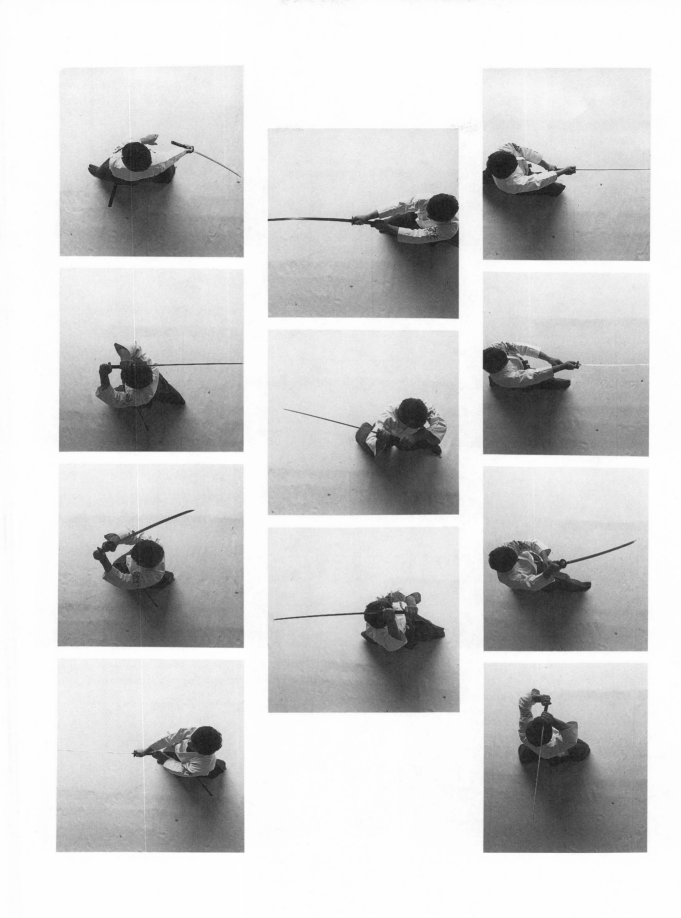

The movement is concluded by cutting the four diagonals.

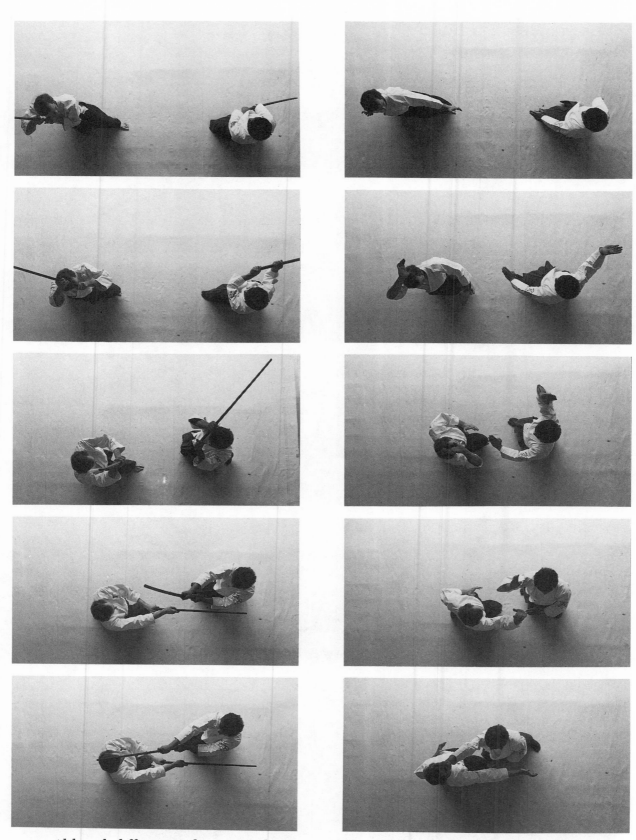

Although different in distance and timing, the basic movement of weapons technique and the basic movement of empty-hand technique are one.

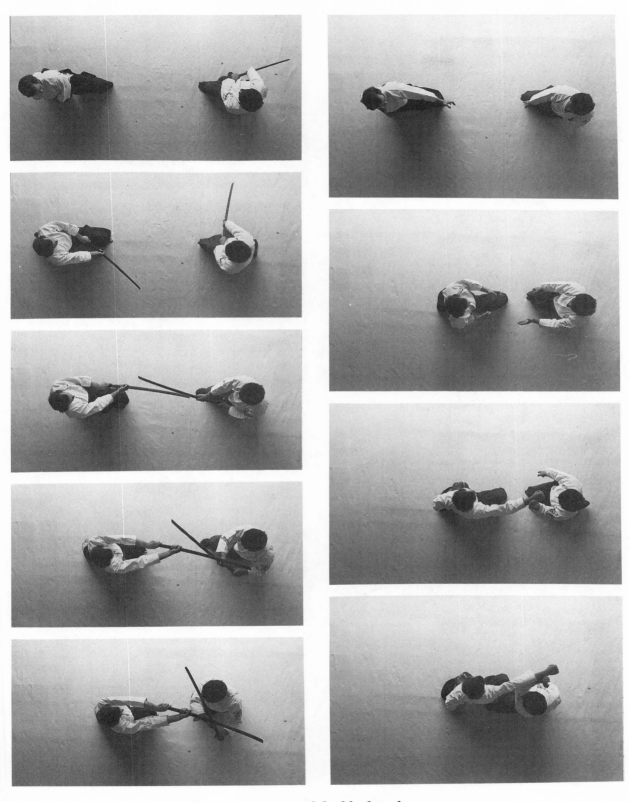

The consciousness of the block is the same.

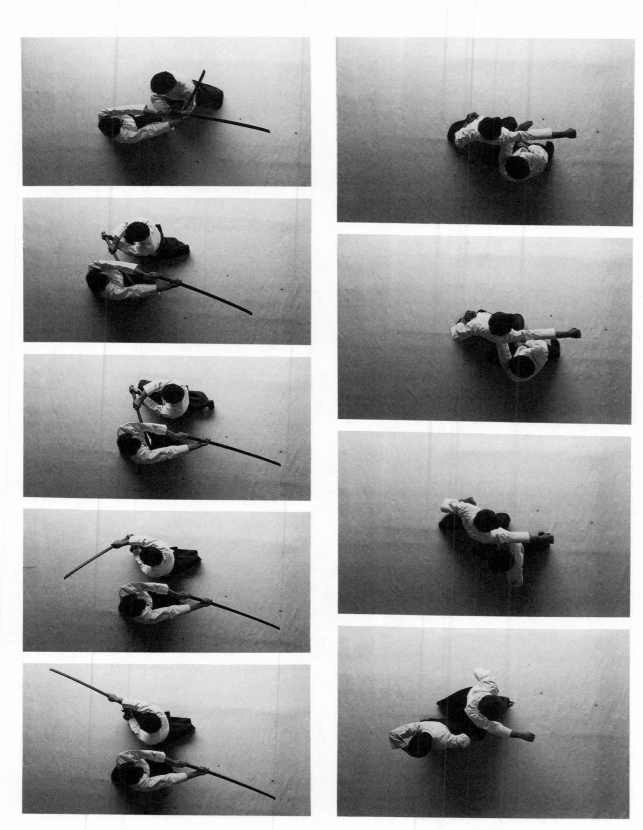

The do cut, just above the waist, and the atemi *to the ribs are the same.*

hand technique training, it is a relatively small pain. But if your partner makes contact while attacking with a wooden staff, a serious injury may occur. When you are standing with a weapon, you are standing at the point of *marubashi*. Your consciousness must hold the intensity of a life-and-death situation at all times. Your awareness must be total. Your responsibility for protecting yourself and your partner is great. There must be no break in concentration. Because of the heightened possibility of injury, strict etiquette and following the exact training process are vital.

Before you begin actual weapons training with a partner, you must spend many hours alone practicing strikes and learning to move in a balanced manner. You must hold the weapon until you are familiar with its weight and balance. You must practice control until you can stop your strike dead within a fraction of an inch of the target. The responsibility of using a weapon cannot be taken lightly.

Beginning partner practice is a simple, prearranged two-person form, *kata*. It is practicd very slowly so that the student can study the correct distance, timing, and proper form and, most important, can develop control. As you become more experienced, the process gains momentum, but the relationship between the speed of the *kata* and your ability to control the weapon is crucial. If your partner misses

his timing, you must be capable of perceiving the break in harmony and stopping the strike before it connects. One small moment of aggression can result in a memorable pain. When your partner attacks with a *bokken* or a *jo*, he is giving you guidance. In the same timing you must defend and attack, following and guiding his next move in one motion.

Training with weapons is the absolute study of communication and harmony in a situation of extreme stress. Your footwork must make contact with your partner's movement. The echo of communication between you must never be silenced. Your bodies must move together; your spirits must breathe together. Each motion must be exact. You must accurately catch the feeling of your partner and make an instant, intuitive decision. There is no time to calculate. Your mind must be empty. Feel your partner's vibration and join with that vibration. Feel the beat of his heart, the pulse in his veins, and blend your timing with his. Perceive his breath and, understanding its rhythm, breathe as one.

I see you walking and I understand your mind. I know the rhythms of your heart, and your spiritual vibration is clear. Why? I am empty. I am a drum. If you hit hard, I make a hard sound. Touch me softly and my sound is a whisper.

ATEMIWAZA

I've heard people say that there are no strikes or punches in Aikido. How can this be true? Aikido is a martial art. The greatest value of training lies in understanding and transcending your aggressive reactions in the face of the stress produced by its martial application. If there is no martial application, there is no conflict. If there is no conflict, there is no reality, and you cannot understand harmony. Too often people misunderstand and practice Aikido as an easy way. Aikido is not an "easy way."

The *atemiwaza* (striking technique) of Aikido training is unlike the focused punch of *karate*. Its purpose is not to kill or destroy, but to distract and confuse, to seize the moment and, with it, the advantage. It is a training aid that, while not an end in itself, can be used as a means to better understand Aikido movement by learning to recognize openings and to further develop a spontaneous reaction. *Atemiwaza* may be used to create a necessary opening or to cover your own opening. It teaches

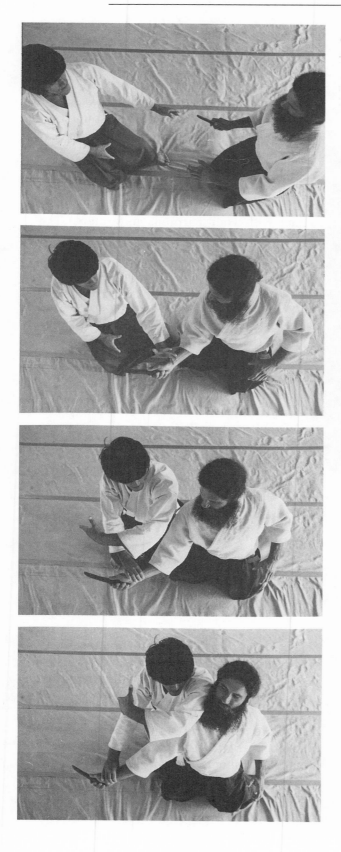

If you have never trained with a weapon, you cannot know the enemy's strengths and weaknesses. Hiroshi Ikeda Shihan, nage, *John Messores,* uke.

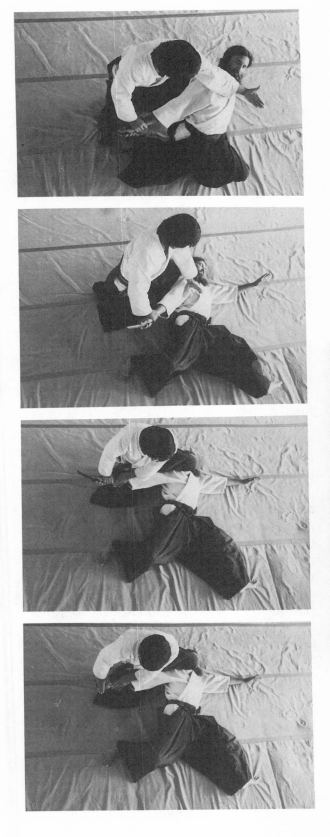

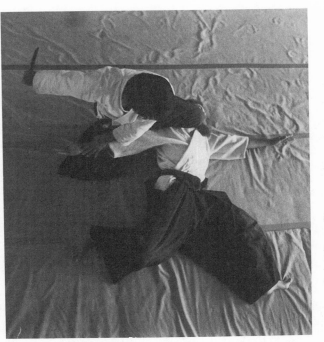

you to continue to see and remain aware of your partner's reaction and situation during the entire process of executing technique.

Atemiwaza

Atemiwaza is not only a training aid for *nage*; it teaches *uke* to respond to the unexpected. I've often seen students attack and stubbornly disregard their partner's *atemi*. Although it is *nage*'s responsibility to avoid making unnecessary contact with his *atemi*, it is *uke*'s responsibility to recognize the strike and respect its authority. When *uke* does not acknowledge and react to this situation, it is but the good graces of his partner that save him from the pain of a cracked rib or a broken nose. If *uke* is perceptive and there is time to block the strike, he must attempt the block. This gives his partner the chance to practice his reaction to a changing situation. Much of advanced Aikido training depends on using the movement and power of this block to execute technique. In the case of a well-timed *atemi* to the face, *uke*'s only chance is often the ability to take a sudden, unplanned fall. This is the saving art of *ukemi*.

Training in *atemiwaza* is not recommended for beginners. It is all too easy to become mesmerized by its power and to neglect the study of form and movement. As in weapons training, exact control and immediate response are necessary to avoid injury. As in training by giv-

ing ever-increasing resistance, it takes many years to discover what is appropriate and what is not. Traditionally, *atemiwaza* is taught only to those of certain *yudansha* level who will not misunderstand its purpose in Aikido training.

In making a fine sword, the iron is continually stressed. Forged in flames, it is softened by the heat of aggression so that shaping and refinement may take place. It is beaten, pounded, folded back upon itself, heated, and pounded until all the impurities are driven away. When it is plunged into water, the temper is set, the fires are controlled, and wisdom prepares to sharpen its edge. The process is very complicated, and no part can be omitted. Its hidden layers number more than a million, but the finished product is simple and pure of line. It is strong yet flexible, and its surface reflects all that is around it.

The study of Aikido, too, is built up layer upon layer. Each layer of experience and understanding ignites the fire of another search for the answer to continually evolving questions. There is no particular style of training that is better than the others. They are all necessary for the fullness of understanding. Hard training and soft training must never oppose each other. They must both be experienced in all their degrees of hardness and softness, and of the hard within the soft, and the soft within the hard.

Your training has its own personal biorhythm, which is different each year, different each practice. If you are always training hard, consumed by fire, you will lose your sensitivity to your partner's reaction, you will begin to ignore the all-important thread of communication between you, and you will never find wisdom. If you are always training softly, immersed in water, you will never be stressed enough to discover your strength. You will lose reality, you will lose the fire, and you will lose the Way. Who will listen if you speak of harmony from a position of weakness? If you are weak, you have no choice. Only from a position of strength, only when you have a choice will your words and actions have meaning.

The desired result of Aikido training is not the physical power of technique; it is the power of wisdom. But solid technique is the first step, the foundation on which to build. The movement and shape of the body reveal and simultaneously affect the movement and the shape of the spirit. I cannot reach inside you and grasp your spirit. I cannot squeeze out the aggression and change its shape. But I can help you to change the shape of your hunched and aggressively tightened shoulders. I cannot make you open your heart and communicate with others. But I can show you how to stand with your shoulders back, your spine erect, open to their movement. I can show you the beginning of the path to communication. I can help you discover a more powerful and compassionate way to react to the aggression of others.

Perhaps instinct cannot change, but the responses of that instinct to fear and stress can and must change. In Aikido training your hand studies God's wisdom. If you have a mental block of fear and aggression, your hand and your body cannot work to produce Aikido technique. Therefore, you must reach into another dimension of understanding, the dimension of universal law, to discover the movements of true power. Your hand, your physical body, begins the revolution. They educate the conscious and the subconscious mind in the way to produce an instinctive response based on patience, modesty, and wisdom. In this way the spirit is refined. This is Shobu Aiki, the wisdom of Aiki.

Within a movement of complete harmony, you cannot see the power, for there is no struggle. Balance, timing, and the use of space and spiritual communication become dynamic art. The image that is visualized is a revolutionary image, pure and simple of form yet strong and flexible, reflecting the world around it. Aikido is a dynamic poem of movement. You must become the galaxy and express it with your body. You cannot imitate the power of an ocean wave; you must become the ocean itself. You must see not just small technique but the entire picture of the movement. You must extend your creativity and create an image of power and reality. Your movement is a poem. You are the wind, the sun, a mountain, and, exactly, you are art.

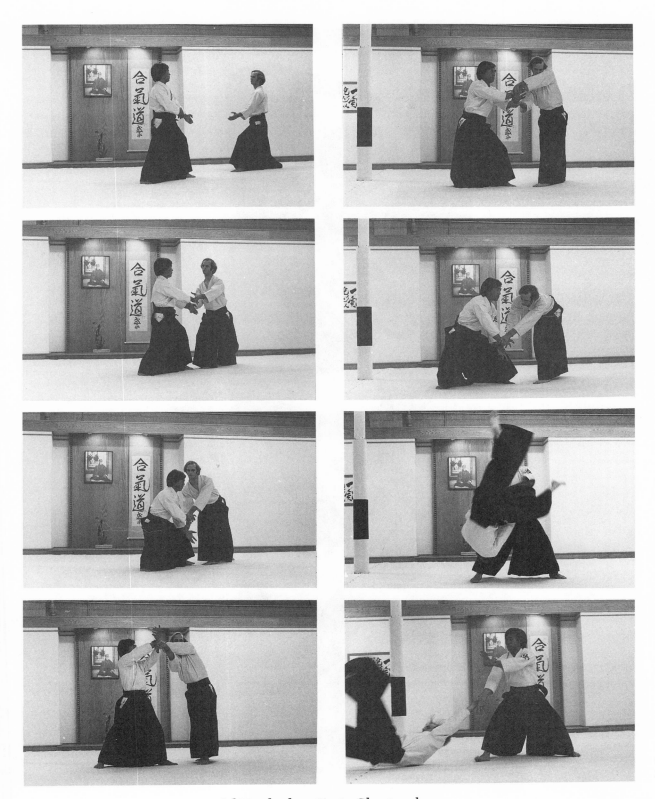

Aiki is rhythm. Kevin Choate, uke.

Hibi Shoshon *is day by day a fresh mind, a beginner's mind.*

13

The
EDUCATION
of an
UCHI DESHI

The objective of Aikido training on the mat is to carry that training into every part of your life. If it stops with technique, it has no real value. This was the education I received from O Sensei, a twenty-four-hour-a-day warrior's education in awareness, sensitivity, intuition, and action. Most important, it was an education in morality and human values.

With time, memories undergo a strange transformation. The exciting and the poignant memories all crowd together, squeezing out the memories of the days that sometimes passed so slowly and the work that was always exhausting. But one thing that the tricks of memory cannot change was the love and concern that O Sensei felt for each of his *uchi deshi*. Although strict and constantly demanding, it was tempered with humor and incredible warmth. O Sensei's laughter was frequent, spontaneous, and deep. Though his anger was sudden and terrifying, it passed quickly, and no judgment of the person or situation remained. He believed that never to

make a mistake was the biggest mistake. Only those who never strive for refinement, who never accept the challenge to surpass themselves, will make no mistakes. He taught that a mistake is an opportunity for creativity; no mistake, only change.

O Sensei did not communicate his orders or requests with words. Just a glance or the smallest gesture had to be correctly interpreted and responded to instantly. If an *uke* did not respond to the slightest signal on the mat, he lost that opportunity to learn and experience O Sensei's movement. Someone else was quickly summoned. There was a correctness, an ordered way of performing even the most seemingly insignificant task. When walking with O Sensei, the student, if only one, always walked behind and to O Sensei's left. The left side was always covered first. The sword, worn on the left side, was drawn with the right hand, making the left rear the most vulnerable in the chance of an attack. O Sensei did not carry a sword in everyday life, and the chance of attack was very small, but by

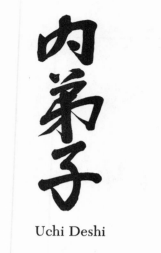

Uchi Deshi

this act the student learned to put himself last and assume the proper attitude of the protection of others.

O Sensei was always accompanied by at least one student who was responsible for taking care of such minor details as carrying O Sensei's luggage or parcels, carrying his wallet, buying his train tickets, paying for anything he might wish to purchase, and so forth. It was exhausting. He walked at a fast clip, never seeming to deviate from his course and never bumping into anyone. I often tried the same tactics, ending up far behind him, lost in apology to passersby with whom I had collided.

O Sensei always arose at 3:00 A.M., bathed, and performed purification rituals before his morning prayers. Before sleeping each night, he observed the same routine. He enjoyed a bath that was hot and steaming, and it was our duty to see that it was prepared and at the proper temperature. Once, while performing this task, my hands had become quite soiled from bringing in the firewood with which to heat the bath water. Wiping them in a rather perfunctory manner, I put one hand in the water to test the temperature. Seeing this, O Sensei growled, "Did you put your dirty hand in my bath?"

Oh no, I thought as I replied, "*Hai*, Sensei. I was checking the temperature."

Angrily he said, "This bath is so important. It is preparation for prayer. How can I pray after bathing in that dirty water? You have no sense. Take out some of the water with that small scoop to test it. Never put your dirty hands directly into the water. Now, hurry. Throw it out and heat some clean water!" But there was the beginning of a smile on his face as he turned away.

The *uchi deshi* all slept in the *dojo*. There was little privacy, and we were always subject to O Sensei's whims. O Sensei only slept a few hours each night. Many times, early in the morning when we were deep in sleep, exhausted from the training and the chores of the day, O Sensei would come into the *dojo* just a bit lonely and looking for someone to talk to. He would often carry his *bokken*, and with a great *kiai* begin *suburi* training. We were shocked right out of our futons into formal *seiza*. Looking around with his most beautiful, charming smile, he would say, "Oh, I'm sorry. Everyone was asleep. Did I wake you?"

Winters were most memorable in the unheated *dojo*, for as soon as he came in, he would throw open all the windows and breathe deeply of the invigorating morning air. And there we'd be, captured in shivering *seiza* with only our thin underwear between us and the snow-kissed air of the *dojo*.

"Well, since you're already awake," and he'd begin. After he had lectured for an indeterminant amount of time, he would just as quickly stop and return to his room. A great sigh would travel through the *dojo* as we shut the windows and dove into our futons in search of another hour's sleep before morning practice.

I always looked forward to traveling to Iwama with O Sensei. Among other things, I could occasionally find the opportunity to be alone and pursue my own studies.

After his evening prayers, O Sensei had retired for the day. Overjoyed at the prospect of some time to myself, I reached for *The Book of Five Rings* by Musashi Miyamoto that I had carried with me from Tokyo. I had just begun when my reading was interrupted by O Sensei's voice outside my quarters. "Saotome, are you there?" And in he came.

"Ah, I see you are reading *The Book of Five Rings*. This book and Confucius's book on military strategy are probably the most widely read works among military, political, and business people. I suppose you've read that, too. Well, be careful, Saotome. Just because you've read these books, it doesn't mean that you understand them."

Glancing at my book and hiding a sigh of resignation, I answered, "Yes, Sensei. I'll keep your advice in my mind."

O Sensei continued, as I knew he would. "It is commendable to pursue literary studies, but make sure that you do not lose sight of the real purpose of your training. Ask yourself: What is the *do* of Aiki? It is the Budo that accepts no enemy. It is the *do* of achieving victory without bloodshed, of ending destructive conflict before it begins.

"Aikido is not the way of weakness or escape, for obviously Budo belongs to those of strength and skill. Yet the Way must lead to a world of mutual concern and respect for one another."

After pausing for a second, O Sensei asked me if I could massage his tired shoulder. Now, rather glad of his company and his relaxed manner, I began to give *shiatsu*.

"Saotome, your massage technique comes from your physical power alone. It is stiff and weak. I can feel no *ki* coming through your fingertips. Relax and blend with the *ki* of this universe. Fill your whole self with *ki* and concentrate it into your hands."

Without any notion of what O Sensei was telling me, I tried my best to follow his advice, pushing with all the strength I could muster. But he just laughed, lying back against my hands until I could no longer support his weight.

Sitting up quickly, he said, "Listen closely to me, Saotome. Reading books will never polish your character, nor will they give you wisdom. Wisdom can only come through experience. Your body and your mind must clearly experience the universe, the nature that surrounds you. Your spirit must accurately reflect this experience. Only through direct experience can you avoid a distorted vision." His voice and his words held the teasing promise of revealed secrets and commanded my full attention.

Searching each word for hidden meaning, my mind was riveted to O Sensei's voice. "Aha!" he said. "Do not lose your concentration. Your mind is drifting away from your hands. My words have diverted your concentration, and there is no *ki* left in your fingertips!"

Even as he spoke about the wisdom of experience, O Sensei had been setting me up to realize how easily words can confuse and distract. He was giving me the chance to discover the power of concentration by losing it. I began to understand that my training ground of Aikido was not confined within the *dojo*.

O Sensei said, "To know Aikido movement is merely the first step in the training process. Without constructive action, that knowledge is meaningless. If a criminal reads Musashi's book, it becomes *The Book of Five Rings* as interpreted by the mind of a criminal, and its knowledge is destructive. Similarly, a reader with a warped mind will turn Confucius's work into harmful and distorted knowledge. Without purity of mind and spirit, you cannot expect to attain the true Way of the Sword. Do you see the connection?"

Everything was at last falling into place, and I nodded.

"*Agatsu* means the victory over oneself through purity of soul. *Masagatsu* is the correct victory, the right Way. *Katsu hayabi* is the spiritual awakening of no time and no space. The combined wisdom of these words is the root of *shugyo*. Without that wisdom, no refinement is possible."

Listening to O Sensei's words, I began to realize the magnitude and responsibility of Budo training.

"I must warn you, Saotome. Unfortunate is he who has never experienced defeat. Without encountering the other side of victory, one is sure to be defeated when he finally meets with someone of superior might. The distorted view of self-aggrandizement produced

(Left) *The Founder's signature.* (Right) Masa Gatsu.

(Left) *The Founder's signature.* (Right) Agatsu.

by only embracing victory can be extremely dangerous, for one will ignore his own limitations. The longer defeat is postponed, the more devastating the defeat when it comes.

"By the way, Saotome, how is the book? Does it interest you much?"

"Yes, Sensei. I can follow the content, but as for understanding, most of it is still incomprehensible."

"That's understandable. Theory alone cannot make you realize *bujutsu*. Your own *shugyo* can be achieved only through the combination of your personal experiences. Speaking of Musashi, have you heard this story? It happened while Musashi was staying in a place called Kogura in Kyushu. As he was awaiting his evening meal, Musashi was approached by a traveling swordsman unknown to him who wanted technical advice. After a very brief conversation, Musashi judged the stranger as a man of skill and honor, and he paid him a small compliment. Accepting the compliment as his due, the swordsman promptly showed off his *bokken*, claiming that it had brought him many awards. 'What a foolish fellow,' Musashi thought. 'With such limited skill, how could he even expect to survive?'

"Musashi then asked for a bowl of rice. When the rice was served to him, Musashi took one grain and stuck it to the servant's hair, just above his forehead. 'Watch closely,' Musashi commanded. And with one lightning move, he unsheathed his sword and split the rice neatly into two pieces without touching the servant's hair. 'Can you duplicate this feat?' he asked.

"The stranger quickly put a little more distance between himself and the rice-splitting sword as he repeated over and over that his skill was much below the level of this masterful display.

"Returning his blade to the protection of its scabbard, Musashi said, 'Even a man with such skill as this is not assured of leaving the *shiai* [contest] in one piece. A true martial artist understands this and will never actively search for a challenge. When challenged, one must try in every way to promptly leave the place of

shiai without fighting.' The stranger apologized for his ignorance and thanked Musashi for the valuable lesson he had received."

O Sensei paused thoughtfully before continuing. "I think the reason that Musashi repelled and survived the threat of death so many times was due to the fact that he not only knew how to win, but also knew when not to fight. By not fighting, he freely admitted defeat. He often claimed that many of his victories were largely determined by luck. He knew his limitations. He had been on both sides of the fence. The only way to close your openings is to stand and acknowledge the fear of death.

"Win over yourself, the Taoist teachings advise. Win over yourself and you will conquer your enemy. The true victor is one who leaves the conflict without encountering bloodshed on either side.

"You know, I was scolded by Kami once," O Sensei said half-jokingly. "It was surely the most frightening moment in my life! Saotome, of what are you most fearful?"

"I have many fears, Sensei."

"Good. The day that you see yourself without weakness and fear is the day of your fallen destiny. Your training will come to an abrupt halt. Do you understand? In the world of competition, when there is a victor and a loser, how can anyone find the truth and reality of life itself? Just picture yourself surrounded by enemy rifles on the battlefield, and you'll see what I mean. If you hide behind the old martial concept of winning, you cannot achieve peace. Competition invariably produces a victim. It is a world without mercy that flourishes on the misery and suffering of others. It is a world of constant insecurity, without freedom or happiness.

"Our society tends to place wealth and physical authority over any respect for human qualities. Certainly it is not a lack of formal education that brought about the problems, but the fear and the greed of so many. Whenever there is greed, confusion, and a lack of communication, there is degradation of human value. Remember, Saotome, know yourself. Without an awareness of oneself, seeking knowledge from any book of wisdom will only add more confusion.

"Follow the wisdom of Kami, and truth will be attained. Polish the mirror of your spirit through *misogi*. You will see the truth within you when you are ready. Truth is eternally present. But do not become attached to *satori*. The moment you think you have it within your grasp, beware. This is only a mirage, an illusion created by your own weaknesses and limitations. If you are always searching for *satori*, you will spend your life trying to step on and capture your own shadow. You must give up this attachment. When the attachment is gone, greed is gone. Then there is emptiness and room for the spirit of truth to enter. Relax and allow your life to melt into space and become a part of God's reality.

"Train and refine yourself. True Budo is within you to discover. Keep this in mind in the course of your training."

Having said what he had come to say, O Sensei retired for the night, leaving me alone with my thoughts.

O Sensei's teachings began with Aikijutsu;
from this it became Aikido and then Takemusu Aiki.
Shobu Aiki wisdom, was its final evolution, and his last message.

The
DOJO:
SPIRITUAL OASIS

Upon first entering a traditional martial arts *dojo*, Westerners are often uncomfortable with the unfamiliar bowing and many forms of etiquette. They may seem overexaggerated, superficial, and unnecessary. Yet each point of etiquette has its origin in a concern for personal safety and general welfare.

Daily life is filled with social manners and customs that allow people to communicate and lessen the possibility of misunderstandings. This is even more important in a warrior society, where violence is tempered only by a strict code of honor and severe social structure. Etiquette is the controlling factor, and in the feudal societies it was often the narrow line between life and death.

When you enter the *dojo*, you are entering a different world, a warrior's world. It can be a place of respect and friendly camaraderie, or it can be a place of paranoia and mistrust. On the Aikido mat we are attacked and attacking, retraining our ability to respond instinctively. It is the underlying current of etiquette and social manner that allows us to practice safely, discipline and redirect our aggressive re-

sponses, and develop compassion and respect.

The following pages are from the training handbook put together by my senior students, which is given as a guidance to each new student that enters my *dojo*. I feel that these rules are necessary to Aikido training.

Aikido is not a sport. It is a discipline, an educational process for training the mind, body, and spirit. Physical technique is not the true object, but a tool for personal refinement and spiritual growth.

An Aikido *dojo* is not a gymnasium. It is the place where the teachings of Master Morihei Ueshiba are studied. It is not a place for the display of one's ego, but a place for uplifting and cleansing one's body, mind, and spirit. The correct attitude of respect, sincerity, and modesty and the proper atmosphere are essential to the learning process, and as Aikido is a martial art, they are essential to the safety of each individual.

The following rules are necessary to the maintenance of this atmosphere and vital to your study of Aikido.

——— RULES OF THE DOJO ———

1. This *dojo* operates in a strict manner following the traditional rules of proper conduct. Its spirit comes directly from the Founder of Aikido, and it is the place for the succession of his teachings. It is the responsibility of each student to honor and sincerely follow those teachings.

2. It is the responsibility of each student to cooperate in creating a positive atmosphere of harmony and respect.

3. Cleaning is an active prayer of thanksgiving. It is each student's responsibility to assist in cleaning the *dojo* and to cleanse his or her own mind and heart.

4. The *dojo* is not to be used for any purpose other than regularly scheduled classes without the direct permission of Sensei.

5. It is Sensei's decision whether or not he will teach you. You cannot buy technique. The monthly membership dues provide a place to practice and provide you with one small way to show gratitude for the teaching received. It is each student's responsibility to pay dues on time.

6. Respect the Founder and his teachings as succeeded and handed down by Sensei. Respect the *dojo*, respect your training tools, and respect each other.

——— RULES OF TRAINING ———

1. It is necessary to respect the Founder's teachings and philosophy, and the way in which Sensei conveys those teachings.

2. It is the moral responsibility of each student *never* to use Aikido technique to harm another person or as a way to display ego. It is not a technique of destruction, but of creation. It is a tool to develop a better society through the character development of the individual.

3. There will be no ego conflicts on the mat. Aikido is not street fighting. You are on the mat to transcend and purify your aggressive reactions, to embody the spirit of the samurai by discovering your social responsibility.

4. There will be no competition on the mat. The purpose of Aikido is not in fighting and defeating an enemy, but in fighting and defeating your own aggressive instincts. The strengths of Aikido are not in muscular force, but in flexibility, communication, timing, control, and modesty.

5. Insolence will not be tolerated. We must all be aware of our limitations.

6. Everyone has different physical abilities and different reasons for study. These must be respected. True Aiki is the proper and flexible application of technique appropriate to any changing circumstance. It is your responsibility to cause no injury. You must protect your training partner and yourself.

7. Receive Sensei's instructions and carry out his suggestions for training sincerely and to the best of your abilities. There is no room for argument.

8. All students are studying the same principles. There will be no conflicts of one group against another or of choosing sides. The *dojo* membership is one family, and the secret of Aikido is harmony.

If you cannot abide by these rules, you will be unable to study Aikido in this *dojo*.

——— PROPER DOJO ETIQUETTE ———

1. Upon entering and leaving the practice area of the *dojo*, make a standing bow.

2. Always bow when stepping on or off the mat in the direction of the *shomen* and the picture of the Founder.

3. Respect your training tools. *Gi* should be clean and mended. Weapons should be in good condition and in their proper place when not in use.

4. Never use someone else's practice *gi* or weapons.

5. A few minutes before time for practice to begin, you should be warmed up, seated formally in order of rank, and in quiet meditation. These few minutes are to rid your mind of the day's problems and prepare for study.

6. The class is opened and closed with a formal ceremony. It is important to be on time and participate in this ceremony, but if you are unavoidably late, you should wait, formally seated beside the mat, until Sensei signals permission for you to join the class. Perform a formal seated bow as you get on the mat. It is most important that you do not disrupt the class in doing so.

7. The proper way to sit on the mat is in *seiza* (formal sitting position). If you have a knee injury, you may sit cross-legged, but never sit with legs outstretched and never lean against walls or post. You must be alert at all times.

8. Do not leave the mat during practice except in the case of injury or illness.

9. During class, when Sensei demonstrates a technique for practice, you should sit quietly and attentively in *seiza*. After the demonstration, bow to Sensei and then to a partner and begin practice.

10. When the end of a technique is signaled, stop immediately. Bow to your partner and quickly line up with the other students.

11. Never stand around idly on the mat. You should be practicing or, if necessary, seated formally, awaiting your turn.

12. If for some reason it is absolutely necessary to ask a question of Sensei, go to him (never call him over), bow respectfully, and wait for his acknowledgment. (A standing bow is appropriate.)

13. When receiving personal instruction during class, sit in *seiza* and watch intently. Bow formally to Sensei when he has finished. When he is instructing another, you may stop your practice to watch. Sit formally and bow to him when he has finished.

14. Respect those who are more experienced. Never argue about technique.

15. You are here for practice. Do not force your ideas on others.

16. If you know the movement being studied and are working with someone who does not, you may lead the person through it. But do not attempt to correct or instruct your training partner if you are not of senior *yudansha* level.

17. Keep talking on the mat to an absolute minimum. Aikido is experience.

18. Do not lounge around on the mat before or after class. The space is for students who wish to train. There are other areas in the *dojo* for socializing.

19. The mat should be swept before class each day and after practice is over. It is everyone's responsibility to keep the *dojo* clean.

20. No eating, drinking, smoking, or gum chewing on or off the mat during practice, nor on the mat at any time.

21. No jewelry should be worn during practice.

22. Never drink alcoholic beverages while still wearing practice *gi*.

You are welcome to sit and observe a class at any time, but the following rules of etiquette must be observed.

1. Sit respectfully, never with legs propped up on the furniture or in a reclining position.

2. No eating, drinking, or smoking while class is in progress.

3. Do not talk to anyone while that person is on the mat.

4. Do not talk or walk around while the instructor is demonstrating or lecturing.

5. At the opening and closing of the class, sit formally at the side of the mat in *seiza* and perform the ceremony with the class. Remain seated until Sensei has signaled everyone to begin practice at the beginning of class or has left the mat at the end.

If you are unsure of what to do in a particular situation, ask a senior student, or simply follow your senior's lead.

Although there seem to be many forms of etiquette to remember, they will come naturally as you continue to train. Please do not be resentful if you are corrected on a point of etiquette, for each one is important to your safety and to the learning experience.

Aikido is not a religion, but the education and refinement of the spirit. You will not be asked to adhere to any religious doctrine, only to remain spiritually open. When we bow, it is not a religious performance but a sign of respect for the same spirit of Universal Creative Intelligence that is within us all.

The opening and closing ceremony of each Aikido practice is a formal bow directed to the *shomen*, followed by clapping the hands twice, followed by another bow to the *shomen* and then a bow between the instructor and students. The bows directed to the *shomen* symbolize respect for the spirit and the principles of Aikido and gratitude to the Founder for developing this system of practice and study. The two claps symbolize unity, *musubi*. The first sends out vibrations to the spiritual world. The second receives the echo of that vibration and connects your spirit with the spirit of the Founder and with the Universal Consciousness. The vibration that you send and the echo you receive is dictated by your own spiritual beliefs and attitude.

There is no right or wrong way in Aikido. If a movement obeys the physical laws of the universe, it is correct. If you obey the physical laws of the universe, your attitude must be correct. By following these laws, you are following the Path (the Will) of God. Therefore, Aikido is not technique training. It is wisdom training.

There are no individual *kata* in Aikido, for Aiki is the harmony of relationships. On the Aikido mat you will find people of different social backgrounds and status, different cultures and languages, different political and religious philosophies. They are coming together not to compete, not to press their own ideas on someone else, but to learn to listen to each other, to communicate through Aikido "skinship." On the mat we cannot hide our true selves. We show our weaknesses as well as our strengths. We sweat together, face stress together, help each other, and we learn to trust. Everyone is studying the same universal principles, and the essence that is the same in each individual becomes brilliantly clear as the mask of insecurity and ego is shed. We are all individuals, but we are a part of each other. If you were all alone in the universe with no one to talk to, no one with which to share the beauty of the stars, to laugh with, to touch, what would be your purpose in life? It is other life, it is love, that gives your life meaning. This is harmony. We must discover the joy of each other, the joy of challenge, the joy of growth.

In Aikido training you do not win. In trying to win you lose. If you see training as competition, you lose, your training partner loses, everyone loses. If you see life as competition, you cannot win, for eventually you must die. But if you see life as a process of universal creativity, you will never die, for you are a part of the process. If you see the growth of your body and your mind as a prelude to spiritual growth, your strength will last forever.

A mind of challenge is not a mind of competition. The greatest challenge is to challenge yourself. You must not spend your life searching for security. If you cover yourself with layer after layer of heavy armor, you will be unable to move, unable to fight and protect yourself or others. You will never feel the warm touch of the sun nor the sharp sting of a hard rain. Joy will be lost. Your freedom and independence will be lost.

If you spend your life in the safety of a cave at the foot of the mountains, you will see only darkness. Your experience will be narrow, and you will never feel the sweet pain of growth. You must leave that protection and security and challenge yourself on the mountains above you. You must climb higher and higher, your vision, ability, and experience expanding with each peak. And as you stand open and unprotected from the wind, with the sun and the snow touching your heart, you will experience the grand panorama of the universe all around you. You will reach out and touch the galaxies, and perhaps you will touch the face of God.

Bushido is challenge and sacrifice. It is the power and strength of an independent spirit. A dependent spirit is weak and cannot sacrifice its own selfish ego and greed. To be truly independent and taste the challenge of freedom, the spirit must be empty. In the final analysis, you and you alone are responsible for your own growth. You make your own reality.

You feel pain, you are afraid, but you are intensely alive. Climbing a mountain of frozen rock, cold, hungry, exhausted, you are alone with the sound of the wind. Give up and you die. Maybe one foot, maybe one inch in one day, but try. Life is the same, cold, hungry, and lonely. You must depend only on yourself. This is Bushido. This is my Aikido world. The search for the top of the mountains.